MW01453434

FOREIGN SERVICE

ALSO BY MARION NAIFEH

The Last Missionary in China

FOREIGN SERVICE

A MEMOIR
MARION NAIFEH

W/W

WOODWARD/WHITE INC.

FOREIGN SERVICE.

Copyright © 2016 by Marion Naifeh. All rights reserved. Printed in the United States of America. No part of this book may be reproduced or transmitted in any form or by any means, electronic or mechanical, including photocopying, recording, or by any information storage and retrieval system, without written permission from the publisher.

Published and distributed by Woodward/White, Inc.

ISBN 978-0-9819862-5-8

For George

CONTENTS

1.	China	13
2.	Mexico	49
3.	Baby Boy	63
4.	Iran	89
5.	Iraq	129
6.	Libya	165
7.	Nigeria	203
8.	Pakistan	225
9.	The U.A.E.	255
10.	Jordan	281
	Acknowledgments	301

CHINA

Beijing ★

Nanjing
Kuling • • Shanghai
Wuhu

Hong Kong

CHINA

I never really belonged anywhere.

My mother Carolyn died a few days after I was born in Wuhu, China. She and my father, B. Woodward, were missionaries. So I was raised by Ru-san, the cook, and Chang-teh, the man who brought the water every day for our bathing and washing—he carried it from the Yangtze River in two huge buckets balanced on a pole across his shoulders.

My earliest memory is of Chang-teh, who had a cyst on his left forehead about the size of a quarter, or rather six quarters stacked on top of each other. When he squatted in the kitchen to chat with Ru-san, I ran around him in circles, pinching the growth on his forehead at every turn.

At age three, I spoke only Chinese: not educated Chinese, but the "gutter Chinese" of the children in our neighborhood.

My father, B. W. Lanphear, and me.

Ru-san / Chang-teh

One day, I'm told, I walked into the dining room, stared at my father, and said: "Ni shi wai guo lao-gun hui lao jiaqu"—"You are a dirty, nasty foreigner, and you should go back where you came from."

So he sent me home, to live with his brother and sister-in-law, Roy and Mina, in Worcester, Massachusetts, to learn both English and manners. Two years later, when I was five, he took me back to China and deposited me in a boarding school in Nanking.

Ever since then, home has been wherever I was living.

My Uncle Roy never really understood my father's attraction to other lands and other peoples, although he put it a bit more bluntly: "Why is he over there with all those goddamn Chinese." Actually, he never referred to the Chinese as Chinese, preferring an epithet similar to the ones he used for blacks, Jews, and especially—because they were so much more prevalent in Massachusetts—the Irish.

Uncle Roy spent his happiest hours nailing down our WASP ancestry, visiting town halls and churches and graveyards, and drawing up elaborate genealogical charts. He traced the Woodward side of my family back to a Richard and Rose Woodward, who left Ipswich, England, in 1634, on the *Elizabeth* for Watertown, Massachusetts— only a few years after the Pilgrims landed on Plymouth Rock. There was also a Joseph Woodward who rose from private to captain during the Revolutionary War. I think my uncle got a little carried away when he claimed a Woodward went over to England from Normandy with William the Conqueror in 1066.

My father, B. W., could not have been a more different younger brother. He was a teacher with wanderlust in his heart. He spent 1915 teaching at the Syrian Protestant College in Beirut—later the American University of Beirut— before he contracted a case of rheumatic fever so severe that he had to return to the States. That set him on a trajectory towards China, where he spent the rest of his life. He met Carolyn March, a YWCA staffer, when they both entered

*My mother, Carolyn March.
I only knew her as this
photograph hanging on the wall.*

At age three, my father brought me to Worcester, Massachusetts, to learn English and manners.

the Language School at the University of Nanking in 1917. She also contracted a disease—typhus—and had to return home to Syracuse, New York, for medical treatment. But when B. W. proposed by telegram, she accepted, and they were married in Wuhu in 1926.

My interlude in Worcester confused matters, but to the extent that I remember a childhood home, it was in China. My first playmates were Chinese—the children of the kitchen staff and other workers in the neighborhood. I distinctly recall a Christmas Eve when everyone else in the house had gone to St. Mark's Church in the compound run by the Sisters of the Transfiguration, and I heard the night-watchman banging his iron pole on the hard ground beneath my bedroom window to let me know I wasn't alone.

I also had 16 Chinese "brothers," all students in Wuhu whose families had been shattered by disease and poverty but who were known to the same Sisters of the Transfiguration. If a boy was particularly bright, the Sisters asked my father, who was the principal of the St. James Middle School, to "adopt" him—although he never formally adopted them, just raised and educated them, most of them all the way through graduate school. There were never more than four brothers at one time living upstairs in the bungalow. But they were more a family to me than either of my parents. My mother was nothing more than a strange woman whose photograph hung above the fireplace. My father was always busy, with a hundred more boarders at the Middle School—and Chinese and Japanese armies marching ever closer to Wuhu.

The four boys who were living in our bungalow when I was there were George, Jimmy, Roland, and William. They teased me constantly. They even devised a little song in my honor, which they would sing at the top of their lungs: "Da-pan-dze, ma-mandi-dzo"—"Little fatty, very slowly walks." But they meant it lovingly, and I remember them very fondly.

Four of my Chinese brothers, with Jimmy at the top, then clockwise, George, Stephen, and Claude.

George's grandmother brought him to Wuhu at age four, after his father died of starvation. Jimmy's mother wanted to become a nun after his father died. Roland somehow made his way to St. James and, when he graduated, refused to return to his village when his parents insisted he marry a girl he could not abide.

The story of "Moon-face" William, as my father called him, almost defies belief. William's father, a farmer, lost all of his money gambling, and William's uncles forced his mother to "remarry," a euphemism for being sold as a concubine. They kept the money.

When William was five, he went with his mother on "Qingming"—Tomb Sweeping Day—to clean the family graves. He got bored and wandered unnoticed back to the village with some friends. Each boy carried a lit torch, and William held his on his shoulder so the flame would not blow towards his face. At one point, the wind shifted quickly and his cotton coat caught on fire. A farmer in a nearby field rushed to put out the fire, but not before it seared much of William's torso and arms.

There was no money for a doctor but, somehow, when he was ten, he arrived at the dispensary run by the Sisters of the Transfiguration in the compound adjoining ours. According to the medical report, he had "a deep abscess in his back and a right arm so badly burned that it is permanently raised parallel with his shoulder." He endured six operations and multiple skin grafts.

When he recovered, he was given a job as a tailor's apprentice. Although the tailor considered him "too dumb" to be of any use, Head Sister Constance forced the tailor to keep him employed during the afternoons so that he could attend St. James. He graduated first in his class at St. James and then first in his class again in college. William was my only brother to flee to Taiwan with Chiang Kai-shek, the leader of the Kuomintang, who lost the civil war to Mao Tse-tung and his Communist guerillas in 1949.

I was only five when my father sent me to boarding school, but the school—the Nanking American School— didn't accept boarders, only day students, so I was the only boarder. I lived with the principal, Mr. Illick, and his family, who couldn't have paid much attention to me, because I remember absolutely nothing about them. I do vaguely recall my class visiting Pearl Buck's husband, John Lossing Buck, at their home. A professor at Nanking University, Mr. Buck taught agricultural economics, with heaps of statistics on rural China. I remember only an old man sitting in a dark, damp corner of a huge living room talking about something. Mrs. Buck was not there because, as I later learned, they were in the middle of a divorce. It was her novel *The Good Earth* that won the Nobel Prize and introduced "her China" to the American public.

That Christmas vacation, I found someone to annoy other than my brothers. Mary Chang was the Chinese nurse in charge at Sister Constance's dispensary. Hour after hour, I trailed after her as "we" inspected the ill and the frail. Mary was young, efficient, and very serious, as well she might have been, since "our" patients were usually one step shy of palliative care. She never made me shut my eyes, even when a poor peasant couple was brought in with severe burns. They had been accosted by some robbers, but had no money, so the robbers burned them all over their emaciated bodies with sticks set on fire.

I was particularly interested in a group of seven female toddlers at the dispensary. When they were only days old, their families had abandoned them, literally hanging them on the fence surrounding the Sisters' compound. Their parents were too poor to feed a girl; a girl couldn't help the family earn money, but still cost money to raise, so they were expendable. Sister Constance was raising the toddlers until young, Christian Chinese families could be found to adopt them. I used candy to bribe the girls to gather round me and listen to my tall tales. Best was when they had colds, and we huddled under an improvised tent with a vaporizer spewing Vicks fumes to clear their clogged nostrils.

I hadn't been at the Nanking American School long before I was sent to a school in Kuling, a mountainous and very picturesque spot where the Chinese elite spent their summers. I preferred it to Nanking, not for the scenery, but because I now had three roommates. Not one of them snitched on me when I found a stray kitten on the soccer field and brought it into our room, using a drawer for its bed. A teacher passing our empty room during supper heard a frantic meowing and expelled the kitten from the school, to our joint sorrow.

I hated the class devoted to stitching French borders on handkerchiefs; everything else was tolerable, although I do remember informing God that if I ever had children, I would never, *never* send them to boarding school.

Christmas back in Wuhu was wonderful. I still have a copy of my father's 1937 annual letter to family and friends in the U.S., which covered our 1936 Christmas in detail: "The day before Christmas, Marion and the boys decorated the interior of the house using much lovely holly with loads of red berries. Ru-san and Chang-teh made arches of bamboo and holly on the front porch, and we had electric lights among these—three lights on each small evergreen tree, on

each side of the porch, and lights in the front window."
Next came presents. Except for paper dolls and books, my presents had an only-in-China feel to them: "nine chickens, five wild ducks, 19 apples, 179 oranges, and 327 eggs; several boxes of writing-paper, silver novelties, a rice pattern tea set (24 pieces), etc."

B. W. then wrote of the "climax to the Christmas dinner when a message came over the radio from Germany that General Chiang was free." Joseph, one of my brothers, rushed into the middle of the dinner giddy with excitement. Apparently, the Manchurian warlord, Marshal Zhang Xueliang, had kidnapped Generalissimo Chiang Kai-shek, who was a hero to the missionaries. But the Japanese were advancing, and the warlord had released him to fight the Japanese. I understood what a warlord was, but little else. We all leapt up from the Mission Christmas dinner to sing a joyous doxology, led by Sister Constance and Sister Louise. Thousands of firecrackers exploded in the streets, and my brothers rushed out to help celebrate. The euphoria reminded B. W. "of the celebrations of 1918." He wrote that "the celebrations continued for a week and ended in a huge lantern procession on the night of January 1, when over 10,000 marched through the streets. They carried hundreds of paper lanterns . . . our chief lantern was a huge lion made of bamboo and paper, but there were arches, boats, airplanes, etc."

Back again to school, back to the beautiful mountains and lush valleys of Kuling. Getting to the school was perilous because there was no road, only a narrow path that crisscrossed along the steep cliffs leading up to the town on the summit of the mountain. We travelled by sedan chairs balanced on two poles carried on the shoulders of four coolies, two in front and two in back. One stumble and all of us would have dropped thousands of feet to instant death.

But a child doesn't take death too seriously—not even with fierce battles being fought near by. Warlords, guerillas, and the Japanese were all fighting. One day, out on the school soccer field where I had found the kitten, I saw a Japanese plane fly overhead and disappear into the clouds. But even that didn't register as a danger. And all of the adults around us, American and Chinese alike, studiously avoided telling us much of anything. When they told me that I couldn't go back to Wuhu for Christmas vacation in 1937, they didn't give me an explanation. It was only later that I learned that Wuhu had fallen to the Japanese on December 5. On December 13, the Japanese bombed the *U.S.S. Panay*, a gunboat of the Yangtze Patrol, which sank in the Yangtze near Nanking. The Rape of Nanking had begun.

On December 26, the school began an evacuation, ordered by the U.S. government. When we reached the foot of the mountain we were taken to Kiukiang, where we caught a boat for Hankow. A train was waiting there, with German, French, British, U.S., and Red Cross flags stretched across the roof of each car, to take 130 of us and other fleeing foreigners to battle-free Hong Kong. "Aunt Alma" was in charge of our class. She stuffed a money belt with our temporary passes and lots of bulky paper currency. At each train stop, I was mesmerized as a Japanese guard marched into our cabin with his gun cocked to check on our papers. Aunt Alma would turn her back to the guard and to us so that she could lift her voluminous skirt to remove our documents for their inspection.

At one stop, a student had decided that he wanted to get

off the train and look around. The whole train had to go back and look for him.

We did find him, but that was hardly the end of the trials that we put poor Aunt Alma through. When we reached our first safe haven, Hong Kong, we went to the storied Peninsula Hotel. After being confined to a single small train cabin, we had the run of the wide, luxuriously-carpeted halls of the entire hotel. We were free; she was frantic. Our table manners horrified her. She was constantly muttering "wobles" to us—elbows spelled backwards—to remind us to take them off the table. We happily ignored her, wolfing down chocolate cake for breakfast, as well as the the other delicacies of the day. We thought evacuation was splendid. For our entertainment, there even was a baby panda basking in the sun on a second floor balcony. Mei-Mei, purchased by the New York socialite Ruth Harkness, was waiting to be taken to the Brookfield Zoo in Chicago.

Then, that same week, we found ourselves in the middle of a typhoon. We were taking the *S.S. Conte Biancamano* to Shanghai when the ship was swept into a fury of swirling winds. Aunt Alma had taken to her bed, seasick. My cohorts and I howled like banshees as we raced round and round on the treacherous slippery decks, dashing into the ship's dining room just as a floor-to-ceiling mirror splintered into a thousand pieces.

I was scooped up from a Shanghai dock and into the arms of a large-framed lady with a cheery face and hair pulled into a tight bun. "You're *here!*" the lady whooped, holding me at arm's length and examining me clinically. "Poor B. W. thinks you were evacuated to Baguio in the Philippines, and you are *here!* And here you will stay with me until the fall term starts. That's soon enough for a boarder."

This, it turned out, was "Aunt" Carol—Administrative Officer of the Shanghai American School and a classmate of my parents at language school. She had married "Uncle" Curly, a British Army officer stationed in Shanghai. Uncle Curly was in charge of protecting all of the foreigners lucky enough to be quartered safely within the International Concession in Shanghai when the Japanese army had taken control of much of the city during the fall of 1937. In spite of the prevailing chaos, Aunt Carol was able to inform B. W. that I was now under her protection.

My new home was Aunt Carol and Uncle Curly's spacious apartment on the school grounds. Their six-year-old daughter Charlotte was delighted to have an instant older sister. She was particularly delighted to have someone else to share the attention of her eagle-eyed governess, Frau Edith. *"Bitte!"* Frau Edith shouted at me, and, rapping me on the knuckles: "You must say *bitte* first, *then* I will pass you the dish!" "No, don't rub your nose! Use the *handkerchief!"* And when we took our afternoon walks, rain or shine: "Stomachs *in!* Shoulders *out!* Step *along!"*

The city we took our walks in was unlike anything I had ever experienced. In 1927, Aldous Huxley had written that "in no city, West or East," had he "ever had such an impression of dense, rank, richly clotted life." Shanghai was a turmoil of people living a life I never knew existed. Occasionally, we would halt our stomachs-in-and-shoulders-out walks to stop in small stores owned by European refugees, where Frau Edith bought cheeses, rye bread, and seasonal fruits. The shoppers in these damp and dingy stores were short, stout, bent, elderly White Russian, Polish, Estonian, Latvian, and Lithuanian ladies, all refugees. They bought eggs, pickles, and salami with copper coins wrapped in tightly-knotted handkerchiefs drawn from their pockets—all commerce conducted in an eerie silence.

We never stopped at the Chinese stalls in the crowded side streets, where shrill voices shouted the bounteous virtues of turnips, cabbages, and scallions displayed in perfect triangular mounds.

When we walked through those streets, Frau Edith's firm hand gripped ours tightly as we made our difficult way through rickshaws, bicycles, and donkey carts.

If we had been especially well-mannered and had displayed sufficiently correct posture, we were allowed to stop at Frau Edith's apartment as she dropped off her purchases and checked on her son Fritz.

A blond-headed teenager in starched beige shorts, Fritz jumped to his feet when he heard the door open and saluted, "Heil Hitler!"

"Fritz, do you *have* to?" she would ask, her voice filled with irritation. "You look ridiculous with your arm sticking out like that!"

"Mother," he replied with scorn, "I am a Hitler youth."

"All the worse," she said, putting up her groceries as we waited by the door.

"Time, girls. Time to be getting *home!*"

"Fritz, I'll be back early," she sighed without turning to look at the outstretched arm.

On our carefully scheduled days, bath time came next. By that time, Frau Edith would have returned home to Fritz. Our nursemaid, or Amah, was in charge. While we happily splashed in an enormous bathtub, she would soak her bound feet in tepid water in a small basin. The water would soon be bloodied from the soles of her feet, cut by the nails growing from her bent toes. Amah, who was in her 50s, had her bound feet as long as she could remember. Sterling Seagrave, an American journalist whose family lived in Asia for five generations, described the practice of binding girls' feet, which dates back to the 10th century: "Bound feet demonstrated the lengths to which a woman would go to make her daughter a desirable sexual object. Foot-binding usually began at age four. A ten-foot-long, two-inch bandage was wrapped around the toes to force them in against the sole. Each day the bandage was tightened until the foot was folded under with only the big toe sticking out, a shape called the 'Golden Lotus' because it resembled a lotus pod with the petals removed. Flesh rotted and fell off, sometimes a toe or two. And the foot oozed pus, until the process of deformation was complete after two years, at which point the feet were practically dead."

When I returned to China in 1980, I saw two women in Shanghai who had bound feet. By 1993, I saw no women left deformed in this horrific manner.

The subject was of particular interest for me at the time, because I had slightly deformed feet myself. The previous summer, my father and a couple of my brothers and I had spent a month during the summer in Kuling, enjoying its cool breezes. My father had bought me a pair of pretty, patent-leather party shoes to go with a beautiful pink silk dress that he had also bought for me. I wore the dress and the shoes to a concert attended by Chiang Kai-shek, where I was allowed to sit at his feet along with several other children. I was so proud of the way I looked and of all the attention I seemed to be getting—I later realized that the crowd was looking mostly at Chiang Kai-shek, not at us children—that I refused to let anyone know the shoes were at least one size too small. This was a little like having my feet bound: My toes were so squeezed they were being bent together slightly.

When I started living with Aunt Carol, she insisted that I wear corrective iron-frame shoes to straighten out my toes. They didn't really work—to this day my toes have a slightly distorted shape—but what really mortified me at that sensitive age was wearing those hideous shoes. There was a lesson about vanity in there somewhere, but I'm not sure I understood it at the time.

After bathing, we joined Uncle Curly in the living room for our tomato juice cocktail before dinner. "What important business have you two accomplished today?" he asked us, sweeping Charlotte up in a tickling embrace. "Marion," he would say to me, "would you please hurry Carol along?" I relished this ritual, for after the masseuse came the manicurist, Eva. Eva always put a touch of pink polish on the nails of my outstretched fingers. Aunt Carol patiently waited until my nails were done before exclaiming in horror that I was much too young for such nonsense. Eva smiled at our worn-out dialogue as she screwed on the tops of her bottles and jars, placed them in her scuffed satchel, and bid us goodnight in Russian. Her route to Shanghai had led her from central Russia across Siberia to Darien and then on down the coast.

We were all refugees.

In the fall of 1939, my classes at school turned suddenly more interesting, partly thanks to a Boston Brahmin social studies teacher who had just graduated from Harvard. Exchanging the streets of Cambridge for the alleys of Shanghai, he was mortified—or delighted—to find each alley filled with Sin.

When even he got bored talking about national social

infrastructures, he would detour into a discussion of what he saw in those alleys, and we eagerly went with him. Somehow Sin, with a capital "S," was always involved, and Sin involved "slothfulness, opium, and sex," in reverse order. This was heady stuff for a class of 11-year-olds. "Now, for example, take an opium den," he would say. "Someone of my height would have to bend low to enter the smoke-filled archway." (It was clear to all of us that the "someone" was none other than our instantly-beloved teacher.) "In these quarters, someone would find tier after tier of bunks occupied by elderly gentlemen. These gentlemen would inhale deeply from their opium pipes as they finger their long, wispy beards. A cloying sweetness would permeate the blue haze, speckled with red burning embers from small bowls at the end of thin long-stemmed pipes."

To what do we owe this state of affairs, our teacher would ask us rhetorically. "The British were the first to exploit the commercial possibilities. From the 1840s on, the British and French forced China to permit the import of opium. For nearly a century, this seed has flowered into the opiate of progress. It has dulled ambition. It has fostered hopelessness!"

Our teacher vented on, with ever-increasing vehemence, in his thick Boston accent, against the ills of man, as we lingered, lost in the sweet smoke of our imaginations.

We thought social studies was great.

English classes were also great. Our English teacher was very young and very pretty. She informed us that, when properly used, English can be as clean and precise as a surgeon's scalpel—and just as effective. Unbeknownst to her, we spent much of each class imagining what we assumed must be her very exciting romantic life, even as she drilled us in the excitement of verb tenses, the virtues of just the right noun, and the horror of unnecessary adjectives. Unfortunately, half-way through the school year, she married Tillman Durdin, the illustrious *New York Times* correspondent, throwing cold water on our vivid imaginations. Our interest in English collapsed instantly, but at least she was better able to explain—in clean and precise English—why we were being hurled into war.

Girl Scouts was almost as good as social studies and English. Aunt Carol, who was the Scout Leader, made me join. I was mortified by the thought that anyone might suspect my relationship with her, so I saluted her smartly and pretended that I had never met her before. My new heroine, after Nurse Chang, was now our Senior Patrol leader, Rita, a towering Latvian blonde. After a session when we worked on a cooking badge, she alone of all the patrol leaders helped us clean up. In the midst of endless instructions on the best way to scrub a dish, she would break into a low, throaty nightclub rendition of "Harbor Lights," then No. 1 on the Hit Parade. A few years later, when I read of the capture of the Riga harbor by the Russians, I remembered those lyrics sadly.

Occasionally, our patrol went on hikes. The war kept us from going out into the countryside, so our hikes were on asphalt city streets. Whenever possible, I would stray from the patrol and explore the streets on my own, especially the Avenue Pétain. Ah, the marvel of hot roasted chestnuts bought from a street vendor on a corner of the Avenue Pétain! The French Club was across the wide avenue, and I would cross over to peek through the slats of the wood fence and thick shrubs surrounding the club. I could peer endlessly at those elegant people doing elegant things.

Tennis on the lawn, tea on the terrace, laughter at a pool's edge: How glamorous life could be in French!

But the larger world around us was anything but glamorous. I may not have been aware of the cruelty of the Green Gang or the scores of Soviet coaches molding the nascent Chinese Communist Party to their benefit, but I understood many of the human tragedies unfolding in front of me. Even a child my age was aware that the city was filled with refugees. I knew some of them personally: Frau Edith, Olga, Mrs. Baum, and Rita. I did not know that, just before World War II, Shanghai was the only city in the world that accepted stateless Jews without a visa, people like Mrs. Baum and my Jewish classmates at the Shanghai American School.

Meanwhile, the fighting in China was getting worse every day, not only the Chinese against the Japanese, but Chiang Kai-shek against Mao and his peasant guerrillas. So, in the fall of 1941, B. W. decided it was time to take me back to Worcester for the third time and deposit me once again on Uncle Roy and Aunt Mina's doorstep.

There I was, getting off the train in Worcester, Massachusetts: a 13-year-old girl weighing 180 pounds, wrapped in a Shanghai tailor's concept of missionary fashion, and wearing my huge, ugly iron-rimmed shoes.

Aunt Mina, who was never one to go to church except on Christmas and Easter and never one to use the Lord's name in vain, later admitted that, upon locking her eyes on me, she had muttered, "Oh, my God."

B. W. did not linger in Massachusetts. He returned to China almost immediately to take care of the school in Wuhu and all of its students. They needed him all the more with the danger approaching from all sides. He traveled first, along with Chennault's famous Flying Tigers, on the Dutch *M.S. Bloemfontein* to Brisbane and the Dutch East Indies. Then he transferred to a French boat in Manila, headed for Shanghai, which was caught in the tail end of another of those infamous typhoons.

Now, at 13, I was much more aware of the changes in my life than I had been as a younger child. Worcester was nothing like Wuhu, Nanking, Kuling, or Shanghai. Walking to school with plowed snow packed tight in seven-foot walls on either side of Willard Avenue was a novelty. So too was eating hot fresh maple syrup poured on newly-fallen snow. Our neighbor, Mrs. Bellows, had her own maple tree farm in upstate Maine.

In my room in Worcester, unlike the school dorm back in Shanghai, Aunt Mina allowed me to plaster every inch of every wall with photos from movie magazines. I earned a meager allowance for washing the dishes and hanging laundry out to dry, just enough to splurge on my new fixation on movie stars. The only time Aunt Mina said no was when I tried to bring home a copy of *True Romance*.

Having grown up in China made me feel a little exotic, a feeling that lasted through Classical High School. I wrote article after article about my life in China for the school newspaper: "Christmas in China," "Food in China," "A Trip in Occupied China."

Twenty-four of our 167 graduating students had gone off to the war, or would be going off soon. War was upon us.

In fact, the war was never very far from my mind. The International Red Cross and the Mission Board in New York did their best to keep us apprised of what was going on back home. We heard that B. W., Sister Constance, and the other Americans in Wuhu had been confined to the Sisters' compound on February 3, 1941. We also heard that on Pearl Harbor Day, Japanese officers ordered Sister Constance to lower the Stars and Stripes and raise the Rising Sun. Instead, she sawed down the bamboo flagpole and walked away, paying no attention to the threats screamed at her by the astonished Japanese soldiers. We heard that in the spring of 1943, all the Americans were sent to ASH Camp at 65 Great Western Road in Shanghai—a concentration camp. By then, B. W. had developed an extremely serious gallbladder infection which sent him back and forth from the concentration camp to the Shanghai County Hospital until the camp was liberated in September 1945. By then he had spent three years, eight months, and one week interned. He had lost 111 pounds and now weighed just 131 pounds. I received a notice from B. W. via the Comité International de la Croix-Rouge, dated November 27, 1944, stating that he was "Getting along okay. Must be so careful. Busy daily. Have lost a little weight. Though late, Christmas love. Greetings. Boys all well. Geoffrey married. Love." Liberation enabled him to return to Wuhu—to a handful of my brothers who, along with Ru-san and Chang-teh, had somehow managed to survive those long, miserable years.

Three years earlier, in the fall of 1943, on my way home from school, I noticed the headline of the *Worcester Gazette* in the drug store: "B. W. Lanphear is being repatriated on the *S.S. Gripsholm*." But that turned out to be only a rumor.

By the time he did return, in 1946, for admission to the Leahy Clinic in Boston, I was a sophomore at Wheaton College in Norton, Massachusetts. That turned out to be a disappointment to my father, who apparently considered Mount Holyoke to be the only college that graduated

My father, released from the Japanese concentration camp, surrounded by his sons and their families.

"ladies." He also despaired of any career choice I might make other than that of nurse or teacher. Of course, I immediately and adamantly opposed both careers, little realizing I would accidently end up being a teacher for over 60 years, all over the world.

For B. W., China and his 44 Chinese sons, daughters-in-law, and grandchildren were his life. They knew him well—far better than I.

For me, he was more than a silent photograph on a wall, as my mother was, but only slightly more. I have only a few intense memories of him. There he is having a huge infected boil under his arm lanced. And there is the moment in 1938 in the Nanking Railroad Station on our way home from picking me up in Shanghai. A group of Japanese soldiers were howling with glee as they pried open my suitcase and dumped my belongings on the filthy station floor, including the underwear of a humiliated 10-year-old. There is the moment when he caught me reading his copy of *Gone with the Wind*, horrified that I was reading such a racy novel. Mostly, there are the moments when I saw him sitting at his desk writing his Christmas letters to friends and supporters back home containing list after list of the year's happenings in China.

Those were the few memories I had of my father when I returned to China in 1980.

My husband George and I had just retired from a life in the Foreign Service and I had begun teaching at the American Language Institute of Georgetown University. Late one Saturday afternoon, I received a call from the Director of the Institute, Sue Peppin, asking if I wanted to go to China. At the last minute, the fourth member of the team that had been assembled to go to China for a semester was forced to cancel, and I was the lucky replacement in this "Gang of Four."

Our gang was under the auspices of the United Nations, the Sixth Department of the Ministry for Economic Relations, and the Beijing Second Foreign Language Institute. Our assignment was to prepare a group of math prodigies who had survived the Cultural Revolution for a stint at Hewlett-Packard in California. They needed to be able to communicate with their new colleagues as they immersed themselves in information technology. They could read English; they could write English. Speaking it was another matter.

Our plane from Tokyo arrived in Beijing late. The designated "leader" from the Second Foreign Language Institute was not there to meet us in the enormous vacuum at the Beijing Airport: The staff had gone home. There were no incoming or outgoing passengers. Sue Peppin and Bennett Lindauer, the only one of us who spoke fluent Chinese, had left to find us a hotel. Sue Bailey and I stared at a handful of bored young police, who had nothing of better interest to do than to stare back. We were two abandoned Western women slouching on our uninteresting luggage. We had no chickens, no bedding, no plastic bags of sticky rice, no bulging baskets of clothing—just Samsonite. For no reason other than boredom, I started singing my "da-pan-dze" ditty of "little fatty very slowly walks." This attracted immediate attention. To the disappointment of our tiny, appreciative audience, clapping for encores, we were hastened away by Sue and an apologetic Institute representative.

Home was now the Friendship Hotel, formerly the site of the Embassy of the Soviet Union. Along with the "500" other foreign experts in residence, we contributed to the babble of languages in the dining-room: Spanish, Urdu, Arabic, Portuguese, Italian, German, and Hausa, among others. Every night we were surrounded by a crowd of squabbling and laughing children, all of them using some form of Chinese as the common language.

On one hand, I was thrilled with our uniforms: a blue jacket with blue slacks, day in and day out. We had a red and white Second Foreign Language Institute pin to identify our "unit." Not once did I have to think about what to wear when I got up. Every morning, there was a tall blue thermos with scalding hot water outside my door for tea or coffee. No thinking necessary.

On the other hand, I had no idea how we were going to teach students who spoke almost no English, just as we spoke no Chinese. All 30 students had been tested with a preliminary English exam, then placed in four levels of English proficiency, and for some reason, I was given the five most proficient students.

Before we arrived in Beijing, we had been informed that the Institute would not be able to give us textbooks for six weeks. None of the four of us knew anything about information technology. And math of any sort? I had flunked it in the third grade, to B. W.'s chagrin. By chance, back in Washington, I had found a book with the promising title *Information Processing* at Reiter's Scientific and Professional Books. I had pored over it day and night until all I could see was a blur of bytes and bauds. But I would have to make do. The five geniuses sitting in front of me—the future leaders of China's technological revolution— were now my students, my charges, my responsibility.

Just minutes before, I had heard Sue Peppin teaching her beginners in Class A prepositions from a very basic English language textbook she had brought with her. She was using every object in her classroom to illustrate what was under what, next to what, and behind what.

The only things I had going for me were that I was old (in my 50s) and a teacher—the Chinese still respected both teaching and old age.

I decided to improvise. I asked my students to sing songs like "Twelve Cans of Tuna Fish" (an American Language Institute classic) to teach them such words as "intonation" and "pacing." And I had them chew Freshen Up gum from the supply I had in my purse to learn words like "shiny," "translucent," "solid," and "viscous."

As it turned out, what was stressing them out about living in California for the four-month training program wasn't the language, but the food. What would they eat? American food, they had been warned, would be absolutely tasteless.

Foreign foods were very much on my mind, as well. As

missionaries in China, we had eaten very well, so well that I weighed 180 pounds when I returned to Massachusetts as a 13-year-old. But to this day, my mind is indelibly stamped with childhood memories of desperately hungry people, scrounging for anything edible on the grounds of our St. James compound. Back in Beijing, I found myself and my fellow instructors from Georgetown being fêted by our benefactors at an early dinner, waiters hovering about, keeping our glasses filled with beer, red wine, and fiery brandy. The appetizers were sweet shrimp, pickles, and carrots sculpted into flowers. Then the good stuff: fat dough purses filled with spiced meat and sweet and sour fish; mushrooms stuffed with scallops; and asparagus. These were followed, mid-meal, by a dessert of fried pastry, dusted in powdered sugar, blistering hot and filled with melted chocolate. Then, after dessert, came a sweet-and-sour fish and, last of all, a delicate fish soup.

We were even invited to the Great Hall of the People for tea. Five thousand people had attended the dinner thrown for Nixon when he went to China in 1972. A mere 3,500 showed up for our tea, which was being held in celebration of International Worker Woman's Day. Bennett, our sole male colleague, had to remain at the hotel. Once inside the cavernous, red-carpeted lobby, we climbed what seemed like a thousand marble stairs to the multi-columned Great Hall, its walls covered in gold wallpaper. We had been told in advance that our table was number 310.

This was the first year that wives of the diplomatic corps and foreign experts were invited to the tea. The other women at our table were the wives of diplomats from Nigeria, where George and I had lived for two years during the 1960s. They had wrapped their heads in extravagant head-ties similar to the ones that were fashionable in Lagos during our time there. Nigerian head-ties have names as interesting as the head-ties themselves. "Shh, Don't Tell Secrets" had been a favorite during our time in the country. My fellow guests told me that they were wearing "Low Profiles," which, they informed us, were now all the rage in Lagos. There on the stage, to my delight, was part of my childhood world, Sun Yat-sen's widow, Soong Ching-ling. One of Madame Chiang Kai-shek's older sisters, she was still vigorous in her late 80s.

While we enjoyed the musical entertainment on stage, a Chinese-American woman arrived late enough to make a high-profile grand entrance. With more than a touch of drama, she lowered herself onto a seat at the table next to ours. Almost all of the women in the room were wearing blue uniforms and ID pins, as we were. Not her: She slipped off a green silk floor-length coat, embroidered with gold medallions and lined with sable. She wore a double strand of pearls so long it reached her waist. Her lips colored a brilliant red, she chatted away with her table of somber Eastern European diplomatic wives.

Back at the Language Institute, our students were almost as concerned about American clothing as they were about American food. They had never worn anything but blue uniforms and ID pins. How would they identify themselves at Hewlett-Packard? All day, non-stop, the campus loudspeakers warned them: "Do not envy! Do not envy America for its technological prowess! Its society is nothing to envy!" Our female students also wanted to know if they should go to the hairdresser for a permanent before traveling to the U.S.

In fact, they were insatiably curious about everything

in America, particularly family life. They could not hear enough about my husband George, and my children Steve and Carolyn. The fact that George wrote me every day was inconceivable to them.

To top it off, I had 16 Chinese brothers!

The minute I told my students about my remarkably large Chinese family, they insisted that they help me locate them. They assured me all I had to do was to contact the highest-ranking Communist Party official in Wuhu and request his assistance.

I wasn't so sure I wanted to contact my brothers. China had just begun to open up to the outside world. I had always feared that, because they had in essence been adopted by an American father and were all highly educated, they must have suffered terribly during the Cultural Revolution. If I reestablished contact with them, wouldn't they just face more problems if trouble broke out between China and the U.S. again? But my students were insistent that I reach out to them.

Liu Wen, the Associate Dean at the Language Institute, was incredibly thoughtful. He knew that at the end of the program, our Gang of Four would head to Shanghai and Wuhu—the latter, an indulgence, obviously, for my sake. First, he offered to help find my father's grave. The Mission Office had informed me that B. W. had died in Shanghai on July 4, 1951. He was cremated and a service was held for him at Holy Trinity Cathedral. It was logical he would have been buried, as so many foreigners in those days were, in the Bubbling Well Cemetery in Shanghai. Liu Wen searched diligently, only to discover that my father was buried in another cemetery, one that had been bulldozed and built over. He was heartbroken as he gave me this news, empathizing that when he himself came to Beijing from the provinces and searched for his own father's grave in the capital city, he too had been unsuccessful.

Each weekend, we explored the usual tourist haunts. We were expected to accomplish this on bicycle, but I had never mastered one. George had tried to teach me, unsuccessfully, before we left for China, in the alley behind our house on Reno Road in Washington, D.C. So my colleagues and I toured by bus and bicycle.

While my colleagues focused on sites such as the Ming Tombs, the Summer Palace, and the Forbidden City, I was preoccupied with the people around me. I was constantly wondering if one of my brothers would appear one day, foolish as it was. The chances were 16 in a billion. Was that one of my brothers who just passed me on Wang Fu Ching Street? Was that George Liang in front of me when I turned into Shop 19 on Liu Li Ch'ang Street, taking a family scroll to be remounted? The owner of that particular shop, who was at least 70, obviously needed bifocals, but had resorted to two pairs of glasses, one on top of the other. Maybe I just needed better glasses, or more of them.

When the program came to a close, we headed first to Wuhu. Traveling as we did by bus, train, and plane, I was constantly reminded of my mother's diary and her account of a 300-mile trip from Chungking to Cheng-du in 1921 on behalf of the YWCA.

"In my sedan chair, I have first the big, yet light, box containing a Pekingese lamp shade for our Cheng-du family. This box goes under the seat of my sedan chair. Then at my feet is my Corona typewriter. A lovely big thermos bottle absolutely the best ever (non-breakable), tied at the back of my chair and resting in the big white granite pail which just wouldn't pack away elsewhere. I'm leaning on a good old quilt and pillow. These two are part of what will be my six nights' bedding in Buddhist temples and Chinese inns. Over my head at the top of the chair is tied my sun parasol and walking stick; also under the top of this water proof chair is my ukulele. Sounds like a lot, but really nothing is heavy except the typewriter. Oh yes, I have my cosmos flowers, writing case, and brown cloth bag with all necessary articles, knife, purse, handkerchiefs, Robinson Reminder, ink bottle & blue silk case for calling cards."

In Wuhu, we were received by a Mr. Chen, the guide appointed by our travel service. Formerly a Red Guard during the Cultural Revolution, Mr. Chen was not pleased with me, nor I with him. He seemed to have little time for my nostalgia.

When I asked to see the hospital where I was born, he took us to the new government hospital, thinking that one hospital was as good as another. "No, not that one," I pleaded. "I-chi-san is the hospital I'm looking for, and it is high on a promontory over the Yangtze."

"This is THE hospital," Mr. Chen replied. He knew he had to be polite to foreign guests as part of the People's Republic of China's "Four Modernizations," but he wasn't going to demean his ideological purity by doing it enthusiastically.

"Yes, but I'm sorry," I said. "*This* is not the hospital I'm looking for, the one where I was born."

Poor Mr. Chen. I may have been a foreign guest, but I was old, obviously a relic of the feudal period.

By pure happenstance, as we toured Wuhu, we turned up a hill, the *right* hill. There was my Methodist hospital, the one built by McKim, Mead & White and opened on December 8, 1927, the year before I was born. At the hospital, every patient, every nurse, every staff member, and every visitor crowded each other at every window to see a rare "foreign devil." Actually, four foreign devils—in person! As far as I knew, we were the first foreign devils to visit Wuhu since China was first Mao's.

Mr. Chen abandoned us to seek the head doctor of this, the Wan Nan Medical College Hospital. Irritated at being posted in the backwater of Wuhu, Dr. Li embraced us with welcoming words and endless cups of scalding tea. When I pointed southeast and asked if there was a large school somewhere in the area, Dr. Li said he knew of the Eleventh Middle School. "That's it!" I cried. Mr. Chan was distraught at these interruptions in his carefully planned 24-hour tour of Wuhu. In spite of his scowls, we drove up to St. James Middle School. Students—this time, hundreds upon hundreds of them—came rushing to the balconies and doorways to watch the spectacle of four foreign devils getting out of a shiny, clean, yellow minivan. I immediately recognized the worn steps to B. W.'s office, now the office of Mr. Tsan, the principal.

It was a stone staircase, and there were deep ruts left by generations of school children scrambling up the stairs. Halfway up, a voice called out, "Marion! Yes, it's you, Marion." He paused. "Maybe you don't remember me, but I'm Chilton, one of your father's students." I did remember. This was tall, lean, wiry Chilton, my brothers' good friend. Behind him was the son of Sister Constance's gardener, another of my childhood companions. He was now an office clerk and offered to bring us tea, his toothless smile full of glee at seeing his childhood friend after half a century.

When I asked to see my home, Mr. Tsan said he thought that was a bad idea, but I insisted and he relented. With a

Standing with George in the shambles of our childhood home.

rapidly expanding escort of students and curious others, we made our way to B. W. and Carolyn's 1920s bungalow. We were enveloped in the acrid smoke from the chimneys of an adjoining cotton mill. Mr. Tsan said the house was now home to four mill-worker families. I ducked in quickly, since some of the sagging bricks on the roof looked none too stable. The decorative glass panels on the front-door were cracked or missing. No one was home but a flurry of chickens and several scrawny dogs. An aging charcoal stove had covered the walls of the small front hall with a thick coat of coal dust.

I stopped and stared at Chilton. With a catch in my throat, and fearing the answer, I asked if any of my brothers were still in Wuhu.

"Why, yes, George, Jimmy, and Joseph, but not Stephen. He died last year. I'll go and find them right now."

This left Mr. Chen positively apoplectic. His days as a Red Guard had been stress-free in comparison. No one had told him how to handle a situation like this, and he had no idea what to do. Our minivan had stopped in an alley off a side street. Chilton had disappeared. It was only a matter of minutes before he would return—and not alone.

Reuniting with my brother George in Wuhu in 1980.

Soon enough he did return, bringing with him my brother George, whose smile stretched the width of his round face, baring his cheek bones and missing teeth. We stood transfixed, grinning foolishly with our arms held out, palms clutching tight.

George and Chilton left to bring Jimmy and Joseph to our hotel, the Iron Hill Guest House, for a banquet ordered by Mr. Chen, who by now seemed to have resigned himself to the new China. There we sat in the courtyard, around a non-functioning fountain, gaping at one another: B. W.'s four aging, balding, wrinkled children. Jimmy, retired as an accountant from the People's Hotel, had shrunk in size with age. Long grey sideburns accentuated his narrow face. Gone was any vestige of the endless, explosive energy that had won him prizes at every provincial sports event: pole vault, broad jump, and discus throwing. Seventy-year-old Joseph, a former nurse at St. James and an invaluable care-giver for B. W. both before and after his incarceration at Ash Camp, had lost his serene, gentle smile.

Although I would never see them again, we remained in

touch through letters.

Our next stop was Shanghai. Sue Peppin asked the waiter at the Ching Chian Hotel in the old French Concession where we were staying if, by any chance, he could locate my brother Roland from the address that George and Jimmy had given us. The waiter knew the location and escorted Bennett and me that same afternoon down two crowded alleys and up a dark, worn stairway. Roland had retired from the Workers' Hospital's dental clinic in 1973. A 1924 graduate of St. James, his eyesight was poor, as was his hearing, but his mind was still quick. Ellen, the educated wife he had chosen against his family's wishes, had died. I knew they had brought what food they could to B. W. at the concentration camp and handed it to him through the barbed-wire fence. They had literally kept him from starving to death. Roland's entire life had been so full of dramatic changes, suddenly seeing me standing in front of him was just one more of life's unlikely occurrences. He was living with his two daughters, Shirley and Paula, and a son. Our ties and memories had faded, but Shirley reminded me that B. W. had taken the two of us to a Shirley Temple movie in the 1930s soon after I had been evacuated from Kuling.

Thirteen years later, in 1993, George, Steve, Carolyn, and I returned to China so that I could introduce my new family to my old family. "Moon-face" William and his wife Grace joined us from Taiwan and it was from him that I learned more details about what had happened to my brothers who had remained in China through the terrors of the Cultural Revolution and the Great Leap Forward.

The Japanese had put fearless Stephen in prison for six months in 1941. Somehow, he was smuggled into Free China where he became a liaison officer for the U.S. Air Corps.

George, a middle school English teacher, "kept off the streets as much as possible." Like Jimmy, he had been forced to wear a dunce cap at the height of the Cultural Revolution when their ties to an American cost them most dearly. Accused of being a spy, Jimmy was sent to a labor camp to break stones. Later, he too managed to escape into Free China and work for the War Area Service Corps.

Since 1993, I have kept in touch with my Chinese family by phone, letters, and emails. I have a picture of my brother George and my husband George walking hand in hand down a Wuhu street. My brother argued that he ranked No. 1, since he was the first George in my life.

As my brothers died, I have remained in contact with their children. George No. 1 died in October 1996 of pancreatic cancer. But his son Jim proudly informed me that his own son Tiger ranked in the top hundred students in the entire province to qualify for Wuhu's best high school. Tiger went on to university in Sydney, Australia. My father had wanted his boys to have good educations, and now their children and grandchildren were benefitting from the start he gave their families.

When I go out my side door here in my retirement in Aiken, South Carolina, and turn East to pick up my newspapers, I always smile. In my mind, I am facing a rising sun, and listening once again to the SFLI loudspeaker: "The East is Red, the sun rises. From China arises Mao Tse-tung. He strives for the people's happiness. Hurrah, he is the peoples' great savior!"

Three times a year Jim reminds me that they have just burned shoe-shaped gold and silver paper, designed for the souls of the departed who were "dearest to us when they were alive:" George, George's mother, and

B. W. The sparkling paper prayer pyre is lit on October 18 to commemorate the day George died. It is also lit on Qingming, or Tomb Sweeping Day; on the Festival for the Departed; and on the Winter Solstice.

MEXICO

Mexico City ★ • Veracruz
         • Puebla

MEXICO

Which was it going to be, Moscow or Mexico City? Smith College had just initiated a Junior-Year-Abroad Program, and students at Wheaton College, my school, were among the lucky ones allowed to apply.

Moscow was very tempting. During my first day at Wheaton in September 1947, I had glimpsed the school's new Russian professor, an extremely handsome Russian émigré named Dr. Nicholas Vakar. It was immediately clear to me that I needed to begin learning Russian, which I did, and equally clear that I should spend my junior year abroad in Moscow. Clear, that is, until the onset of the Cold War, and all student travel to Moscow was canceled.

Mexico City, my second choice, became my first. As a Spanish major, logically, I should have chosen Mexico City from the beginning, but at that age logic wasn't much of a factor.

I knew little of Mexico, but I started reading books by writers such as Gabriel García Márquez, often known as Magical Realists for the way they embraced a feeling for the magical and infused it into their experience of the rational world. Sixty years later, Mexico's magical reality has stayed with me. I saw the country the way Chile's illustrious poet Pablo Neruda did. "I came to the Anahuac plateau," he wrote in 1940, six years before I arrived there, "to breathe what Alfonso Reyes hailed as the most transparent region of the air—Mexico with its prickly pear and its serpent; Mexico blossoming and thorny, dry and lashed by hurricane winds, violent in outline and color, violent in eruption and creation, surrounded me with its magic and its extraordinary light."

An esteemed writer and intellectual, Alfonso Reyes, was president of the Colegio de Mexico when he welcomed Neruda, the newly appointed Chilean Consul, to the country. He was still president of the Colegio when 14 college juniors from different colleges on the East Coast, including me, arrived under the auspices of the Smith College Junior-Year-Abroad Program for a year at his school. Reyes had founded the Colegio in 1940 as a think-tank for a group of intellectuals exiled from Spain's terrible Civil War. It

The first Smith College Junior-Year-Abroad group in Mexico, with me at upper right.

is still astonishing to me all these years later that he was able to gather Mexico's most illustrious artists, historians, archaeologists, and journalists into a single institution, and even more astonishing that he gave us American kids real access to them.

Most of us could read and write Spanish passingly well, but none of us could speak even the most rudimentary Spanish. Only two words came easily off our tongues: *platano* (banana) and *chocolate*—hardly the foundation for intellectual discourse with our elite "professors" at the Colegio on subjects ranging from Tenochtitlan to the Mexico's muralists.

To force us to learn to speak the language, we were divided into small groups and sent to Puebla, in the hinterland, where English was not spoken as widely as in Mexico City. Three of us—Suzy, Betty, and I—were deposited at the front door of 6 Sur 306. Our carefully chosen hosts, Judge Sarmiento and his wife, and their daughter Conchita— who would soon be graduating from law school herself— welcomed us warmly to their lovely home in Spanish. We were also bombasted with Spanish at a formal class in town for an entire month. Learning to conjugate verbs was certainly one method of increasing fluency, but far more valuable were our informal conversations on the patio of the Sarmiento home. The family lived on the second floor, at a safe distance from our rooms on the first floor, where they opened onto the patio. More to the point, across the patio, we faced the rooms of eight handsome young medical students who spoke not a word of English.

One night, not long after we arrived, we were woken by a mariachi band, courtesy of our new patio friends.

It wasn't long before Betty had selected a med student

Toni and me and Betty and Armando.

named Armando as her private tutor, and I had selected one named Toni. All of this was actually quite innocent—it was, after all, 1948. We explored every church, every plaza, every nook and cranny of Puebla de Los Angeles. The beautiful, ice-capped, but still-active volcano Popocatépetl could always be seen in the distance.

Our preferred haunt was the Agua Azul, a swimming pool and dance hall on the outskirts of Puebla. Named after the sulfur-rich hot springs nearby, the Agua Azul—the Blue Water—was as enchanting as it was inexpensive. Toni, who was not only studying but working overtime at the Comisario de Policia, was short on both money and time. He always seemed to have one more gun wound to sew up or one more autopsy to review before we could head to the Agua Azul. So I spent many evenings outside the police morgue waiting for him, engaged in my own schoolwork. It all seemed very romantic.

The four of us also became regular commuters on the

two-hour bumpy bus ride between Puebla and Mexico City. By the time Betty and I and the others returned to the Colegio in the capital, we had an inkling of what lay ahead for us.

One day, Betty and Armando and Toni and I drifted leisurely around the lake of Xochimilco in a small boat named the *Yolando*, surrounded by flowers and romantic music. Another day, we took canoes to the *chinampas*, ancient floating gardens grown on shallow lake bottoms. We stopped at the market place in Milpa Alta, where the people were still speaking a language called Nahualt. We visited an old woman in her ramshackle hut to see weaving done "as it should be." In a dark corner of the hut was an altar with the usual profusion of images of Christ and the Virgin, along with an offering to Tlaloc, the ancient God of Rain.

How does one fall in love with a city—the *Nueva Grandeza Mexicana*, the New Mexican Greatness—overnight? There before me was the entire capital, "stretched out among the centuries, alive, and eternal," in the words of the Mexican poet Salvador Novo López.

Our language instructor was an energetic young man named Felipe Barraza, who was much better at teaching grammar than at telling the time. Day after day, he showed up to class late, moaning about so much to do and so little time to do it.

One brave student eventually asked him why he didn't just get a watch.

"Never," he replied. "It would remind me of the hour of my death."

Obviously, Barraza's thinking was infused with as much magic as realism.

Each of the professors that Alfonso Reyes had somehow brought into the Colegio was a leader in his field, if not *the* leader. Our literature instructor was Agustin Yañez, the novelist, essayist, and politician. One of his most brilliant and beloved novels *Al Filo de Agua—The Edge of the Storm—* had been published the year before we arrived in Mexico. There was enough Indian in his DNA to date his ancestry back to precolonial days. And those were the days he concentrated on in class, including his favorite, the poetry of Sor Juana Ines de la Cruz, a 17th-century nun in the New Spain. Yañez would go on to become the Governor of the state of Jalisco from 1953 to 1959 and the Minister of Education from 1964 to 1970.

Daniel Ruben de la Borbolla was the country's top anthropologist and archaeologist. It was at his urging that 14 of us climbed the pyramids and other ruins at Teotihuacán, Tlalmanalco, Chimalhuacán, and Papantla. If we couldn't pronounce it, that's where we went.

We visited Papantla, just slightly north of Veracruz, during its annual festival. We walked through the narrow cobbled streets, darting between swerving buses with their roofs piled high with potatoes and vegetables. We swarmed past Don Hernando's fragrant vanilla warehouse, a small bullfighting ring, and a whirling pink Ferris wheel. Graceful Indian women in starched white cotton dresses and intricate lace shawls stopped to stare at us. We were the only ones not dressed for the fiesta. The air was filled with deafening chatter, the cries of vendors, and the beats of marimba bands. A couple of us plopped down on a bench in the town's main plaza, sipping a mixture of Teohuacán water, red wine, and fruit juice, waiting for the day's pageantry to unfold.

Long before white men had arrived on the shore of Veracruz, each year the most exemplary youths from the surrounding villages had been chosen to honor the Gods of Wind and Rain. Beginning a week before the festival, they had to agree to abstain from alcohol (a local brew called *pulque* made from a plant called *maguey*), tobacco, and sex. Of these youths, the five most impressive had to climb a thick rope attached to a 100-foot pole located just outside the town cathedral. When they accomplished this feat, the cathedral bells rang for noonday mass.

While continuing to honor these ancient rituals, Mexico was rushing full-throttle into the future, and I felt its energy. In the morning, we would read about Aztec rituals and punishments; in the afternoon, Professor Zavala took us from the fundamentals of Aztec religion and society into the whirlpool of communism, socialism, and anarchism brewing around us in modern Mexico. I had actually heard Alexander Kerensky, the exiled chairman of the Russian Provincial Government, lecture in Boston on a weekend visit from Wheaton. I knew that Leon Trotsky, the founder of the Red Army and the leader of the Menshevik division of the Russian Communist Party, had sought asylum from Stalin's wrath in Mexico in 1936. Instead, he had been assassinated at his home in Coyuacán on Stalin's orders. Trotsky had been a neighbor of Diego Rivera, who was the person who had convinced President Lázaro Cárdenas to give him refuge in Mexico. The busy labor leader, Vicente Lombardo Toledano, even received Betty and me and gave us a lecture on his efforts to raise workers' hourly wages in a uniquely practical Mexican brand of Marxism.

I sat riveted, listening to the master himself, Rivera, at a conference at the Universidad Nacional. He was a large, messy man, with eyes the shape of saucers, hair that flipped behind his ears, and an enchanting smile. His subject was supposed to be modern Mexican art, of which he was one of the three leaders, but he began his lecture by condemning General MacArthur and the rest of us imperialists from the United States, and went on to harangue the existing Mexican government for the terrible social conditions in the country at large.

Our own professor of modern art, José Chávez Morado, made no secret of being a communist himself and showed us that social dynamics were a significant force behind the contemporary Mexican Renaissance in mural painting. Since the Revolution, Mexico had been examining its indigenous and colonial pasts in order to discover an authentic future. So, in addition to creating paintings of great beauty, the muralists—Rivera, David Alfaro Siqueiros, and especially José Clemente Orozco—were providing a civil education for the populace. Morado and his fellow artists were convinced that art could help enhance an emerging modern Mexican identity.

When I was assigned Orozco as the subject of my most important paper—a kind of mini-dissertation—I was actually upset. I had requested to interview Luis Barragán, the architect. Many years later, in 1980, he would win the the Pritzker Prize, the most important prize in the field of architecture. But I was already mad about Barragán's work, mostly residential buildings with stucco walls in sculptural geometric forms, often painted with the country's intense blues, reds, and oranges—intensified by Mexico's cerulean blue skies. His landscaping often included pools of water, filled continuously by water falling from rooftop sources. He had a flair for combining intellectual rigor with a touch of the unexpected, the monumental with the charming. Orozco's name, by contrast, meant almost nothing to me. I pleaded with Morado to let me switch to Barragán, but he told me that his decision was final. It would be some time before I fully realized my good fortune, since arrangements would be made for each Smith Program student to interview the subject of our paper one on one. Orozco was already seen as the towering genius of the Mexican artistic renaissance, and his stature would only grow with time. Barragán himself had designed the studio where I interviewed Orozco. That he agreed to spare time for a 20-year old American student speaks volumes about the humility of the most illustrious of Mexico's three illustrious muralists. He had even been commissioned to paint major murals in the United States, including "Prometheus" for Pomona College in California, "Quetzacoatl" for Dartmouth in New Hampshire, and a cycle of five politically-charged murals for the New School for Social Research in New York City.

I was so clueless that I didn't even follow up with the other two most prominent muralists, Rivera and Siqueiros, even though Morado had given me their phone numbers. I had seen both of them in public spaces. I knew their political thinking. I knew what a mural was. I foolishly decided that was enough.

At least I followed up with Orozco himself. I don't remember much about that hour-long interview other than a long window stretching behind an old man. He wore large, round, black-framed glasses. I didn't even notice that his left hand was missing.

Orozco had begun his career as a political cartoonist and had gone on to study at the European-style Academia de Bellas Artes on the assumption that every artist should know the basics. Still, he lamented that Mexicans seemed able to paint only in a European style. He sought liberation from that "foreign tyranny" and believed academia itself was "nothing but a warehouse storing mummies and fossils." So Orozco, like his fellow muralists, combined aspects of European painting with subjects and stylistic elements from Mexico's precolonial past to create works that targeted the plight of the poor in a postcolonial capitalist system.

My own professor of art, Morado, was also communist, but he was somewhat less political than his three more famous colleagues. Always calm and relaxed, he saw "reality and fantasy as the most profound elements" in his own painting—the visual extension of the Magical Realist tradition in Mexican literature. I was able to interview him for an article in the *Summer Bulletin of the National University,* in his home, over tea and toast with orange marmalade. We students, he told me, should not be blinded by the exoticism of our temporary home. Mexico, he told me, was "not a nightclub or a fairground where tequila, chili con carne, and hot tamales are the main attractions."

But it was an impossible mandate, with the tequila, champagne, wine, and *posadas*—a frappe made from red wine and rich cream—available everywhere. And certainly not with the bullfights.

I saw my first in Puebla, but in Mexico City, whenever I had enough pesetas, I went to sit in the cheaper, sunnier, hotter side of the bull ring. I was obsessed with the famous matadors of the day—Armillita, Procuna, Fermin Espinosa, and Arruza. I had seen *Blood and Sand* starring Tyrone Power and Rita Hayworth way back in the early 1940s, but a real bullfight was no movie. It was exotic, true enough, but *real*: first, the picadors, equestrian toreadors, thrust their lances at the snorting bulls from the comparative safety of their stout mounts, working the bulls into a frenzy of rage, then the swift-footed matadors, twirling their enormous red capes further tormented the creatures, with the cheering crowd releasing its own pent-up energy.

It was all very gruesome, but somehow amoral in the way that Ernest Hemingway described it in *Death in the Afternoon*: "I know only that what is moral is what you feel good after and what is immoral is what you feel bad after and judged by those moral standards, which I do not defend, the bullfight is very moral to me because I feel very fine while it is going on and have a feeling of life and death and mortality and immortality, and after it is over I feel very sad but very fine."

This was heady stuff for the daughter of a missionary, as electrifying as the nightclubs we seemed to go to every night. One might wonder how much studying we managed to do, and the truth was very little, but our Spanish was becoming absolutely fluent. One night, I sat blissfully listening to Agustin Lara, the forlorn popular pianist and songwriter who sang tenderly of his love for the wondrously beautiful film star María Félix, his then-wife. Another evening, at Ciro's, there at the next table was Tyrone Power, in the flesh.

Professor Morado would not have been impressed, but my reality was being imbued with the magic of celebrity.

Christmas brought me back to reality in the form of my missionary father, B. W., still recovering from his four-year nightmare at the Japanese concentration camp in Shanghai. Medically evacuated to Boston by the U.S. Navy, he was, two years later, still a sick man, but well enough to pay a visit to me in Mexico—the strongest memory I have from my entire relationship with him. He literally hitchhiked his way down to Mexico City, lecturing at one church after another about China and the importance of the missions, in order to see me.

As tour guide, I escorted him to "my" Mexico. We visited all the main tourist attractions, but, to my astonishment, B. W. even joined Toni and me for a glass of champagne at one of the nightclubs.

When I gave my father a goodbye hug at the airport, I had no idea it would be the last time I would see him. He was happy to be going back to his Chinese family, and I was happy at the thought of visiting China again—his college graduation gift to me. But I never made that trip. With Mao tightening his hold over China, B. W. was tasked with closing down the operations of the Episcopal Church in the country. Heartbroken, he was scheduled to leave China only weeks before he died on July 4, 1951. At least he knew that I was about to marry someone named George Naifeh in February.

As my days in Mexico dwindled, I often wandered into a contemporary art gallery, the Galeria de Arte Mexicano. Although I had no money for a work of art, the gallery allowed me to browse freely. However, one look at "The Horseman"—a man's body with an abstracted horse's head—by Guillermo Meza and I *had* to own it. Meza had drawn a perfect embodiment of Magical Realism in charcoal and crayon in preparation for a backdrop for a ballet.

With Guillermo's blessing, the gallery promised not to sell the drawing until I could earn the $100 asking price—something it took me an entire summer soda-jerking in

Massachusetts to accomplish.

In 1995, when George and I took a trip to Acapulco, we stopped in Mexico City. I found Meza's gallery, which informed me that the artist was still alive, and, when they called him, informed me that he remembered my purchase from almost half a century earlier. Meza invited George and me to come out to his studio. Before leaving it, he gave me an etching of a young man, his head covered by a mask, based on the skeleton of what had probably been an eagle's head. His message was that we all wear masks to protect our identities, unless magic has reconfigured our reality.

My reality would soon turn to yet another completely different part of the world.

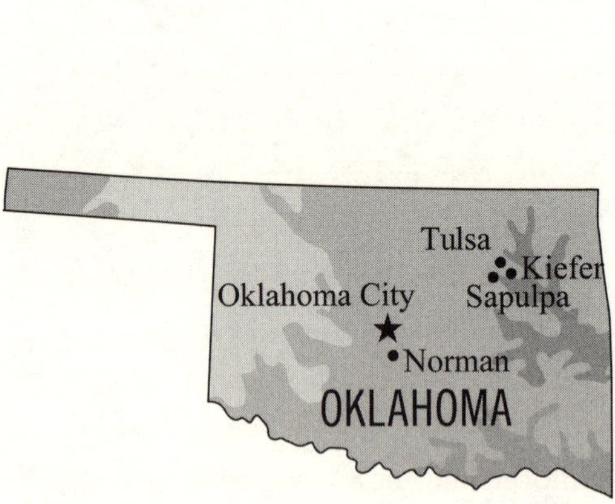
Tulsa
Kiefer
Oklahoma City
Sapulpa
Norman
OKLAHOMA

BABY BOY

When I graduated from Wheaton, my grammar instructor in Mexico City offered me a job at an English-Spanish newspaper there. Toni had been writing me obsessively and had even proposed marriage. I got as far as the Worcester Greyhound bus stop. Waiting on a high stool, I took one sip from the cup of coffee on the counter in front of me and had an epiphany that was I not cut out to be a doctor's wife in Mexico, I jumped down from the stool and took the bus back to No. 10 Willard Avenue.

The front door was open. Aunt Mina was upstairs cleaning. I yelled, "I'm home." Aunt Mina never said a word.

Now, I couldn't even be a soda-jerk at the Tatnuck House, my job in previous summers. The owner had offered the job to someone else. My graduation gift—a trip back to Wuhu—was out, now that Mao had sealed his grip on China. There was nothing to do but go to graduate school, the inevitable goal of the aimless and the uncertain.

The School of Advanced International Studies (SAIS) of Johns Hopkins was located in Washington, rather than the main Baltimore campus, a location selected for its proximity to the government we were studying and the source of the jobs we hoped for when we graduated. SAIS was the brainchild of Christian A. Herter and Paul H. Nitze, both of whom were in the middle of distinguished government careers. Both realized that, in America, a graduate program in international relations only existed at Tufts, in Boston, far from the hands-on government professionals who could serve as tutors and mentors. Great Britain's world dominance was slipping dramatically in the aftermath of World War II, and America was stepping into its place. We needed lots of foreign experts, and we needed them quickly.

The problem was that to most Americans, much of the world was basically terra incognita. Missionaries and missionary children were practically the only exceptions. But though we knew other languages and other countries, most government officers considered us hopelessly idealistic.

In 1949, President Theodore Roosevelt's grandson, Kermit Roosevelt, made fun of missionaries, describing the first clumsy steps of the U.S. in the Middle East as those of "a comic juggler, a ventriloquist's dummy, a somnambulist, or a real-life missionary who suddenly finds himself plunked down before Broadway's footlights playing opposite Tallulah Bankhead." Mr. Roosevelt took the stage himself in Tehran three years later, when he helped engineer the fateful and ultimately counterproductive overthrow of the duly-elected Prime Minister Mossadegh.

On my first day at SAIS, I found myself seated with men, men, and more men. Our 1950 student body comprised 60 men and only three women. Most of the men were veterans of the recent war and were married, but some boarded at the school. I had my meals with the boarders. I arrived in Washington by train the first night, but the train was late, so I had to rush to dinner. There was only one empty seat, and it was all the way across the dining-room. With my head bowed in embarrassment, I steered myself in that direction. To my horror, every single student in the all-male room stood up, and stayed standing, while I walked the gangplank. Wheaton, in my day, had still been all female, so the SAIS culture shock was severe.

Given my childhood ties to China, I could have chosen to take Paul Linebarger's courses on the Far East and possibly his course on psychological warfare. He had spent many years in China, where his father had been a legal adviser to Sun Yat-sen, and he had been a close friend of Chiang Kai-shek. But he made it clear that he didn't want women in his class. He considered us, however few we were, a "distraction." According to school lore, he could be pretty distracting himself. He had a glass eyeball which he would scoop out of its socket and throw on the floor to "get the attention of daydreaming students."

Linebarger was an academic, but like most of the faculty at SAIS, he was intimately involved in the management of postwar international matters. Francis O. Wilcox, my lecturer on international organizations, had been Chief of Staff of the Senate Foreign Relations Committee. John Loftus was currently serving the State Department as an expert on petroleum. From him, we learned how the petroleum concessions had been awarded largely at the direction of Calouste Gulbenkian, a British businessman and imperialist who had been prominent in former Ottoman days. My thesis adviser at SAIS was Spruille Braden, former Ambassador to Colombia, Cuba, and Argentina, who was deeply involved in lobbying for Anaconda Copper in Chile and for United

Fruit in Central America, which would later come to be considered among the worst excesses of American imperialism. Both the faculty of the Colegio de Mexico and all the young Mexican students I had befriended would have been appalled that I was now one of his students.

But I had far more important things on my mind than imperialism, British or American.

Now that Toni was miles far away in the past, I found myself spending a lot of time with Dillard Spriggs, who was also in the Latin American Section. His roommate, by chance, happened to be a George Naifeh. Theirs was one of the dormitory rooms above the classrooms and dining room in the large SAIS building on Florida Avenue. When I mentioned the two of them in my letters to Aunt Mina, I referred to George, who was an Arab-American, as "el Arab."

Dillard was Texas born and bred. We seriously discussed getting married; fellow students assumed we would. Dillard's parents were professors at one of the state colleges. However, a day came when Dillard told me that we would have to live by his rules, then literally itemized them in a manner that was more that of a boss than that of a husband. The conversation went south from there.

It didn't help that I was quickly finding his roommate more interesting than I found him. Six months after graduating from SAIS, I called Aunt Mina to tell her that I was going to marry "el Arab." She was hostess that night for her bridge group. I could hear her hold her breath for a second before asking me if I thought I could adjust to living in a tent. The next morning a friend from Worcester called and said, "Ye Gods, what did you tell Aunt Mina last night?"

So I called Aunt Mina again and informed her that although George was of Arab origin—his parents had

George - Baby Boy.

been born in parts of Syria that had become Lebanon and Jordan—he was born in Kiefer, Oklahoma. In fact, I was the one with the problematic background. When George applied for a marriage license from the Maryland County Clerk in Rockville, the clerk pointed to my birthplace and said he could not marry someone of the "Yellow" race; actually, Maryland was one of the states that had just repealed its miscegenation laws. So the bureaucrat was uninformed as well as a racist. George told him that my parents were missionaries, and with some suspicion, he decided to give us the license anyway.

George's childhood was much more "American" than mine. He was the youngest of six children, which is why his family called him Baby Boy. His three older brothers shooed him away when they played marbles or poker with their friends behind the gas station. His brothers knew how to jitterbug and were known to wear zoot suits to a honky-tonk. George had played clarinet in the school band. Benny, his older brother, had bought it for him on an installment plan. George had been on hay rides; he had watched floats in holiday parades. He had been to State Fairs. He had eaten hot dogs hot off a grill.

He had also had days when there was nothing to eat. Nothing. Thanks to the Depression, his father Charlie lost not just his Kiefer grocery store, but his jobs at Morning Dry Goods and at Sooner Wholesale. He took orders on credit and was known for writing those orders with a singular, confident flourish: He was the most literate of his fellow Kiefer immigrants from Lebanon and Jordan (then still known as Syria). But much of the time he couldn't collect from his customers or pay his suppliers. So even though he was in the food business, there was never enough food to feed his own family.

One morning, when George's mother Saida was home and Baby Boy was busy doing nothing, he saw a welfare wagon pulled by a weary horse starting to climb up Standpipe Hill, where they lived in a ramshackle hut. The wagon stopped at every house and the driver offered flour, sugar, prunes, and cooking oil for free.

"Mama, come quick!" he said, racing into the house.

Saida followed him to the edge of the embankment to take a good look.

"That is not for us, Baby Boy. Shame on you! That's for the poor people." He was too young to understand why pride could be more important than food.

He was still hungry when he grew old enough to attend school. He watched carefully as other children ran into Mr. Easley's grocery store with long lists on scraps of paper. Minutes later, they came out with bags bulging with cans, vegetables, and fruit. A few days later he marched into Mr. Easley's with his own long list. He could barely print the letters: peanut butter, plums, candy, and grapes. He loved the big red grapes with seeds he could spit out, far out. Mr. Easley read the list carefully, his glasses slipping down on his nose. His large white apron flapping, he walked to the full shelves and barrel bins and returned with the magical load to pile on the counter and add up the prices.

"Where is the money for all this, Baby Boy?" he asked kindly.

"I don't know."

"But Baby Boy, you need money to get all this."

"The other kids come in with lists and no money," he said, his lips quivering. "I've watched. And you give them what they want."

A neighbor named Junior Mitchell had a mom who was always yelling for her wandering cows—"Mabel," "Martha," and "Minnie"—that grazed on the hill behind Baby Boy's house. Year after year, Junior never crossed Baby Boy's path without yelling out: "Sheenie, sheenie, bob-tail wienie." Baby Boy had no idea what the words meant, but they sounded mean and nasty. He decided to ask Mrs. Adams, his Sunday school teacher. She was sweet, and like all of the church workers in town, except for Mrs. Jones at the Methodist Church who played the slot machine on Sunday afternoons at Minerva's Drugstore, Mrs. Adams seemed to know everything. She gave him the gold star every Sunday for the best Sunday school attendance.

"Sheenie? Why, Baby Boy, of course—you are sheenie. You're Jewish." His skin was brown. The people of Kiefer called Standpipe Hill "Jew Hill." Sometimes in the dark of night, if one stood on Standpipe looking across to another hill, one could see fires burning. People said hateful men were putting up crosses to lynch Jews and blacks. And possibly brown-skinned people like him. In fact, one night,

George at left with his sister Julia, brother Sam, mother Saida, and father Charlie.

the Ku Klux Klan burned a cross in front of *his* house.

Baby Boy somehow knew that it was useless to try to explain to Mrs. Adams or Junior Mitchell what a Syrian Orthodox Christian was. But he had a plan.

When there was flour, his mother made large loaves of *maroof*, a very thin, flat Middle Eastern bread. She would take balls of raised dough and flip them onto a plow disk placed over the gas stove burners to cook. One day, Baby Boy took two of the loaves to class—a class that included Junior Mitchell.

"See this bread," he told his classmates. "I'll give you each a piece. Then you will have eaten the same bread Jesus ate. When they were little, my mom and dad lived where Jesus lived."

George's older brothers, who played football for Kiefer High, had a more direct response to the anti-Semitism they were experiencing. Kiefer had a population of fewer than 200 people, so they easily figured out who was wearing the sheets of the Ku Klux Klan and paid them a very serious visit. A few fisticuffs later, the Kiefer branch of the KKK ended its policy of cross-burning.

Actually, the town was a weird combination of intolerant and tolerant.

George's mother was terrified that those same three eldest sons, who were star football players, would injure themselves on the football field. It was understood that if there was an injury during a game, the game couldn't be started again until Mrs. Naifeh came onto the field and could be assured that no one had suffered serious harm. When she died in her forties in 1938—George was only 14 at the time of her death—Mrs. McGinty, the Post Mistress, flew the flag over the post office at half-mast. The entire school was let out to attend her service at the Methodist Church.

So, when George entered high school, he was pretty much on his own. Then came Pearl Harbor. His oldest brother Sam's deafness kept him out of the war, but Benny was already in the Navy and Jimmie left for the Army. George knew he would be drafted and wanted to join the Army Air Force. But he also knew that you had to pass

George in the Army Air Force in World War II.

some relatively stringent tests to get into the Air Force and that his A average at Kiefer High didn't really mean much. He was also a half-credit short of the language requirement in Latin. So he got himself transferred to Tulsa Central High so that he could graduate from a better school with a better education.

He befriended the Latin teacher, and convinced her to tutor him, and talked the admissions officer at Tulsa University into admitting him to T.U., all to improve his chances of being admitted into the Air Force. His number came up in August, and he got his wings by passing the obligatory I.Q. test at Fort Sill.

Trained as a tail gunner, he was assigned to the 490th Bomb Group of the Army 8th Air Force in England, flying over enemy targets in Germany. While stationed at Diss Air Base in Norfolk, he took a three-month course to become a radio operator. Unlike most of his fellow airmen, he blew his pay not on poker, but on the theater in London. He saw Noel Coward in "Private Lives" at the Apollo. He saw "Happy and Glorious" at the Paladium, "Something in the Air" at the Palace, and "The Lisbon Story" at the Stoll. Much of his new life in the Air Force was welcome to him: new skills, affordable theater, and three square meals a day.

But there was also fear. A flight crew got fresh eggs and bacon each morning they flew on a mission. On the morning of February 6, 1943, he enjoyed a full meal of scrambled eggs. His B-17 was headed for a bombing mission that day. As the radio operator, George was usually tasked with throwing the chaff—a cloud of confetti-like pieces of aluminum that confused the radar on enemy antiaircraft— from the plane window. On February 6, the mission was going to be so complicated and George was going to be so busy on the radio that an extra man was added to George's radio room to throw out the chaff. In spite of the chaff cluttering the sky and the particularly heavy enemy fire exploding all around them, his plane accurately hit its target, some railroad tracks in Cologne.

On the return flight, over enemy-occupied Strasbourg, France, another plane collided with his, splitting it in two just behind George's seat. Because his radio space was cramped, his parachute was on the floor. Instinctively, even as the plane collapsed around him, George picked up the parachute and snapped it on. He missed one of the two snaps as he crawled out of the ragged hole, watching the chaff thrower, who hadn't had time to put on his parachute, fall to his death. Then George lost consciousness. He came to, not far from the ground, falling diagonally because he was missing one of the two snaps. He had enough wits about him not to try to fix the missing snap, and left things alone, hoping for the best.

As he landed, he saw a group of peasants running towards him wielding hatchets and knives, and he panicked. His Air Force briefing had been very clear: "Do not give yourself up to an enemy civilian; he hates you and he will kill you. It is OK to hand yourself over to enemy troops, who are governed by the Geneva Conventions. But civilians are another thing." George tugged at the parachute, which caused him to fall into a tree and then onto the ground, severely spraining his ankle.

But fortune was on his side. The peasants were members of the French underground. After treating his ankle and hiding him in a cave until the way was clear, they got him back to safety in Free France.

Eight months later, he was honorably discharged as a

Staff Sergeant, earning a Purple Heart, an Oak Leaf cluster, an Air Medal, and four battle stars. Soon he was accepted into the University of Oklahoma, all four years paid for by the GI Bill.

But what to do with that degree? Even with his efforts at Central High School in Tulsa, he basically had a Kiefer education, and that meant pretty mediocre grades at OU. But he wanted to try to obtain a graduate degree at SAIS, the same School of Advanced International Studies in Washington where I was headed. With such a mediocre academic transcript, he had to bank everything on the interview.

As he entered the interview room, he saw the SAIS admission committee—six intimidating professors—poring over his papers and appraising his qualifications.

"Listen," he said. "If you base my admission on my grades in college, you will never let me in. Could I please ask you to close your folders for a minute and let me explain to you what an excellent diplomatic envoy I will be to the Arab world?"

It worked. They admitted him with his C average from OU.

On the first day in language class, his Arabic teacher asked if anyone in the class knew any Arabic. George would later say, "I was a fool to raise my hand."

"Let's hear some of your Arabic," said the young instructor, who was from Iraq.

"Hut el laham fi el stuuv."

"And what does that mean?"

"It means 'Put the meat in the oven.'"

"And where did you learn this Arabic?"

"At home, listening to my mother."

"It sounds like it. That's some garbled combination of Arabic and English. Maybe you better *forget* your Arabic and start from scratch. Now, let's all turn to the text."

Among the professors invited to give a guest lecture at SAIS was Colonel William A. Eddy, and George was fortunate enough to be appointed his student guide while he was at the school. Col. Eddy had worked in the Middle East, like his father and grandfather before him, both of whom had served as missionaries in Lebanon. His grandfather went to Lebanon in 1854—in fact, he offered the prayers at the 1866 opening of the Syrian Protestant College (today's American University of Beirut). A century and a half later, I can think of no single initiative by the United States in the Middle East that has had a better impact on our relations with the region. In Col. Eddy's papers, which he donated to Princeton, he is listed as "educator, diplomat, minister to Saudi Arabia, intelligence agent, and college president."

Col. Eddy had served as translator when FDR met King Abdul Aziz on the *U.S.S. Quincy* on February 4, 1945. He had enough command of Arabic—and enough sensitivity to Arab sensibilities—that he was able to convince Abdul Aziz that, instead of the 100 sheep he wanted to be brought on board each day to be slaughtered for fresh meat, seven sheep each day would suffice. He later wrote that he was "the only link in language and customs between the 269 Naval personnel and the 48 Saudi Arabs on board." He had "a 24-hour job interpreting and mediating: I had to stop Arab servants from making coffee on charcoal burners over the dynamite."

Col. Eddy's visit to SAIS was in the spring of 1950. George and he had such an instant rapport that, since Col. Eddy was still a full-time consultant to ARAMCO, George applied to him for a job. George got the job, but at the time ARAMCO wasn't allowing dependents to accompany employees to Saudi Arabia—there wasn't any family housing—and George planned to ask me to marry him.

Col. Eddy was very understanding—in fact, he suggested that this son, Bill Eddy, Jr., who was an Episcopalian priest in suburban Maryland, perform the marriage ceremony. He did, and Col. Eddy came to the wedding on February 3, 1951.

I was having some problems of my own finding a suitable job. Spring was the season for prospective employers to come to recruit. Because I was in the Latin America section, I signed up for a job interview with the representative from Eli Lilly, a pharmaceutical company, for a position in Latin America.

When I entered the office, he gave me a startled glance: "What are you doing here?"

"I'm a student here. I am looking into possible jobs in Latin America."

He started eyeing at me, beginning with my feet, rising inch by inch, until he locked eyes with me. "We prefer our women in the home," he said, bringing the interview to an end.

This was hardly unusual at the time. Just for perspective, Supreme Court Justice Sandra Day O'Connor, who graduated from Stanford Law School in 1952, wrote that she spent a very long time "trying, without success, to find a job as a lawyer." The concept of diversity hiring did not yet exist.

But after knocking on closed doors for months, the Organization of American States—or the Pan American Union—let me in. I was appointed Reference Librarian, which basically meant that I sat at a desk in the corner of a gorgeous flower-filled, palm tree-shaded atrium. There was even a brightly colored parrot darting about. The only question I remember having to research was from *National Geographic*—someone wanted to know how many fish were in Lake Titicaca in Bolivia.

Adding to my delight in finding a paying job was finding a new place to live. On a bulletin board at the Pan American Union, someone named Emma Reyes had listed a room in her second-floor apartment on Girard Street. Emma, it turned out, was a painter from Colombia who was working at the Pan American Union on a UNESCO-funded project to combat illiteracy in Latin America. Her glorious drawings were used to illustrate such texts as *Vacunaron a Los Otros Niños* (They Vaccinated Other Children), *Quieres Saber Algo de la Historia de America?* (Do You Want to Learn Something about the History of America?), and *San Francisco de Asís*. I applied, and she let me into her apartment and her life. Emma understood English, but chose, on principle, not to speak it. Rooming with her was very good for my Spanish.

Emma was slightly exotic, slightly mysterious, slightly masked. She had the striking dark good looks of her largely Indian heritage and long black hair. She had piercing black eyes that missed nothing. Listening to me talk on and on about SAIS, the world, and my former classmates, she suggested that my friends and I were too "intellectualized," that we talked about ideas and not emotional realities.

Emma had been abandoned at birth by her parents, who left her and her older sister Helena under the care of a woman named Maria, who kept them virtually locked up in a shack without windows and with little food. When she turned four, Emma was allowed to leave the shack, but only to empty a heavy chamber pot at a dunghill on the far edge of town. At the dunghill, she met another impoverished child, a handicapped boy she called El Cojo, Spanish for 'lame.' The two of them built a statue made of sand and filth that represented a deity they invented, whom they called General Rebollo. After playing "a thousand and one games" that they invented around the General, one day El Cojo announced that the General had died. They decided to bury him, but he was too heavy, so they had to whack him into pieces and then bury each piece.

Emma said that, in a childhood lived at the edge of a dung heap, one "grows to understand hunger, cold, and death."

Yet, the worst was still to ome. After moving Emma and Helena briefly to a new town, Maria abandoned them at a railroad station. Emma was five years old. A policeman and a priest found the two sisters and turned them over to a convent that cared for the poorest of Bogota's abandoned children—if one could call it caring. The nuns employed the girls as child laborers to sew and embroider garments for Bogota's elite. When she wet her bed, she was told that the soup she was given was made from boiled rats—the rats she had seen scurrying about in the kitchen.

The girls received no education whatsoever, except in religion. They were told all about El Niño, the baby Jesus, and especially about El Diablo, the devil, who would punish them for not following the convent's rules. Emma was jealous that, whereas she had no father, El Niño had three: a carpenter; a wealthy, older man who owned the entire world and lived up beyond the clouds; and the Holy Spirit. One day, she and Helena talked each other into climbing a tree in the patio to see if they could see the old man who lived up above the sky. They got caught in the tree and could not climb down. When Emma pricked her finger on a needle, she was terrified that the Holy Spirit, who lived inside her, would leak out.

The convent orphanage was so tightly closed that the girls were never allowed to leave the building. A priest—the only man they ever saw—came every Sunday to say Mass. He opened the convent door from an unfathomable outside world, locked the door behind him, and hung his key on a kitchen wall. Alone in the kitchen one day, Emma, who was 18 by then, yet still totally illiterate, took the key, unlocked the convent door, and walked into the streets of Bogota for the first time.

Somehow, she soon found out that her father came from a prominent family. In fact, *his* father—Rafael Reyes—had been President of Colombia. She sought her father out, but he would have nothing to do with the daughter of some long-forgotten mistress. Emma traveled as far as Argentina and Uruguay, where she married a sculptor, Guillermo Botero Gutierrez. They had a son who was killed as an infant during the political chaos raging between Uruguay and Paraguay, and she and the sculptor divorced. Fortunately for me, she made her way to Washington and to the apartment we now shared.

Our days fell into a comfortable routine. Emma worked on her own canvases every free hour she had, day and night. She had a friend who was an Argentinian priest and dropped by frequently. They spent hours arguing about history and life and death. They had to climb over my body stretched out on the floor in the apartment's short hallway to get to her living room: The phone was on a stand there, and I spent hour after hour sprawled on the floor talking to George.

One night, as usual, I was blocking easy passage in the hall, talking endlessly with George on the phone. Emma paused a minute while stepping over me to tell me that I was going to marry George. She repeated it: "You are going to marry him." "I am not," I said. But she was right. Several months later, she received special dispensation from the Catholic Church to participate in a Protestant wedding. I have a photo of Emma, my maid of honor, with a bemused expression on her face, leaning against a wall at the reception, observing the goings-on. Among her wedding presents was one of her paintings, which shows her with her feet propped up on a table in a room filled with her paintings of simple peasants. Years later, when she had moved to France and achieved considerable acclaim, someone would write that Emma had the "clear eyes of a child."

We kept in touch for close to 20 years through letters and Naifeh family visits to Rome and Paris. She knew when Steve was born in Iran in June 1952 and couldn't decide if he resembled me or George. I knew that she had an exhibition in Mexico City that same October at the Galeria Arte Contemporaneo, with others to follow in Rome, Milan, Jerusalem, Haifa, Bogota, Brussels, and elsewhere. I knew she had married a French doctor from Périgueux.

I recently Googled Emma and was amazed to learn that this woman, who was illiterate until she was 20, had achieved acclaim not only as an artist but as a writer. She had become a close friend of a highly respected Colombian historian, diplomat, and journalist named Germán Arciniegas, and had written him 23 letters about her extraordinary childhood in Bogota. Emma had requested

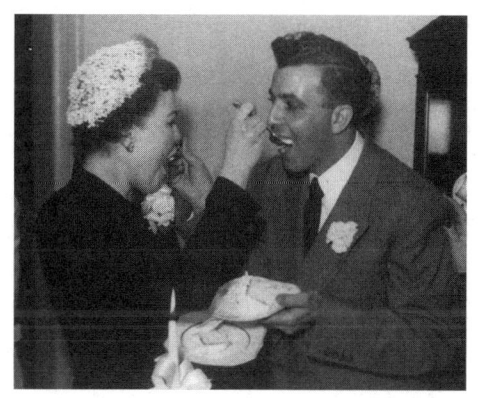

George and me sharing cake at our wedding reception in Washington.

that the correspondence remain private. He only broke his promise of confidentiality once, when he showed her letters to Gabriel García Márquez. Márquez, winner of the Nobel Prize for Literature in 1982, called Emma to congratulate her on the emotional intensity of her story and the beauty of her prose. She was less pleased with the praise from Márquez than she was displeased by the violation of her privacy. In 2012, after both Emma and Arciniegas had died, his family had the letters published as *Memoria por Correspondencia*. This memoir, in the form of a series of private letters, galvanized the literary and art worlds not only of Colombia but all of Latin America.

I had handled George's proposal to me with something less than aplomb. We were having lunch at a crowded restaurant on Connecticut Avenue when he asked me if I wanted to go to Iran with him. His security clearance had just come through, and he would be leaving Washington relatively soon. I said that would be great, but I was pretty sure that in 1950 a couple couldn't live together without being married. "I'm *asking* you to *marry* me," he said, kindly leaving off the words "you dummy."

I was even less adroit at some of the practical aspects of marriage. To begin with, I didn't have a clue how to cook. Long ago, Aunt Mina had given up trying to get me interested in the wonders of preparing a good meal.

The first home that George and I shared was a one-room apartment with a kitchen but no bathroom. We shared a bathroom, which was upstairs, with five young Mexican Embassy employees. Our landlord was a cook at the Colombian Embassy. Our first dinner guest was Bob Harris, George's roommate from the University of Oklahoma. Bob had a degree in petroleum engineering but was following his true passion, singing. Bob, who had sung at our wedding, eventually sang for several television shows, including the Fred Waring, the Gary Moore, and the Carol Burnett shows. Having decided to make fried chicken for my first meal, I took one look at the sputtering oil in the frying pan, panicked, and abandoned it. I've forgotten what I managed to serve in lieu of the intended meal.

My social skills were also in short supply, and George loved entertaining. In Kiefer, his family had far too little food for the family to even consider offering food to guests. It was a very painful memory for him, a defining one, almost, especially since the Syrian Orthodox priest, a travelling minister of Irish heritage, would only baptize a child whose family offered a banquet in exchange. So George went unbaptized for years, fearing that his soul was in danger until he was old enough to arrange a baptism at a more accommodating and less greedy house of worship. Kindly ignoring the catastrophe of my first efforts at the stove, he set up a regular series of dinner guests to entertain while we waited for our trip to Beirut by ocean liner en route to Iran.

Not that we had the money to serve anything approaching an appropriate meal to our sometimes socially prominent guests. A woman with a Fortune 500 last name commented one evening that the wine we were serving was absolutely marvelous, and wanted to know the winery and vintage. I ignored the question about four times, as best I could, before I finally got exasperated enough to go to the kitchen and get the gallon jug of Gallo wine for her inspection. She promptly had to use the "powder room." I was so rattled that I went to our tiny linen closet and grabbed a bath towel, explaining that the "powder room" was upstairs—and was shared with several other apartments. The next day, at his office, George received a thank you note for me along with an elegantly wrapped box of delicate hand towels.

Luckily, I had taken a secretarial course as a form of insurance in an uncertain job world for women, before I landed my job at the Pan American Union. So the State Department hired me to work as a secretary in the small American Consulate in Meshed, the city in Iran where George and I were heading. We were the fourth—and, I later heard, the *last*—couple hired by the State Department for an overseas assignment. I listened carefully while George received his lessons in Farsi at our apartment from a Mr. Fatoui. He counseled George and me that Iranians, like other Middle Easterners, would be incredibly generous. You had to be careful not to compliment the items in their homes too much or they might give them to you. George's eyes brightened at the thought of a Persian carpet or brass pitcher. We learned more about the culture of our new post from a retired OSS officer, Al, who had been stationed in

Leaving for Beirut on the Excalibur.

Iran. He spent most of the time telling us how really filthy everything would be: "If someone offers you a cup of tea and you don't know who prepared it, just slosh some of the boiling water over the side of the cup, and sip from that somewhat-sterilized side."

George and I sailed to Beirut on the *Excalibur* of the American Export Lines, a trip that doubled as the honeymoon we couldn't afford. For 10 days, we ate breakfasts, elevenses, lunches, teas, and dinners. Each of us gained 10 pounds and swore we would never again take long trips on boats.

My father was supposed to meet me and my new husband when we anchored in Beirut—he had just finished closing down the Episcopal Diocese in China. But the night before we arrived, while still on the board the ship, I received a telegram from Aunt Mina: "B. W. died July 4th in Shanghai at St. Elizabeth's Hospital." I later learned that B. W.'s death certificate said he died from complications of the liver and the esophagus—he had never really recovered from his four years in the concentration camp. But when I received the telegram, it was hard to believe he hadn't died of a broken heart after having to leave China.

The Beirut harbor was magnificent, embraced as it was by a series of mountains crested with the cedars of Lebanon. B. W. had arrived at this very harbor in 1910 to begin his first mission in Lebanon. Now I was here, and he wasn't.

Our first impressions were abruptly interrupted. "Mr. Naifeh?" someone called out. "George Naifeh?"

Mansur, a heavy-set American Embassy driver in full uniform, had come to meet "the three new diplomats headed for Tehran:" George and me and a woman named Janet Sutherland, an experienced secretary. Janet was a very proper lady, down to her spotless white gloves. This was 1951, some ladies still wore white gloves.

"Naifeh?"

"Yes, I'm George Naifeh."

Mansur could not take his eyes off George, all six feet of him, his skin bronzed even darker than usual from hours spent at the edge of the ship's pool; his thick, greying black hair a tumble of curls and waves. Mansur grabbed George and gave him a bear hug. Mansur was about to give Janet the same bone-crushing squeeze when George saved the day: "No, she's not a Naifeh," he said. "*This* one," pointing to me. "*This* one is." I got the embrace.

George had warned me that Beirut was famous for the speed and recklessness of its drivers. After 10 unnerving minutes racing through crowded streets, we came to a screeching halt, not in front of the Embassy, but in front of a small neighborhood grocery store. There, precariously perched on an upturned yellow Coca-Cola case, yet totally relaxed in the early afternoon sun, was a middle-aged man, obviously the grocer. His arms were folded on his heavy stomach, which was resting on his knees. His head bobbed up and down on his chest as he slipped in and out of sleep.

"Shakeeb, wake up, you lazy, good-for-nothing bum," shouted Mansur in Arabic through the open window. George gave us a breathless simultaneous translation. Mansur continued: "See what I have brought you from America. This is your cousin Saida's baby boy. Wake up. Look at him. Feast your eyes."

By nightfall there was a Naifeh everywhere we looked. After checking into the Embassy, Janet escaped to a hotel, but George and I were packed with six other Naifehs into one car, while another car followed, similarly weighted down with yet more Naifehs. We were headed for Marj Uyun, the town where George's mother was born. I sat half on George and half on a relative named Ramziyeh.

Ramziyeh was celebrating our arrival by blowing into a hollowed-out gourd, which produced a very loud kind of music. The others joined in a very off-key song. The car behind joined in with a round of its own—also off-key. We careened at high speed and at high decibels all the way to Marj Uyun, just this side of the Israeli border. I could see an Israeli farmer quietly examining his heavily-laden lemon trees. Our entourage, still pressing against each other, tore around two corners and screeched to a stop at Saida's family home. The front garden was filled with tidy rows of grape vines. The house was solid brick, had a wrap-around porch, and was full of still more relatives eager to welcome us.

I was at a total loss as I moved through a tidal wave of hugs and kisses. The kisses were a shock. Never once in my childhood had my Aunt Mina ever kissed me.

George and I were both seated at the men's table, a very

long table that was instantly covered with mountains of food. I looked at the women serving it, all of whom seemed to be looking at George with abject pity—pity and confusion. How could this Prodigal Son, wealthy enough to have crossed the ocean to pay his respects to the town of his origins, ended up married to this mute, bespectacled woman—rather than to an eligible young lady from Marj Uyun.

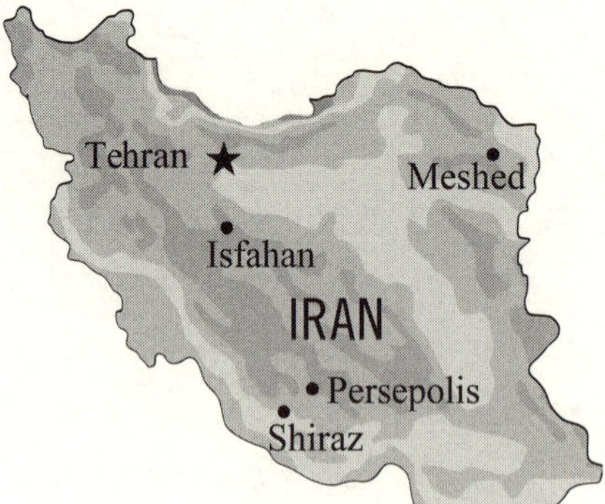
Tehran
Meshed
Isfahan
IRAN
Persepolis
Shiraz

IRAN

In 1969, the brilliant British historian and travel writer James Morris described Persia as the "most sensuous country." For him, it was "Persia that has so enslaved the imagination of foreigners for five centuries or more." The day we landed in Tehran, the heat was blistering, but relief was as close as the luxurious green trees in the gardens of the Middle East Pension on Avenue Pahlavi, where we were to stay for orientation before leaving for the eastern city of Meshed. Massive flowering bushes shaded the pathways throughout the garden—long, sinuously curved brick pathways, laid out in intricate decorative patterns. Water lapped the sides of a small tiled pool. I could even refresh my eyes by looking up at the snow-topped Mount Damavand, only 45 miles outside the city.

Reality struck the next day, July 15, 1951. Before our assignment in Meshed, George was to go to Isfahan for a month's training in the provinces under the watchful eye of Consul Kay Bracken. I was to report to the Consular Section of the Embassy in Tehran.

Walking down the hall to my assigned office, I literally

bumped into Walter J. Levy, the American oil guru, and Averell Harriman, the prominent businessman and diplomat. Secretary of State Dean Acheson had asked them to try to straighten out the increasingly ugly dispute between Britain and Iran over oil.

I had just heard of Levy's and Harriman's harrowing ride to the Embassy from the airport. Raging crowds had assembled to demonstrate against the two Americans. Sponsored in part by the communist Tudeh Party, this was obviously an inaugural skirmish of the coming Cold War. Blood was flowing in the streets; 20 were dead and several hundred injured.

The problem was very simple. Britain had controlled Iran's oil for decades and, even though its military empire was crumbling in the aftermath of the War, it was holding on tightly to what remained of its economic empire, and the Anglo-Iranian Oil Company—which consisted, largely, of Iranian oil providing English profits—was an important part of it. It was feared that Iran would follow the lead of countries like Mexico, which had expropriated British and American oil interests in 1938. The Mexican expropriation had led Secretary of State Acheson to announce that it was "the sovereign power of a state to take such property" as long as it paid "prompt and just compensation."

Therein lay the problem.

The story began in 1872, when the profligate ruling Shah had granted Great Britain the right to exploit Persia's mineral resources in exchange for a sum of money. In December 1951, Saudi Arabia had demanded 50 percent of the profits of ARAMCO, the Arabian-American Oil Company. Why wouldn't Iran make a similar demand?

Acheson was worried. He knew that "throughout the

Near East lay rare tinder for anti-Western propaganda" and that, even though "this tinder would be, and was, lighted everywhere," it would flare up "first in Iran." President Roosevelt had said that he was "rather thrilled with the idea of using Iran as an example of what we could do by an unselfish American policy." Iran, he sincerely believed, could develop into "a pattern of self-government and free enterprise" and thus a prime example of how the U.S. could help in the development and stabilization of other "backward areas." But Great Britain, not the U.S., was the country with something to lose.

Moreover, in 1950 and 1951, Iran was becoming a theater in the developing Cold War between the U.S. and the Soviet Union—the Soviets were busy stirring up chaos on the Korean Peninsula and opening up a worldwide "hate America" campaign. Acheson was concerned that if the British didn't work out a satisfactory division of Anglo-Iranian Oil Company profits with Iran, Prime Minister Mossadegh might actually invite Soviet intervention to strengthen his hand against Great Britain.

Even on days when crowds weren't raging in the streets, we could feel the underlying tension in the country over the oil issue. Harriman returned in July to help the intransigent sides reach a compromise. He failed, and matters only deteriorated.

This was the Iran that George and I had been posted to in July 1951. George was over 200 miles away in Isfahan while I labored in the Embassy's Visa Section. Day after day, the waiting area was crowded not only with wealthy Iranians trying to flee the political turmoil in the streets but also with refugees from Russia, fleeing Stalin's wrath and seeking safe haven in America.

All the time I was filing visa applications for these desperate souls, I was trying to make sense of this political tornado, twisting all in its path. I knew that Mosaddegh, or "Mossy" as the foreign community called him, was the eye of the storm for us, the Soviets, the British, and, not least of all, the Iranians themselves.

Mossy was a canny politician stirring every available pot, playing every angle, and gaining headlines all over the world. Born in 1882, the son of a wealthy landowner and, on his mother's side, the great-great grandson of a Qajar ruler, Mossy had attended the Ecole des Sciences Politiques in Paris. He had also received a Swiss doctorate in law in Neuchatel. He understood a West that did not understand him.

I was eager to catch a glimpse of this reviled and adored magician. I pestered Mr. Shabbaz, an Embassy interpreter, until he relented and let me tag along with him one day when he went to the Majlis, or Parliament, to cover the day's session. I was not disappointed. There, reclining in striped pajamas on a thin cot on the Majlis floor lay a balding, pelican-nosed, wrinkled old man with white-parchment skin. He had the stage presence of an Academy Award-winning actor as he reported the status of the oil negotiations to the members of his Parliament. His long, tapered fingers punctuated the air as his faltering voice crept from a hoarse whisper to a screeching falsetto. I was mesmerized. Mr. Shabbaz kindly gave me a running translation, since my three-week immersion in Farsi had progressed no further than "Mother does not have bread in the basket."

I also pestered Cliff Linch, the Labor Attaché, into taking me along with him and his wife Sally to Isfahan for an extended weekend so that I could see George.

On the way to Isfahan, the Linches and I stopped at the

holy city of Qum, with its shrines, *madrassas*, and *sayyeds*, descendants of the Prophet Mohammed. Shiite religious scholars—tall and short, skinny and fat—were bustling about with loud green sashes for girdles. Cliff mentioned that the largest shrine, the one with the largest gold dome, was the Shrine of Fatima the Immaculate, sister of the Eighth Imam, Reza. Fatima's tomb, Cliff added, was enclosed in an enormous sandalwood box. We infidels would not be permitted to enter the Shrine's portals or enjoy the fragrance of that sandalwood.

From Qum on, we were enveloped in sand—on us, in us, and around us. With all that infuriating sand everywhere, it was no wonder that the people who lived there were enchanted by every blade of grass and every fragile leaf. No wonder they listened with delight to the sound of moving water, whatever its source, from a small stream to the rush of water from a *qanat*. These *qanats*, or underground irrigation canals, were sometimes thousands of years old. They could be 100 feet deep. When they opened to the surface, they released water from nearby mountains with a thundering roar, allowing the sand to breathe life.

We made a quick stop at Yussefabad to use the "facilities," or lack thereof, and found a group of village elders perched on broad wooden benches covered with Persian carpets, which straddled a small stream. Men, long in years and in beards, were happily savoring small glasses of hot tea, which they sipped through huge chunks of block sugar, clenched between their teeth—or what was left of their teeth. But mostly they seemed to be enjoying the sound of water trickling from that stream.

Quietly stretching along beside us all the way to Isfahan were old mountains, fat mountains, scrawny mountains, worn down from the endless shifting and blowing of the sand. Only years later would those mountains at Fordo (outside of Qum) and at Natanz (outside of Isfahan) contain, buried deep beneath them, the nuclear enrichment centrifuges that would be the cause of future diplomatic stand-offs and yet another proxy war with Russia.

Little did James Morris realize the irony he was spinning when he described the view from across the river in Isfahan: "There behind you the great domes of the mosque stand above the city like reactors, radiating inexhaustible energy, as though their golden tiles are actually glowing with heat."

But for George and me, Isfahan wasn't about diplomacy. Our three days there were a second honeymoon. We glowed with romance among the wonders of Isfahan, as well as Persepolis and Shiraz.

Isfahan was magical. It was there that the greatest of the Safavid rulers, Shah Abbas the Great, who lived from 1571 until 1629, laid out his new capital, known at the time as one of the world's most glorious cities. Swathed in black robes, the Shiite religious teachers, the *mullahs*, scurried about in the hushed courtyards of the Royal Mosque. The *mullahs* had stained their beards and their fingernails a rich, deep, dark orange. Somehow they were the perfect accent to the Mosque's famed bulging blue dome and dazzling explosion of glazed blue tiles.

At the center of ancient Isfahan was the Maidan-e-Shah, the royal plaza, seven times the size of the Piazza San Marco in Venice. Built by Shah Abbas the Great at the beginning of the 17th century, the grand, open space was surrounded by a series of monumental buildings—each an architectural masterpiece—linked by a series of two-storied arcades to the Royal Mosque, the mosque of Sheikh Lotfollah, the magnificent Portico of Qaysariyyeh, and the 15th-century Timurid palace. They are an enduring testimony to the extraordinarily high level of cultural life in Persia during the Safavid era. But the Maidan-e-Shah was also used to play the ancient Persian game of polo. It didn't require much effort to imagine the hooves of horses thundering in heated polo matches there half a millennium ago for the entertainment of the Shah and his court.

Martin, the American Consulate driver with a tweed Scots cap covering a very bald head, paused near a scattering of stones that marked the site of an ancient Zoroastrian temple where bodies of the faithful were left for the sun and buzzards to dispose of.

Next was an excursion through the bazaar, something that George took to with an enthusiasm that escaped me. I always disliked shopping, anywhere, anytime—even in a Middle Eastern bazaar as thick with history and exoticism as this one. A mass of ancient stalls covering a vast area, honeycombed with alleyways and barely lit by shafts of light entering through tiny skylights, whole sections were devoted to a single trade, such as carpets or copper vessels, triumphant mounds of spices or sparkling shelves of silver jewelry. The narrow passageways were crowded with an impossible number of men, their beards and hair dyed red, this time, not orange. There were scores of chatting, chador-robed ladies clutching the sides of their robes in their teeth when they had to pay for a purchase or pick it up.

But my favorite glimpse of what life in a Persian province might be like was dinner at Consul Kay Bracken's. She was a statuesque, no-nonsense American. Her principal guests were a famous tribal chief named Yaya Bakthiari and an assortment of his cousins, male and female. I was proudly informed by the Bakthiari ladies, each of whom had decorated her hands with an intricate henna arabesque, that Soroya, the Shah's new bride of six months, was also a Bakthiari. Led by two of Kay's American staff, the handsome Khan made a one-of-a-kind chorus line doing the Charleston in his broad black satin trousers. He was tall, dark, and smolderingly handsome, his opium-stained teeth only making him a more romantic figure. George had told me that Kay frequently rode out to Yaya's encampment to discuss political matters. In my romantic state, I was convinced that there had to be more than political interest on the part of the attractive, strong-willed American Consul—and on Yaya's too.

Kay let George and me have her driver take us down to Shiraz, stopping in Persepolis on the way. Since we were there, it has become a major tourist attraction. In 1971, the late Shah chose to honor the 2,500th anniversary of the Persian Empire there. More than 500 bottles of champagne were served to the 600 guests, along with a meal prepared by Maxim's de Paris, which closed its restaurant in Paris for two weeks to accommodate the Shah. International guests were housed in tents with marble bathrooms and crystal chandeliers. The Shah's own tent had a gold bathtub with solid gold faucets. But even today, the Ayatollahs are cashing in on Persepolis as a prime tourist attraction for Iranians.

But when George and I stepped out of the Consulate car, there was not a tent in sight—nor a single human being. We had the place to ourselves. Until Alexander the Great left Persepolis in charred shambles, it had been the glory of the Achaemenid kings for centuries. Ghosts were turning the pages of my college art text as we walked up a crumbling great double stairway lined with friezes and panels of subject nations bearing tribute all the way to the gigantic altar, with its broken columns decorated with tiers of horses and lions.

It was hard not to be affected by the incredible beauty and echoes of a long and glorious history.

Shiraz even cast some of its romantic spell over Gertrude Bell, the Middle East expert, better known for her ties to Sunni Arab Iraq. The British "Desert Queen" spent much of 1892 in Tehran as the guest of her aunt, the wife of Ambassador Sir Frank Lascelles. There, she discovered what she called paradise. It must have helped that she was falling in love with a junior British diplomat, Henry Cadogan, whose prospects of marrying her were eventually dashed by her adored father, who deemed Mr. Cadogan unsuitable. Gertrude had also fallen in love with the Persian language and Persian poetry. In 1897, she published an annotated translation of the *Divan of Hafez*, Shiraz's famed 13th-century poet.

I am proud that a friend and American Middle East expert, John Limbert, with whom we served in Abu Dhabi many years later, wrote what may be the best book on Shiraz: *Shiraz in the Age of Hafez: The Glory of a Medieval Persian City*. His book is a eulogy to 14th-century Shiraz, a place where "poets composed, scholars studied, and princes and their courtiers played deadly games of power." John, who later became an ambassador, became a pawn himself in deadly games of power: In 1979, he became one of the Americans held hostage in our Embassy in Tehran for 444 days.

We found Hafez's austere tomb set in the middle of equally austere gardens. It was in distinct contrast to the tomb of Sa'adi, another renowned Shiraz poet. Sa'adi's tomb, set in a ring of rich green grass, was a sparkling jewel box of blue tiles, gilded by a late afternoon sun. Sa'adi's *Gulestan (The*

Rose Garden) and *Bustan (The Orchard)* are quoted today for their earthy humor and practical advice. Referring to a miserable marriage to the daughter of an Aleppo merchant, Sa'adi wrote, "A bad wife is hell on earth."

As George and I drove back to Tehran, we had the good fortune of seeing hundreds of Bakthiari tribes moving south to their winter quarters, where they could find grass for their animals. Among their vast herds of bleating brown goats and sheep was a small group of rare white camels. Keeping them in line were the Bakthiari tribesmen, who kept coming and coming in a seemingly endless line across the dusty plain, prodding donkeys and horses and camels laden with their tents and all of their earthly goods. The women, bronzed as walnuts, followed with their crying babies.

George and I made our own migration north in September to Meshed, our new home—our first real one as a couple. Meshed was the storied capital of the province of Khorasan. Even the name Khorasan—which had once encompassed Afghanistan, Turkmenistan, and Uzbekistan—captured the "roses, nightingales, and poetry" of Isfahan and Shiraz.

George and me arriving in Meshed, our first assignment in the Foreign Service.

Our squat, rather ugly cement house didn't bode well, nor did the front yard storage pool, or *umbar*. The pool was replenished from the city's open *jubes*, or open roadside water ditches, and provided all of the water for bathing and cleaning. I insisted that we install proper pipes with actual faucets. Our drinking water came from the Consulate, which got its water from the Imam Reza Shrine. We were told to boil all of our water, not just the drinking water, for 10 minutes, so I boiled it for 15. I seemed to spend almost every hour of every day boiling water.

The Consul's house was a former Ottoman palace, with 14-foot ceilings and intricate moldings everywhere, magnificent old-fashioned blue-tiled stoves built into the walls, and large formal gardens. George and I made do with two nasty, smelly, wheezy kerosene heaters—and, instead of gardens, a patch of brown dirt and sand around the *umbar* pool. (Always a devoted gardener, George eventually remedied that.)

In fact, George and I were the only Americans assigned to Meshed who lived in an Iranian neighborhood, far away from the "togetherness" of our five American colleagues—the Consul, who was a bachelor, and two couples—in the Consulate compound. Working next to each other, and living next to each other, they had absolutely no privacy. Before I even met the two wives, I had heard of their raging feuds. They lived in adjoining houses and had their windows open one fine, crisp afternoon. One of the two women smelled something the other was frying in genuine butter and was furious that she had not shared any of that butter. The wound was deep, for sweet butter was almost impossible to come by. For George and me, away from the compound, it was "out of sight, out of smell, out of mind."

We were also lucky with our servants, an essential part of living in such conditions. Even though the Consul was a bachelor, his cook was known by each of the feuding ladies to have used 30 eggs in a single day. Obviously, the cook was pilfering eggs. One of the two women, a gorgeous red-haired, fiery-tempered woman named Molly, was convinced that her cook was helping himself, not to her eggs, but to her cigarettes. She laid a trap for him by leaving piles of carefully counted cigarettes in every room. The temptation was irresistible and the culprit was caught red-handed and fired. Then there were *real* fireworks when Molly's husband, a phlegmatic man named Mike, discovered that the driver he had just fired had wrecked Mike's car by pouring salt into the engine. We had an all-purpose maid, or *bache,* named Mirium, who was a Christian. She was sufficiently all-purpose that Jahangir, our cook, scolded me when I questioned her food consumption. "She *work* a lot. She *eat* a lot."

Most cooks hired by Westerners were not very good at cooking. Barely out of his teens, with a crown of pomaded jet-black hair and a fine moustache, our cook Jahangir paused to admire his reflection in every mirror he passed. I hired him not because he could cook—which he couldn't—but because he was literate. After a few hands-on demonstrations and translations, I dictated all my favorite recipes from *The Joy of Cooking* to him and left him alone. It worked.

Meshed is famous in particular as the home of the Imam Reza Shrine. Ali al-Reza, the eighth Shiite Imam, for whom the Shrine was built, was "martyred" in 818 A.D.—supposedly by poison.

Martyrdom has always been a factor in Shiite Islam. When the Prophet Mohammad died, his cousin and son-in-law Ali ibn Abi Talib became the first Muslim Imam. When he died, his son, Hasan ibn Ali, became the second Muslim Imam. But when Hasan died, there was a disagreement whether a descendant should become Imam (the Shiite solution) or an elected official should assume the position (the Sunni solution). The dispute was not unlike the dual Catholic papacy that lasted from 1309 to 1377 and resulted in one pope ruling from Rome and another from Avignon, France. But the disputed line of succession created a schism in Islam that never healed and is on full murderous display today.

The Battle of Kerbala, where the Shiite Imam was martyred, is memorialized each year in a celebration called Muharram, which usually turns violent, with celebrants flailing themselves into a frenzy of bloodletting. Muharram began soon after we arrived in Meshed, and George and I were spectators to some of the more frenzied celebrations. Molly and Mike invited us, for security reasons, to spend "Tasu'a" and "Ashura," the ninth and tenth days of Muharram, at the Consulate compound. We played bridge, sipped martinis, listened to Ravel's *Bolero* on a phonograph, and peeked through cracks in the Consulate garage walls at the parade of wailing mourners headed for the Shrine. Bitter cold as it was, the mourners were stripped to the waist. They thrust heavy iron chains high in the air, flinging them with full force against their own bare flesh. Occasionally, a mourner would unsheathe a sword or grapple with a knife to slash his head until blood splattered his face and body.

In the office the next morning, I got even more uncomfortably close to the violence when I slipped into George's office next door. Some of the visitors to George's Information Bureau, who regularly leafed through whatever materials lay on George's reading tables, cornered me. One removed a long knife from its sheath, sharpened it, and cut his scalp until blood dripped from the cut. He told me that he might even kill himself so that he could have the honor of showing me the depth of his faith.

Fortunately, Muharram lasted only a few days, and life in Meshed immediately turned more banal—but also more benign. George often showed documentary films in the open-air space located beneath his office. This dark, damp space—it felt like a dungeon—was an irresistible draw for the impoverished of Meshed, who were as astonished by American newsreels as we were by Muharram. George, who remembered his own childhood hours spent at the Criterion and Yale theaters in Sapulpa, Oklahoma, had a hard time excluding any child who wanted in, so from time to time, he called on Molly to help with "crowd control." Six-foot-tall Molly was basically his bouncer.

Her former colleagues at Elizabeth Arden in New York City would have been as horrified by her new job as they would have been by her Meshed coiffure. The four of us, Molly and Mike and George and I, all went to the same open-air barber, who placed the same bowl on each of our heads to cut our hair, producing a look exactly like that of Moe from the "Three Stooges." With her fiery-red cap of hair, giant Molly positioned herself along with her enormous black German shepherd at the entrance of the office basement and, in an instant, the chaos was under complete control.

Then there were the English classes that George and I taught, 12 a week between us. Showing films—propaganda films, really—and teaching English were two of the most practical tools of "public diplomacy" in the Consulate arsenal. George had seen films and language classes used effectively in Isfahan, and he replicated them in Meshed. Before his office space in the Consulate was ready, George held classes in our home, itself hardly ready. Moreover, there were as few texts for teaching English as a second language in 1951 as there were texts for teaching Arabic as a second language. In other words, *there were no texts*, only magazines from the reading corner in George's office: *Time*, the *Saturday Evening Post*, and, inexplicably, *The Journal of Venereal Disease*.

Soon, I was a conscript just like Molly.

I woke up one morning to the thunderous chant of every known word for a toilet: "stool," "head," "john," etc., and soon I knew immediately that this was not a suitable vocabulary for a respectable Meshed lady, especially if taught by a man. Meanwhile, George was receiving multiple requests for language classes from his male students, who were the husbands of such ladies. George knew, and I knew, that a woman was needed to teach the women. That meant *me*, even though it meant that I would be breaking a lifelong promise to myself to defy B. W.'s lifelong intent that I should become a teacher.

I somehow succeeded in fooling myself that, under these circumstances, I wouldn't be *teaching* the ladies, I would be *chatting* with them. Actually, I began each "class" with strenuous calisthenics. We did jumping jacks; we bent and touched our toes; we climbed onto our chairs and down from our chairs over and over. When I actually began an attempt at language instruction, I used my fingers to point at the objects in the room or used pantomime with exaggerated sound effects: I sang, gargled, coughed, and whispered. If I had been able to ululate, I would have.

It was probably because of the entertainment value, but our English classes were a hit. One late afternoon, there was utter bedlam in one of George's classes. A classroom intended for 20 students was packed with 60. Two long tables were scattered with the usual assortment of magazines and pamphlets. George had given dire warnings about "not removing—repeat NOT removing" any of the material on the tables. Just as the class itself began, the electricity went out, as it was wont to do. With the room in total darkness, George heard the scrunch of magazines being stuffed into pockets and sleeves. He burned his tongue on a few choice expletives and his fingers on some sputtering matches before the lights came back on. When the 20 most mischievous students were expelled, they locked the rest of us in on their way out. Jahangir, who was taking the class, had to climb through a window to unlock the door and release us.

The people of Meshed did not despise Americans nearly as much as they despised the "Englisi"—the English—who were portrayed in the daily newspapers as cheats and deceivers. But we were still *ferengi*, or foreigners, and, as such, suspect. Somehow our immediate neighbors had a much more positive view of the new foreigners in their midst. We won a Persian lottery with our neighbors on Kusangi Street: the Ghanis, the Ziais, and the Samirods. Mr. Ghani, our landlord, was the first and only landlord we ever had and would ever have who actually *lowered* our rent. The fact that he owned half of Khorasan may have been a contributing factor. In his own home, he had layer upon layer of carpets, some so big they unfurled up the walls.

"Oh, what a lovely carpet," George noted, eyeing the top one, and hoping that the advice he had been given back in Washington about Middle Easterners offering you any possession that you complimented was true.

"Yes, isn't it!" was Mr. Ghani's only response, to George's mortification.

Dr. Ziai and Dr. Samirod were among the most respected physicians in Meshed. In fact, the patrician Dr. Ziai was the leading surgeon at the Reza Shah Hospital. Dr. Samirod was the head of the medical school—and a bridge fanatic. An unassuming, self-made man from the northern village of Bujnurd, Dr. Samirod was the wealthiest doctor in town. He had studied in Paris for nine years, where, it appeared, he had practiced his bridge skills full time, while squeezing his medical studies into his spare time. He taught Dr. Ziai the game, as well as all of the students and residents he currently supervised. Every Tuesday afternoon at the hospital there were marathon bridge matches. Because I was the wife of his honored teacher, Persian etiquette required that I play on his team, regardless of my total lack of skill. He spent every game scratching his scruffy beard and eyeing me worriedly through his horn-rimmed bifocals.

Perhaps an even more valuable neighbor lived just behind our home: the city's police chief.

All the ladies of Kusangi Street were in my classes, and my gracious students showered me with roses, jasmine, and caviar. George wouldn't touch the caviar. His mother had warned him when he was four to be aware of the bones in the fish his brothers caught in the creek, fearing that he might choke to death. For the rest of his life, he absolutely refused to eat fish. The fact that caviar has no bones made no difference to him—the word "caviar" was used too often in the same sentence as the word "fish." That just meant more caviar for me. Morning, noon, and night, it was the snack of choice in Meshed: I spread a fat, glossy, black layer of roe on half an inch of local bread, or *nan*, and happily munched away.

The first months we were in Meshed, I tried to learn Farsi, but soon gave up. We were so close to Russia, and there were so many White Russians in Meshed, I decided to go back to improving my Russian. Our proximity to Russia was highlighted one afternoon when we were having a picnic high on a nearby hill, staring idly at some drifting clouds. Mike and Molly were with us, and Mike announced that one of those clouds had just been floating over the Soviet Union. The local communist Tudeh Party had, if anything, grown in strength since we first arrived in Iran, so it seemed that it might be of some value to improve my Russian. I was soon racing through narrow cobbled streets to the home of a woman named Mrs. Schanpour, who lived near the British Centre, for lessons three mornings a week.

Yet the mornings were becoming increasingly difficult. I had started out with a "T. T." or "Tehran tummy"—a sort of dysentery—not long after we arrived in Meshed. Soon I was in serious trouble. It seemed that, no matter how carefully our maid Mirium, our cook Jahangir, and I scrubbed all of our fresh food—soaking each leaf of lettuce in Tide and permanganate—a chemical compound with a strong oxidizing agent—then carefully rinsing and drying it, I got sicker and sicker.

Aunt Mina wrote from Massachusetts that we seemed to have a lot of meals with our neighbors and friends, and maybe they were not as careful as we were. But I was sure. I had inspected their kitchens, and they took all same the precautions we did. Besides, I only ate cooked food and drank straight gin (no ice cubes). I sought medical help, of course, but nothing Dr. Cochran at the Presbyterian

Mission Hospital offered seemed to help.

One day, when I was there, a female German doctor had been admitted to the Mission Hospital for the delivery of her first child. She told me that, in her provincial village, when an expectant mother was about to deliver, all the lady's friends gathered around, inspecting and commenting on the event as it unfolded. About an hour before the birth, the mother-to-be drank a quart of lukewarm mutton fat. She then got in the middle of the floor to squat, and, assisted by a midwife, proceeded to deliver. By the next day, the new mother was up and about.

Molly had told me that she had an extrasensory insight into the matters of expectant mothers. Not long after, when I happened to mention that I was driving down to Tehran with George, who had been called there for a consultation, she ordered me not to ride in the mobile film truck. "You're pregnant," she said.

"I am *not*," I sputtered.

"You listen to me. Taking that dilapidated, ridiculous vehicle all the way to Tehran is out of the question. I just know these things. You have an "I'm pregnant" look. Trust me."

I went back to Dr. Cochran, and, to my amazement, he confirmed Molly's diagnosis.

As a consequence, though George drove down to Tehran with a driver in the mobile film unit, I flew. Across the aisle from me in the prop plane, a heavily-veiled elderly woman glanced out her window as we were taking off. When she realized her feet were not within reasonable proximity to the ground, she let out an unholy shriek. She struggled to her feet, clutched her chador, staggered to the floor of the aisle and promptly lay face down. She screamed, flailed her arms, and kicked wildly all the way to Tehran.

George's trip was even more noteworthy. He had to spend one night on the road, and a village teahouse was the only hostelry of any kind available. The place was hardly spotless, but he was pleased to be shown to an enormous room with one lone cot, whose twine-braided frame was bare of any bedding. Gratefully, George lay down in all his clothes and luckily fell asleep immediately. When he woke at the first flush of dawn, he found himself surrounded by at least 50 men, including his driver, stretched out over every square inch of the packed earth floor around him.

We had expected to spend the three days of our trip at the Middle East Pension, but Alan Jackson, an Embassy bachelor, kindly invited us to camp out in his apartment. It was a good thing, for reports soon surfaced that Meshed was soon to be enveloped in *hub nist,* or bad weather, and we were compelled to spend three weeks in Tehran, including our first Christmas in the country. On Christmas morning, George found a suitable tree down on Naderi Street by the British Embassy, the walls of which had recently been serving as a urinal in a display of the public's ire. George also found some decorations and lights at a small Armenian shop nearby. By the time Alan woke up, the tree was properly decorated, and we could wish him and ourselves merry Christmas in proper style.

A couple of weeks later, jokes about why we didn't just use a couple camels to get back to Meshed were getting irritating just as an Iranian Airways prop plane took off for Meshed with us on board. Meshed, in its pristine winter finery, had never been so beautiful—or so cold. Intent on not wasting money, Jahangir had kept only one small kerosene heater on during our absence, and had lit it only occasionally. It took days for us to thaw out. Mirium laughed when we discovered the faucet in the bathroom had cracked because of the freeze. "Now, you will have to use the water from the *umbar*, just like us. You will have to crack the ice and then scoop the water to wash your face." We used the kitchen sink instead. We were back in full swing.

The British were not. After more than a century, they were on their way out.

The trench warfare between Mossadegh—Mossy—and Great Britain had heated up. Negotiations over compensation for the nationalization of the oil company had hit a final impasse. On January 14, the British Consul in Meshed was informed that he had one week to pack up and leave.

The citizens of Meshed celebrated the announcement of the provincial expulsion of the British "propaganda" office with a flourish of national pride. Iranian flags were flying high over every shop, stall, and teahouse.

I was focusing on our family, soon to be a threesome. But I was very much aware of the unfolding of the political drama. I had read that Mossadegh was named *Time*'s Man of the Year for 1951. He had been selected over such luminaries as Eisenhower, General MacArthur, and Churchill. It was not surprising that Mossadegh's "antics" were being described as "grotesque" in the West. But I should have paid a little more attention to the statement in *Time* that "the U.S., which will have to make the West's policy in the Middle East whether it wants to or not, as yet has no policy there."

Things were moving fast on all fronts: U.S. foreign policy, my pregnancy, my job. I was expecting my third boss in my five months in the Consulate. The first had been in Meshed two years before his alcoholism became too severe for the higher-ups in Tehran and Washington to continue to ignore.

The second, Robin, was the ideal boss and diplomat. However, he was crippled by a sudden paralysis and had to be flown back to the U.S. Robin was full of amusing comments: His host in Torbat-e-Hedairi, he said, was "a generously proportioned chest of drawers supported on spindle legs;" a luncheon rice pilau had been "so drenched in mutton grease that a thick coating of grease" lined his mouth for hours. The fine art on the walls of his Consulate residence consisted of huge framed pictures of Rita Hayworth, Veronica Lake, and Judy Garland.

The new Consul's plane had not yet arrived. The baby was not due until June. Life was beginning to seem almost normal. I raced over to the home of the British Consul and his wife, who had just been expelled, not just to commiserate, but to buy their playpen and baby carriage. Their stately residence was a sorry remnant of yesteryear: The balconies were sagging, the painted shutters cracked and chipped. There were no turbaned guards at the gate to usher me in. No elephants lingered on the front lawn to impress me with the might of the Raj. We had tea by a charcoal fire in a brazier. Their toddler son William was just starting to wobble about. He touched every item within reach with jam-smudged fingers.

Then there was a trip to the tailor for some skirts that would allow for my expanding waist. Jahangir and Mirium were working furiously to prepare for a dinner on February 2 for Charlie Gidney, our *third* new Consul. George had invited two bank presidents and the new police chief for the dinner with Gidney. The police chief regretted, saying he was getting ready "for possible disturbances on the streets." I was more interested in the fact that the wife of one of the bank presidents was a Qajar princess. Since she was a student of mine, should I call her Fatima or Your Highness during a

FOREIGN SERVICE | 111

dinner at our home? Their acceptance had read: Prince and Princess Kakuvoussi would be delighted to accept."

Time's profile of Mossadegh had mentioned that "the dizzy, old wizard" was also a Qajar Prince. It had warned, ominously, that, "For all its power, the West in 1951 failed to cope with a weeping, fainting leader of a helpless country; the West had not yet developed the moral muscle to define its own goals and responsibilities in the Middle East."

Mossadegh was not waiting for the U.S. to flex its moral muscle. On February 7, we got the word. This time, it was not the British; it was us. All USIS provincial "propaganda posts" were to be shut down immediately. We were to be gone within a week. "The government doesn't mean *you*," friends told George over and over again. Mr. Tehranian, editor of the daily *Khorasan*, assured him that it was all a mistake. Even as we boarded the plane, he told us, "You will be back soon."

As it turns out, we did go back—but not for 20 years. When we were evacuated from Karachi to Tehran during the India-Pakistan War of 1971, we flew up to Meshed for the day, just to stroll down memory lane. George peered over the wall of our old squat house on Kusangi Street. I suggested, helpfully, that he was crazy, and that it would serve us right if we were shot on the spot. The lady of the house soon emerged from the front door to confront this enormous invasion of her privacy. George smiled with all his considerable charm as I apologetically explained in English that this had been our first real home, our honeymoon home, one that we cherished.

"Please, won't you come in," the unveiled lady asked. "My husband is a psychiatrist who teaches at the medical school, and he will be home in a minute. I know he will want to invite you to stay here with us." With a smile, she added, "You can, you know, have your old bedroom back for the night."

"You are so kind," I managed to stutter. "Thank you, but we can't stay. We have to catch the plane back to Tehran this afternoon. We just wanted to take a peek into the past."

Back in Tehran, the simmering political situation was rising to a boil.

Mossadegh was now more concerned about the Americans than about the British. He couldn't decide if we were trying to prevent the British from undertaking aggressive action or if we were *encouraging* them to take action—action to get rid of him. Neither George nor I nor anyone else in the Embassy who didn't work for the CIA had any inkling that the top British MI6 spy in Tehran, "Monty" Woodhouse, had already devised just such a plan. It was called "Operation Boot" and the purpose was to overthrow Mossadegh's democratically-elected government. At the time, the Soviets were whipping up anti-West demonstrations, but under cover, we and the British were also whipping up anti-West demonstrations in the hope that, out of the turmoil, a coup against Mossadegh could be justified. The recently-departed CIA station chief in Iran, Roger Goiran, the epitome of a gentleman's gentleman, didn't question America's and Britain's need to challenge the Soviet Union in Iran. But he was worried that a coup against Mossadegh would do us geopolitical damage, forever associating the U.S. with imperialism and colonialism. His replacement, Kermit Roosevelt, had different ideas.

I had more immediate concerns. At least for me, being an evacuee was nothing new. But what was next for George and me? What would be our new assignments? Where would we live?

The answers came quickly. George was reassigned as Assistant Cultural Officer in the Embassy. Days later, he would be named Radio Officer. I started out in the Economics Section but was soon transferred to the Administrative Section, only to resign two months later as the birth date neared.

We easily found a two-story home on Takhte Jamshid. It felt like a skyscraper after our squat cement house in Meshed. Fortunately, the kitchen, which was on the first floor, had plenty of space for three huge tanks for boiling water. Jahangir, whom we sent for, would take care of boiling the water and cooking. He was delighted to be in the capital, which he had never visited before. The only negative was that a lifetime of drinking tea through cubes of sugar had so completely ruined his teeth that he had to go to the dentist for a complete set of false teeth.

The view from the living room, which was on the second floor, increased my paranoia about hygiene, especially with a baby on the way. From that height, I could see into the courtyards of the neighbors on each side. Their *umbars* were filled with water that ran down through *jubes*, open-air canals, from the foothills of the mountains to the north of Tehran. Those *jubes* were used by passing Iranians for every possible need. The *baches*, maids, on either side washed the clothes, the dishes, and themselves in that same water.

Just as my paranoia was reaching a fever pitch, we received a dinner invitation from our next-door neighbor. That very afternoon, I had seen the lettuce, obviously headed for our dinner, being washed in their *umbar*. Furthermore, our hosts were Colonel and Mrs. Sarhang. He was a well-known and highly respected, high-ranking Tehran police official. It would have been imprudent to refuse the invitation, as well as rude.

"No salad?" asked the good Colonel. Up to that moment we had had a delightful evening. They were charming. We were charming. George had them spellbound with his stories of life in America. I had been nervously trying to discuss babies in my limited Farsi with Mrs. Sarhang. George and I raved over the *khoreshe fesenjan*—chicken with pomegranate juice and walnuts—as we piled our plates with generous second helpings. But not a bite of salad.

"You can eat the salad," said the Colonel.

"Oh, I have eaten too much. I can't possibly eat another bite. I just had more of your delicious *fesenjan*."

The Colonel eyed us and then our plates: "You really *can*, you know, *eat* the salad. It has been washed in permanganate just the way you do it. Your servant Jahangir washed it himself."

I blushed permanganate purple, but we clung to our excuse of satiation.

Jahangir got an earful when we got home.

"Why, *why* didn't you tell us?"

"But that is how you like it."

I considered firing him, but only for a split second.

Having no teeth was hard on his vanity. His thick black hair was still impeccably trimmed and his beard closely shaven. But the constant grin was missing. His self-esteem in tatters, he no longer took any pleasure at the sight of his reflection in every mirror—at least not until his dentures were ready. I needed our faithful, bright-eyed, inexhaustible, if none-too-bright Jahangir more than ever.

For one thing, now that I was months pregnant and couldn't bend easily, only Jahangir could handle the kitchen sink, which was a proper Persian one, only inches off the floor. Persian sinks were constructed that way to make it easy to wash rice. And we needed a lot of rice, since our home had almost immediately become a travelers' caravanserai. Mike and Molly came on their way out for reassignment. We insisted on keeping their dog until they finished driving around Europe and sent word for us to ship him to them. Then we had Rocky and Ahme Stone, newly assigned to Tehran. Rocky was a fellow SAIS Middle East graduate and George's best man at our wedding. We knew Rocky was in the CIA, but at that moment even he didn't know what his role would be in Operation Ajax/Boot.

Rocky was scrappy, tough, and determined. When he was a teenager, his father had walked out on the family. In his 20s, serving on an army base, he was standing near a munitions depot when it exploded, and he lost much of his hearing. Because of that hearing loss, he learned to read lips and always focused on others with a disconcerting intensity. If I didn't know him so well, I would have been uncomfortable when those brown eyes of his bore into me. It was a little hard to be too scared of him when I had seen him and George acting like idiots during our SAIS days, putting on Lebanese dance performances, *dubkis*, for my entertainment. Ahme was a true South Texas 20th-century frontier woman. With a lilt to her step and a contagious laugh, this Corpus Christi native was a Texas beauty. Every morning when she came to breakfast, she would greet us with "soapy hair"—as close as she could come to "*sohb beh khair*," Farsi for good morning.

I wasn't the only nosy neighbor on our block. I may have spent hours looking out our second-floor living room window, but our neighbors—and all passersby who happened to take a look our way—were entranced by our *ferengi* ways. Whenever Jahangir took a break from his labors, he went straight to the open front gate and chatted with everyone:

every peddler, every beggar, every tradesman. When George brought a film home from the office for us to review, we became an open-air cinema: Crowds squeezed onto every balcony of every second floor across the street. Music from the Boat Club, a nightclub of sorts at the end of the street, often clashed with our film's soundtrack, but no one cared.

As the days warmed up, and every balcony window was left open, we were all one happy family. The woman I waved to every morning was married to the government authority on steel for the Iranian Five-Year Economic Plan. The gentleman on our right was a poet. He gave us copies of his odes to the marvels of petroleum. Jahangir had to translate for us as best he could the words of this self-proclaimed Hafez of carbon-based fuels.

That no one heard a thing the night we were robbed seemed incredible. We had two houseguests spending the night. Jahangir and his wife Razi, who had just arrived from Meshed, were sleeping in their quarters behind the house. Even Molly's dog was still staying with us. George and I were in the master bedroom with the balcony open to the world. We woke up to see four legs flying over the front wall. Two pairs of George's trousers, which had been hanging in the closet in our room, were gone, as were my two specially-tailored pregnancy skirts.

I was lucky that all the British had not yet been kicked out of Tehran. Dr. Cohen, my OB/GYN, maintained a lonely outpost at the British Nursing Home. He waited patiently for my birth date before packing his bags and fleeing. Poor Ahme, who gave birth to her first baby six months later, had to make do at the Varjevan Hospital, which was staffed with Russians. When I went to visit, unflappable Ahme was in tears because the nurses had placed the new-born infant over a rigid wood board and bound her to it tightly using lengths of cloth—a technique that ensured, she was told, that her child would grow up with good posture. "My poor baby! Her legs! Her back!" Ahme was inconsolable. I tried to address the situation with the head nurse in my college Russian, but to no avail. Fortunately, an Iranian doctor came to the rescue.

For weeks prior to my delivery, Dr. Cohen made it clear that I should continue to walk—and then to walk some more. It didn't do anything to slow my weight gain, because my favorite morning walk was to the Russian bakery to get some *Amerikanski* loaves and to sample the hot, sticky, raisin buns, the flaky croissants, and the enormous star cookies. I was elated one morning when a fellow shopper mistook me for a Russian, although my accent eventually gave me away. From Saisi Street down Maucheri, I usually stopped to admire every display of strawberries, apricots, and honeydew melons. I can still smell the mixed fumes of kerosene lamps and damp cement at nearby metal-soldering repair shops manned by Iranians and Russians and Armenians.

Tehran was a wild mix of displaced 20th-century refugees. Many Armenians, who fled during the chaos of the disintegrating Ottoman Empire, preferred life under the Shah to life under Stalin. A surprisingly large number worked at our Embassy. Vahram, who worked for George in the Radio Section, invited us to their Orthodox Easter service. Carefully walled away in a corner of town, their Armenian cathedral was a non-descript white plaster building on the outside, but inside it was ablaze with a thousand burning candles and thick with the smell of incense. A priest thundered the litany from behind a gold-leafed screen, then stepped forward to lead an outdoor procession. We all filed slowly around the church holding icons and lighted candles. The priest paused before re-entering the church. He turned to face us and joyfully announced: "Christ is risen."

There was even more of an ethnic mix in the Tehran American Boy Scout troop that George founded—the first one in Iran. Within months, he had the sons of U.S. Army colonels, Armenian cab drivers, Lebanese merchants, Czech construction engineers, Jewish shopkeepers, and Yugoslav doctors all swearing allegiance to the same youth organization. If some of the younger ones had trouble with their merit badges, they came over to the Scout Den, our home, where they consumed mountains of Jahangir's hot dogs, potato salad, and chocolate cake—and were still hungry.

It took a while for them to understand scouting. The first time they had all gathered to set out on a camping trip, George noticed that many were carrying heavy three-tiered lunch pails full of food. Others just brought their servants. The assembled mothers saying goodbye to their precious ones were nonplussed by George's comment that Scouts did not need servants.

"Why, of course my son will need a cook. How will he eat?"

Toward late May, as my due date approached, George had concerns other than helping the boys become Scouts. The demonstrations near his office were increasing in size, in fierceness, and eventually in violence. New water pipes were being laid on Naderi Street, turning much of the road into stones and clumps of cement, which made excellent missiles. The government eventually imposed a curfew from either 8:00 p.m. or 10:00 p.m. until dawn. Since the hours shifted from day to day, you could never be sure when the curfew began. The streets were in constant turmoil between the supporters of Mossadegh and the supporters of the Shah.

The streets of Tehran were in turmoil leading up to the ouster of Mossadegh.

Through the Embassy and the Tehran police department, George obtained a curfew-breaking document stamped with an awe-inspiring array of official black stamps and red seals. This document announced that he was escorting his wife to the hospital because she was about to deliver a baby.

We needed that document the night of June 19. The streets were eerily silent and empty of all but the police, who were standing guard with bludgeons and guns. When George showed them his magical document, they waved us on. Already alerted, Dr. Cohen and his nurse were waiting at the nursing home, literally ready to flee the country as soon as our child was born. Waiting for the delivery, we smoked—and we smoked a lot. My cigarettes were Benson & Hedges. I can't remember what brand Dr. Cohen smoked, but he had a long cigarette holder, and since he was already scrubbed, his nurse was in charge of taking it out of his mouth from time to time and flicking off the ashes for him. George was waiting anxiously upstairs—this was long before the time when husbands were invited into the delivery room—on a lumpy chintz sofa reading *Ride a Pink Horse*, the first and last mystery he ever read.

The first born was a son! That was as it should be in the East. One of the first visitors to the British Nursing Home to congratulate George was an Iranian general, another of George's English students. I heard the boots clicking down the empty hall before a trim dandy in a shiny white sharkskin suit appeared in the waiting room. He was close enough for me to see that he was carrying a *kashkul*, or dervish alms bucket, carved out of a coconut shell from the Seychelles—filled with red roses for George to give to me. Two days later, the main headline in all the Tehran newspapers was that this same general had been executed for having shot a man two weeks before. The murky circumstances were never adequately explained.

George and Steve.

We took Steve home three days later, along with the *kashkul* from the general.

I knew absolutely nothing about taking care of a baby. All of my Chinese brothers were a good four years older than me. I had been a babysitter during high school, but I had never cared for an infant. Babies terrified me, and now I had one of my own. My lack of experience was so obvious to our Iranian friends that I was showered with advice. Even though it was summer and hot outside—Middle East hot—I followed one friend's advice to stitch a flannel tummy-band for Steve. I clutched my Dr. Spock's *Baby and Child Care* all day long and remain forever indebted to its incomparable index.

Jahangir and Razi had the nursery waiting for us when we returned from the hospital. It was as sterile as a Mayo Clinic operating theater and remained that way as much as was humanly possible.

Dr. Spock recommended a daily outing so that an infant's lungs could be filled with fresh air. I had the splendid baby carriage we bought from the British Consul and his wife back in Meshed ready. I was prepared to dodge the loose cows, sheep, or goats that I had met on the daily constitutionals that Dr. Cohen had recommended before the delivery. More worrisome than an animal or two was the graffiti everywhere saying, "YANKEE, GO HOME." We were quickly being seen as having replaced the British as the force behind the Shah's street demonstrations.

Animals and graffiti were one thing, kisses another. A kiss was what we encountered one afternoon as the petroleum poet's *bache* was squatting outside their gate. Lowering herself to Steve's level, she made a grab for him and smacked him with a noisy, saliva-rich kiss on his lips.

Only some deep maternal wisdom kept me from boiling his lips to decontaminate them.

Thank God for Steve's long-suffering pediatrician, Dr. Ahari. His office was just behind the Majlis, the Parliament building. Despite the increasing danger from the street crowds, he never once hesitated to race over to Takhte Jamshid out of concern for Steve and his mother's strange ways.

Less than a month after Steve's arrival, Mossadegh resigned in a disagreement with the Shah over his choice for Minister of Defense. The mobs went wild, whipped up by the Ayatollah Kashani in alliance with Mossadegh's National Front and the communist Tudeh Party. Kashani was calling for a holy war against the imperialists. In this latest uproar, more than 500 demonstrators were reported killed and 4,000 hospitalized. For five days, until the Shah reinstated Mossadegh as Prime Minister, the whole country was torn apart. Radio broadcasts blared night and day from our neighbors' radios with sobs and mourning for the dead. It made one shiver.

By February 1953, it was rumored that this time, Mossadegh was forcing the Shah to leave the country. Once again mobs roamed the streets. A relatively small earthquake rattled everyone's nerves, with Iran on a physical fault line, as well as a political one.

On March 3, 1953, Stalin died, which demonstrated the strength of the Tudeh Party. George barely managed to navigate through the thousands gathered by the Russian Embassy on his way to work. Women were sobbing hysterically before the black- and-red-draped gates. One encounter with a Soviet had been enough for me. At a cocktail party for a newly arrived American Embassy Air Attaché in December, I was roped into a very one-sided conversation with three officials from the Soviet Embassy. "Who is your husband? What does he do? How long have you been here? Where did you learn Russian? Why did you learn Russian?" I forget what innocuous replies I stuttered, but it was clear that my dossier at the Russian Embassy was getting thicker.

Foreign correspondents, particularly American correspondents, were descending by the planeload to file their stories about the smoldering "rare tinder" that Acheson had warned would catch fire first in Iran. At the time, there were few people I held in higher regard than journalists. One day, George brought home *Time's* Middle East bureau chief, who was stationed in Beirut. I spectacularly failed to impress him with my culinary skills, attempting to make a fiery Mexican *mole poblano*. An Embassy secretary and neighbor encouraged me as I added more and more cocoa as a substitute for unsweetened chocolate, which wasn't available in the markets. The mole was inedible. A can of tuna fish came to the rescue.

There was Clifton Daniels, the courtly North Carolinian, who was then chief correspondent for the Middle East for *The New York Times*, operating from a base in London. He later became managing editor of the *Times* from 1964 until 1969—after marrying President Truman's daughter, Margaret, in 1956.

There was the irascible Nate Polowetzky, the Associated Press correspondent, who would become AP's longtime foreign editor. He was known to have barked at complaining correspondents that if they thought it difficult to cover war, they should try covering peace. We saw him regularly in the apartment of a stunning blonde named Anna Karoline

Lohman—we called her Carrie—who was an endless source of delight: spontaneous, honest, unpretentious, curious, and besotted with baby Steve. She married Nate soon after we left Iran, to the consternation of her high-society father, who didn't know what was more upsetting, the fact that Nate was Jewish or the fact that he was a journalist.

There was also Mark Purdue, who spent many a night at our house. To our distress, he was expelled in May. The Tehran press explained that he was kicked out for "having sent abroad false and provocative news against the interests of Iran." Mark was the fifth foreign correspondent and the third American to have been expelled since the nationalization of the Anglo-Iranian Oil Company was announced two years before.

But in even the most extreme situations, life seems to go on. In March 1953, Norouz, the Iranian New Year's celebration, was celebrated without any seeming regard for the danger on the streets. The customs were a little bizarre, but charming. Our neighbors placed small earthen pots—each containing a coin, a piece of charcoal, and some seeds—on top of the walls overlooking the street—and then proceeded to knock them down, so that they would shatter on the ground. By breaking the vessels, the celebrants were warding off all the evils that might befall them in the New Year. Our neighbors also built piles of dried thorns and set them on fire. Members of their families along with guests proceeded to jump over the smoldering piles.

Mrs. Ahari, the wife of my pediatrician, explained Norouz to us. The holiday is of ancient Zoroastrian origin, and every year it coincides with the Spring Equinox—and the return to earth after a long, cold winter, of Rapithwin, the Zoroastrian Lord of Noonday and Heat. It was also the day Jamshid was lifted into the heavens on a magnificent throne to reign like the sun for more than 700 years. Just as we decorate Christmas trees for Christmas, people prepare for Norouz by filling seven trays with symbolic offerings to yet another Zoroastrian deity over a period of several weeks. Somehow the Shiite *mullahs* put up with these pagan rituals. All the offerings that filled the trays begin with the letter "s": *sekeh* (a coin), *sanzee* (greens), *sonbol* (hyacinth), *seer* (garlic), *senjed* (dried fruit), *samanu* (a sweet), and *serkeh* (vinegar). These offerings represent truth, justice, good thoughts, good deeds, prosperity, virtue, generosity, and immortality.

But it was only a matter of time before the political violence would begin to consume our lives. At first, Rocky and Ahme were the only members of our circle who knew what was going on right before our eyes. Rocky told us bits and pieces about what happened over the years, but it was a *New York Times* article published in April 2000 that told us many of the details of the CIA plan to overthrow Mossadegh, an operation that took roughly from November 1952 through August 1953. Robert Fisk, for nearly 30 years the Middle East correspondent for *The Independent* of London, had revealed more of the British side of what Fisk calls the "Persian skullduggery" and "regime change on the cheap."

The planning for the coup began as early as November 1952, but it wasn't until May 1953 that Dr. Donald Wilber, our own spy, met with his British counterparts in Cyprus to make final preparations. On July 11, the day we left Tehran, President Eisenhower gave his approval for the operation. Shortly later, on the evening of August 15, the coup started. Kermit Roosevelt was in charge. Fortuitously for Roosevelt, Mossadegh dismissed Ayatollah Kashani from his position as Speaker of Parliament, which triggered a bedlam of riots and counter-riots. In the evening mayhem, the Shah fled first to Baghdad and then to Rome. Mossadegh tried to get control over the situation by ordering his police chief to quell the disturbances. Instead, the police chief sided with the royalists in the army. It was Mossadegh who was arrested after a pitched tank and rifle battle on Kokh Avenue where he lived, only 100 yards from the Shah's Winter Palace.

Three days later, on August 18, the CIA headquarters in Washington was filled with "depression and despair." Nothing was going according to plan. The Shah, who was feckless and very nervous, seemed to be changing his mind every day about whether a coup would succeed. Mossadegh's forces held the streets one day, the Shah's forces held them the next. But the Americans were forging ahead. Roosevelt smuggled General Fazlollah Zahedi, the Shah's newly declared Prime Minister, lying on the floor of his car, into the safe haven of the American Embassy for consultations.

And there in Shimron, in the foothills of Tehran, sat Ahme, the beauty from Corpus Christi, guarding Zahedi's son Ardeshir with a gun hidden under the afghan she was knitting. She sat outside a closed bedroom in their home where he had been told to hide. Ahme just sat there calmly knitting the afghan and watching over her eight-month-old baby.

Rocky was in another hideout with the General, who, upon learning that he was indeed the new Prime Minister, was so nervous his fingers shook as he tried to button the buttons on his uniform. Rocky had to button them for him.

While Mossadegh was being placed under house arrest, Rocky then took General Zahedi to the Radio Tehran building in a tank to proclaim the new government. But in all the confusion, the broadcasts only discussed the new cotton crop—not the coup that was taking place. By 2:20 p.m. on August 19, the coup was a *fait accompli*, and the Shah was on his way home from Rome. In the scramble at the radio station to provide appropriate music for the announcement of a new government, someone grabbed a recording of "The Star-Spangled Banner."

Mosul

Baghdad
★

IRAQ

Ur
Basra

IRAQ

Our new post was Baghdad, where we arrived on April 5, 1954. We spent the first two weeks at the famed Zia Hotel, perched on a high point next to the Tigris River, which had recently flooded, drenching the entire city in mud.

I was pregnant again—seven months pregnant—and I was busy chasing Steve around, keeping him from jumping into the Tigris. One of our fellow guests was an elegant Florida lady who was never seen without her perfect pearl necklace. She even maintained her composure when the Zia gardener forgot to switch taps and, as she lay in her bathtub, watched it fill with muddy river water. She chatted happily on about how this exotic adventure had to come right out of the *Thousand and One Nights*. Other Zia guests included Yankee helicopter crews who were spending their days dropping food and clean water for victims of the flood and spending their nights in the hotel bar, where a bartender named Jesus served up his famous fiery drink called a "Desert Dream."

Everyone loved telling the story of the little English girl who, on returning to England, was asked in Sunday School if she knew who Jesus was.

"Oh, yes," she said proudly. "He's the bartender at the Zia Hotel."

George was out searching for a home and an office, since we no longer had the Embassy to fend for us. After leaving Tehran, George had resigned from the Foreign Service and had been hired by the American Friends of the Middle East (AFME) to set up an Iraq office. Dorothy Thompson, the famous American journalist who founded AFME in 1951, had met George in Iran and had been impressed by his intelligence, his energy, his sincerity, and above all his singular effectiveness in communicating with Middle Easterners. Ms. Thompson was convinced that it was vital to the postwar world that the U.S. and the Middle East understand each other, and she chose George to take up this mission in Iraq.

Our new house on Seif Al Islam Abdullah Street was quite beautiful, a wonderful Bauhaus structure with huge floor-to-ceiling windows everywhere. In a country that had summers hovering about 130 degrees, with even worse humidity and no air-conditioning, it may have been a beautiful house, but it was also all but uninhabitable. Those windows trapped the summer heat and roasted us alive. We were on the west side of the Tigris, still swollen with filthy flood water. The parkway across the street was a concourse of mud, jammed with ragged tents, huts made from battered sheets of tin, and other makeshift hovels.

Although we didn't have the Embassy to help us begin our new life in Iraq, we had Father Connell, one of the New England Jesuit Fathers who taught at either Baghdad College or Al Hikma University. He was able to answer all of my most urgent questions about our new home. Fortunately for us, he frequently dropped by on his way back to the campus from a trip into town. Living in Iraq, my main concern was the fauna: lizards, crickets, sand-flies, frogs, mosquitoes, and scorpions. Father Connell reassured me that the scorpions were the only ones that could kill us—suggesting, helpfully, that we shake out our slippers in the morning before putting them on. People had actually died from bites from scorpions lurking in their slippers.

Then there were the diseases: malaria, smallpox, sand-fly fever, schistosomiasis or bilharzia, cholera, typhus, and typhoid. I had also heard of another common ailment in Iraq, one absurdly difficult to spell—leishmaniasis, also known as the Baghdad boil, which was a lesion left by a sand-fly. I had seen someone who had one, and it left a terrible scar. Disfigured for life from a bite by a microscopic sand-fly.

I was particularly concerned about how to protect Steve, who was thrilled with the frogs and lizards, from all of these hazards without turning him into a lifelong paranoiac.

That was a few weeks into our stay; we hadn't been in the new home three days when George had to fly to Beirut for a Muslim-Christian Convocation sponsored by the American Friends of the Middle East. No Jahangir, yet. No English-speaking workmen from the Embassy's General Services section to call. I knew Michael at the Zia at the Hotel and

Steve at the gate of our second home in Baghdad.

Jesus at the bar, but virtually no one else.

I was determined to be okay. Steve, however, was miserable. By the end of the first day with no Daddy to play with, he was driving me crazy, especially in the evening.

During the day, he had the refugees and their scrawny cows and mangy camels to watch from the walls of the garden. Occasionally, one of the workmen George had hired to work on the house and the garden, with its three struggling date palms, took pity on him. He helped Steve turn on the faucet to the garden hose to provide water to a veiled refugee. She was using one arm to carry a baby and the other to lead a cow with a rope—all while balancing a bucket for water on her head. Steve was mesmerized.

After dark, however, the show ended. When Steve had finished his supper, we took a walk in the courtyard where we heard shrieks of laughter from children playing next door. He would not budge, attempting to bore a hole with his eyes through the two-foot-thick wall separating our two houses. With some difficulty, given the advanced stage of my pregnancy, I hoisted Steve onto the top of the wall, making sure his legs dangled on the other side.

My stratagem worked.

Within seconds, nine-year-old Ma'ad Saffar and his father were banging on our gate to invite us next door and into their lives. The father, it turned out, was a doctor—Dr. Samim Saffar—a tall, skinny man with a wonderful heart. His wife Aliyeh was strikingly pretty, and her mother, who lived with them, had obviously lived a long life and learned much from it. In addition, to Ma'ad, nine, there was Ra'ad, seven, and Muthir, two. Although only the good doctor and Ma'ad spoke any English, and only a smattering at that, it didn't matter. We were instant friends.

Steve's best friend, Muthir.

Steve and I went to the Saffars the next morning and almost every morning thereafter. I sat on a stool in the kitchen, sipping steaming-hot Turkish coffee while Aliyeh and her mother squatted comfortably on the floor, washing, scraping, cutting, frying, steaming, and stirring the day's meals. Aliyeh's mother was a toothless delight, her faded yellow curls escaping a tight black silk scull-cap. She chain-smoked perfumed Turkish cigarettes. Ismet, the maid, dashed about making sure the peelings and the rest of the waste were swished down the drain in the middle of the floor. Steve and Muthir raced and raced around the house, screaming and laughing with pure joy.

Once, when Muthir paused to lick at an open crack in the plaster, I looked at Aliyeh.

"No problem," she said, anticipating my concern. "Don't worry. Actually, it is healthy. His body needs it."

"Healthy?"

"Of course. It's natural. There is something he needs

there in the plaster. Probably a mineral or two. I don't know which ones."

Aliyeh patiently coached me in Arabic, which was proving a nightmare. The ostensible reason for learning Arabic was to immerse myself in Arab culture. The real reason was that I didn't want to miss anything, especially the gossip among the women. But my pronunciation was ghastly. I was increasingly jealous of Steve, who was beginning to speak Arabic as easily as he spoke English. His grammar was sometimes off, but his pronunciation in both languages was perfect. His vocabulary was filling with useful phrases in English, with an Arabic translation ready for the neighbors: "Look me," "Go away," "Me no do," and "Me no want do." Aliyeh was non-judgmental and determined to keep me sane as she gently taught me conversational Arabic.

Nevertheless, I took great solace in the misery of others who found learning Arabic as difficult as I did. One of the first New England missionaries in the Middle East, Pliny Fisk, wrote that he was quickly discouraged by Arabic's "13 conjugations, 20 ways of forming the plural, and 33 ways of forming the infinitive; with its consonants without vowels, and its unnumbered dialects." Nearly a century later, another American missionary, Z. M. Zwemer, wrote that "the gutturals [in Arabic] belong to the desert and were doubtless borrowed from the camel when she complained of overloading."

My gutturals were safe with Aliyeh and her mother. They never once laughed at me.

Poor Aliyeh did complain, however, about the endless supply of chickens, goats, and sheep that her husband received in exchange for his medical services. She was fed up with slitting the throats of scrawny chickens and plucking their feathers.

"Another chicken! What to do? And you saw; yesterday, there was another sheep." Another of Samim's patients had paid him with an unshorn sheep. "I don't need another silly sheep. The boys need shoes, not sheep. Samim will accept anything in payment. What can I do?"

Our social life began to pick up—starting at the top of the social and political ladder. One day, Sarah Jamali, wife of Prime Minister Mohammed Fadhel Jamali, came to call. Sarah, who was of Canadian and American origin, had met Dr. Jamali at Columbia University in New York City in 1932. Before accepting his marriage proposal, she came to Baghdad for a year to teach and to decide if she could adjust to his family and to an entirely different culture. From the time she rang our doorbell to the day she died in 2008, Sarah Jamali remained a close friend. Simple in dress and manner, she didn't wear a speck of makeup and never descended into idle chatter.

I learned that, in 1940, their first-born son, Laith, was diagnosed with encephalitis and suffered severe brain damage. There were no schools for the intellectually challenged in those days, but when Laith was 10, Sarah managed to place him in a Rudolf Steiner school in Scotland, which had the expertise to address children like Laith. And "eventually," as she would say, "all necessary things seemed to fall into place of their own volition." The first school for those with similar challenges, the Ramzi School, was started in Baghdad.

Laith's medical challenges were hardly the only battles Sarah would have to fight. Her husband Dr. Jamali was caught in the political mayhem of the late 1950s and sentenced to death by hanging. Morocco interceded on his behalf, and after three years in prison, he was able to go into political exile in Tunisia in 1962. While her husband was in jail, Sarah Jamali later told me, "I suddenly found myself confined to home in Baghdad with lots of time on my hands." Instead of bemoaning her fate, she tapped into the rich oral tradition of her heavily-veiled mother-in-law to write a wonderful book: *Folktales from the City of the Golden Domes*.

Enjoying our tea that afternoon and discussing the problems of female education, I suddenly felt something crawling up my left leg. I had shaken out my slippers and shoes in the morning, but my nine-month girth was such that I had considerable difficulty bending over far enough to see the creature that was determined to climb the length of my leg. I soon realized that it was a dreaded scorpion. I flicked it off, less fearful of instant death than of losing my composure in front of the Prime Minister's wife. I even managed to kill it unobtrusively with my shoed foot.

About to give birth again, I had hired a stony-faced Syrian Catholic woman named Almas to take care of Steve while I was at the Seventh Day Adventist Hospital downtown beside the Tigris. We had sent back to Iran for Jahangir, who, as a Shiite, was thrilled at the thought of being so close to the holy Shiite shrine of Karbala. But until he arrived, I had also hired a man named Mansur to clean the house.

On June 16, three days before Steve's second birthday, one of the worst experiences of our life overseas began. Two days earlier, my obstetrician—a Dr. Semikova—had found me "ready and healthy as an ox." If I didn't have the baby within two days, she would induce labor.

Muthir was visiting, and he and Steve were seated at a small red children's table in the kitchen eating a snack when

Mansur, who was removing a cabinet from the wall over the sink to check for mold, jumped as a mass of water bugs rushed into the room from the space behind the cabinet. He tried stomping on the horde, to little avail. In the second it took to avert my eyes from the horrific scene, I felt the fetus stiffen, and I knew something was very wrong.

Within minutes, George, who had been working in his office down the hallway, was rushing me to the hospital.

I blacked out, not to wake up until I had been transferred to a bed in the hospital, with George standing there beside me, tears streaming down his face. Dr. Semikova was whispering in my ear: "God has saved him. God has saved him from another Korea." There on a small white table to my right, lying on his right side, was a dead infant boy with a crown of tight, black curls, just like George's.

I heard people scurrying around me. I heard them talking. "Don't give her any plasma. She's gone as well. We need the plasma for the living, not for the dead." I was hemorrhaging badly.

I was now fully aware of what had happened and what was happening. But somehow it seemed as if it was happening to someone else—not to me. I was moved out of the delivery room and into a very large and very empty hospital room—basically to die.

Throughout the long night, an exhausted Seventh Day Adventist nurse from Canton, Ohio, held my hand—her glasses slipping off her face, her head nodding to sleep. I later found out that George was on a frantic mission to find the Rh-negative blood I needed but was not being given. He had been offered all that was available in Baghdad in 1954: blood from inmates in the insane asylum. George, who hadn't slept for more than 24 hours, had alerted the

U.S. Embassy and he and the Embassy staff contacted every American in Baghdad looking for someone with the right blood type. Luckily for me, two of the Jesuit Fathers—Father Fallon, an Irishman, and Father Olson, who later became the Bishop of Iceland—had the right blood type and rushed to the hospital, either to save my life or to ready me for the next. Aliyeh and her mother happened to be visiting me in the hospital when I had the infusion of Father Fallon's blood. Even though she was a doctor's wife, Aliyeh was astonished: In Iraq, it was almost unheard of for a non-family member to donate blood.

George was still tragically busy, looking for a coffin for the boy we had planned to call Roger. Muslims wrap their dead in a clean cloth and bury them within 24 hours. But we weren't Muslim. The hospital administration was of no help, so George ended up calling the Royal British Hospital. After George explained the circumstances, the British matron on the other end of the line asked if a six-foot coffin would "do."

"Oh, yes," she added. "I forgot. I can't let you have one. They are only for the British."

The young American Consul, Mr. Wolfe, intervened at that point. He arranged for a carpenter, probably from General Services, to make a coffin. He also managed to have Roger buried in the British Civil Cemetery.

With each transfusion, I went through a thousand emotions: fury, guilt, and despair, then joy for a new day, before I collapsed again into misery. I was riveted by a lizard crawling across a crack in the wall, then by the shadows of old palms dancing on the walls, as I made out the muffled sounds of boat traffic on the Tigris below. My room, which looked onto a deep balcony, could well have served as offices for Ottoman generals or for British generals as they kept a tight rein over the "benighted Mesopotamians." Then again, the enormous building with its wrap-around balcony was typical of the missionary houses I had lived in and played in so many years ago. My worlds were blending into one.

Three days after I was admitted to the hospital, George brought Steve to visit. It was his second birthday. Clutching a bouquet of tiger lilies and bright yellow and red zinnias, Steve stared at me from the end of the bed and kept on staring. We didn't share a word as I stared back, disbelieving that any of this could be real.

I was released a week later. George helped carry me down the hospital stairs, but not before a clerk dropped the hospital bill in my lap.

"You forgot to ask," he snarled as George gave him a dirty look.

George's reply—minus a few four-letter words—was: "I'll teach you to be missionaries if it's the last thing I ever do."

I was released on the condition that I received a daily liver shot.

Every day for two weeks, our overworked neighbor, Dr. Samim, tended to me along with the hundreds of patients at his clinic. I later learned from Aliyeh that he was shocked that I shamelessly threw aside my sheet so that he could give me the shot in my hip. Male Iraqi doctors rarely had much direct contact with their female patients. The norm for him was to hand his stethoscope, equipped with a special attachment, to a maid or family member to place on a female patient. No matter how clear he tried to be in his instructions, he was never quite certain if the stethoscope was being positioned on the patient's head, foot, or abdomen. With me, he had no such problem. I was happy to bare my hip in all its naked glory.

I never quite understood the Arab attitude toward modesty. On the one hand, a male doctor could not inspect a female patient. On the other hand, during the hottest summer months, all of Baghdad slept on their roofs to escape the blistering heat, including us and the Saffars, whom we had not yet met. One morning, I was embarrassed to wake up, sleepy-eyed in my pajamas, to see Dr. Samim, in his pajamas, eyeing me less than a couple of feet away.

Similarly disorienting was an experience with Selma, the wife of the Army Captain who lived on the other end of Seif Al-Islam. I had met her at one of the neighborhood gatherings that Aliyeh had on the seventh of each month. One day—after chatting with me in our sitting room—she walked to the front door of our house instead of to the side door we all used. George was at his desk, and I'm sure he didn't look up. Even so, and even though she was almost entirely covered up in her *abaya*, she was mortified that he might have seen her toes in her open-toed sandals. This same Selma asked me to walk her home to her carport one day. Already married for three years, without a single child, she had convinced herself that she was pregnant. Aliyeh called it a "ghost" pregnancy. I was dumbstruck when Selma, facing the street, opened her *abaya* and lifted her breasts up for me to confirm that they were the breasts of a pregnant woman.

I wasn't brave enough to remind her of the ancient Iraqi superstition that I was already familiar with—namely, that a woman who was having trouble getting pregnant had several options. She could crawl under a camel's belly; she could walk around town, enter a cemetery, and jump over seven tombs; or she could collect water from seven cisterns and have it poured over her head through a broom.

These wild cultural differences were astonishing enough for me, but they were downright overwhelming for the scores of naive American women who had met and married Iraqi students studying in the States, then come back with their new husbands to become Iraqis. They were caught in a vise of culture shock. By default, I often became their guide and counselor. Sometimes, just a spoonful of peanut butter could help. I could afford to buy a jar from Orosdi-Backs or Spinney's. They could not. The monthly stipend a bursary student received in the U.S., which was approximately $3,000 a month, dropped to about $150 when he returned home. But the shock of living on an almost nonexistent budget was nothing in comparison to shock of adapting to life as an Iraqi wife and mother.

George had an American secretary named Jane who destroyed and ditched her capri pants before she even left Texas to come to Baghdad. I always knew when her in-laws were going to show up because she would erupt in a nervous rash. There was no problem with her father-in-law, who was a respected *mullah*, but her mother-in-law was a henna practitioner. Henna has played a role in Middle Eastern societies for centuries. The leaves, flowers, and twigs of the henna bush are ground into a fine powder and applied to the skin or hair to improve a woman's health, to act as a conditioner, or simply to beautify. Her mother-in-law's specialty was the latter. She not only drew henna swirls on the hands and feet of a bride the day before a marriage was consummated but also on the front of the bride's body, making a luxurious path all the way down to the private parts. Jane was aghast. I was, too.

There was also culture shock for non-Iraqi Arabs settling into Baghdad. Rabob Chaderchi was one. An Egyptian dentist, Rabob's husband was a gentle Iraqi Foreign Service officer named Hekmat. He had been posted for the past 16 years in the West, predominantly in New York City. Rabob and their 14-year-old daughter Lubna were miserable in Baghdad. Lubna threatened daily to flee to New York, or even to Cairo, where her older brother Mohsen was in boarding school.

I was a safety valve for the Chaderchi women. Each one could pour her heart out to me. In return, Rabob helped me with my Arabic. Aliyeh gave me daily practice in conversation, including discussions about how terrible it was to marry a daughter off at 14 and expect her to start being pregnant year in and year out. But Rabob could help me with Arabic declensions.

One day, Rabob talked me into accompanying her to call on Princess Rajiha, the aunt of King Faisal II—the reigning King of Iraq—and the daughter of King Faisal I. I knew the Princess was married to a commoner who was an Air Force pilot. He and George had worked together to start the Baghdad Rotary Club. George really liked him, and I was curious. A Qajar princess had come to dinner in Meshed, but she was my student. I had never formally called on a princess, a member of a reigning royal family.

"Just do as I do," Rabob prompted. "Follow me."

But she faltered as we drove up the driveway.

"Here, put this in your purse. I've got a drippy nose, and I might have to open my purse. The gun might show. You don't have a cold."

It was too late to stop her. She thrust her small pistol with an ivory-inlaid handle in my purse.

"Why do you need a gun? This is insane," I said in horror. "Now I'll be the one to get arrested and deported for carrying a gun—your gun."

She paid me no heed. Her gun was already in my purse. I kept uncharacteristically quiet, trying to avoid calling attention to me and my purse. While Rabob happily chatted away in a mixture of Arabic, Turkish, and French, I surveyed my surroundings. It was early February and each lady, excepting the Princess, Rabob, and myself, was covered in mink and diamonds. We were sitting in huge chairs upholstered in silk brocade as we drank our Turkish coffee and nibbled Swiss chocolates. Silver bowls filled with violets were everywhere. The Princess herself was plain, plump, very sweet, and soft-spoken. Her eyes were heavy-lidded, like her father's, and her lipstick and fingernail polish were the same bright shade of vermillion. I managed to get out of the house without anyone discovering the gun I was carrying.

The first dinner party at our house was every bit as awkward.

I had not yet heard that a Bedouin in the desert was expected to honor an unexpected guest by slaughtering a camel, then stuffing it with three sheep, each sheep stuffed with five chickens, and each chicken stuffed with 10 eggs, all on top of a mountain of rice. According to H. R. P. Dickson, a seasoned British Political Officer who served in Mesopotamia and Kuwait in the 1920s, "a Bedouin, however poor he is, and however lowly his dwelling place . . . will slay his last camel or sheep to do honour to his guest . . . (he) would ruin himself rather than be stingy to his guests."

But I still had Aunt Mina's New England parsimony ringing in my ears: "Waste not, want not." There would be

12 of us at the dinner, so I had prepared 12 lamb shanks. And I had mounds of rice, vegetables, and salad. I had even asked Omar, the bearer of an Embassy friend, to come serve.

The conversation was sparkling, the food delicious, the evening a success—until Omar bent down to whisper in my ears: "the chauffeurs."

"What do you mean, the 'chauffeurs?'"

"They have to be *fed*."

"Fed?" I had no idea what he was talking about.

"It is *expected*, Madame. It is our custom. You have to serve food to the guests and to their chauffeurs as well."

I left the guests and prepared food for five hungry, disgruntled chauffeurs.

Lesson learned. The Naifeh family honor was kept intact with the help of three cans of tuna fish.

We were soon invited out for dinner again, this time to the home of Sheikh Abbas Kashif Al-Gita. George was very friendly with the Sheikh's brother, Mohammed, who had recently returned home from the University of Michigan with a Ph.D. in nuclear physics. Because the wife of a visiting Fulbright professor had hounded George about visiting a "real, honest-to-goodness" Iraqi home, he had talked Mohammed into having his brother, the Sheikh, invite us all to his home for dinner.

At no point in the evening did the Sheikh's wife appear in our mixed gathering. But throughout the dinner, unbeknownst to the Fulbright wife, Mrs. Al-Gita stood behind a tiny window that allowed her to survey the dining room and direct the servants to bring more food to this guest, more soft drinks to that guest. The Fulbright wife was taken aback by the mounds of food being served—food that both looked and tasted strange. She had anticipated not liking the dinner and had settled on what she clearly thought was the brilliant stratagem of putting a plastic bag in her pocketbook so that she could dispose of the food on her plate without eating it. I watched, horrified, as she furtively slid the food on her plate into the pocketbook—all in full view of Mrs. Al-Gita. Every time the Fulbright wife slid another morsel from her plate into the bag, our hostess directed a servant to replenish the plate. I could only assume that Mrs. Al-Gita thought the Fulbright wife was stowing the food away for an impoverished family at home—although she must have been dumbfounded when her guest added vanilla pudding to the pocketbook's jumbled smorgasbord.

Even at weddings the sexes did not mingle. I attended one wedding so large it had to be held in King Faisal Hall. There were 300 guests—all women. The only men were the musicians in a seven-piece band, and they were hidden behind a screen in a corner. The bride sat alone in the middle of the stage in a voluminous, frilly white wedding gown. Under two naked light bulbs, she sat between two pedestals holding enormous bouquets. The orchestra provided loud background music for two singers and two belly dancers. Midway through the proceedings, the bride slipped out backstage to change. When she returned, she was wearing a long, form-fitting, pink-sequined gown. This wedding was, in some ways, like countless others I would attend throughout the Arab world: a presentation of the bride to female family and friends, with the actual marriage finalized a few days before when the groom and the bride's father signed an agreement in a local mosque.

One evening out was far more modest than the grand wedding, but ended up being even more memorable. It was a simple enough dinner at the home of the head of the Baghdad office of what would become known as the Agency for International Development. The family's daughter was home from an archaeological dig at Nimrod, north of Baghdad, directed by the famous British archaeologist Sir Max Mallowan. George was seated next to a woman in her early 60s who was simply dressed, without makeup or any jewelry other than a wedding band. She and George had an animated conversation, although he must have missed her name when they met at the table.

When we rose from dinner and started to mingle, a short trim British gentleman introduced himself to George as Mallowan—the famous archaeologist himself.

"I understand that you are married to Agatha Christie," George said, "and that she has been up at the dig with you."

"Yes, she has. My wife was sitting next to you at dinner."

Aunt Mina had devoured *Murder on the Orient Express*, *Murder in Mesopotamia*, *They Came to Baghdad*, and every other mystery from the pen of the famous mystery writer. To think that George had spent an entire evening chatting with Agatha Christie was almost inconceivable to her.

Most of the archaeologists working in Iraq in the mid-20th century were, like Mallowan, British. But there was an American archaeologist making important discoveries in northeastern Iraq, and George and I heard him give a lecture on his discoveries. Dr. Robert J. Braidwood was a professor at the University of Chicago; he had just come down to Baghdad from working in a small village called Jarmo. Braidwood credited events in a village like Jarmo with launching human civilization: "Somewhere in one of perhaps a dozen places in the Middle East about 12,000 years ago, someone made a remarkable observation—a common weed, which had been collected for eating, was growing where he or she had previously spilled seeds. That was the beginning of agriculture, which was the beginning of civilization."

Not long after meeting Mallowan, I joined a group from the American Embassy on a trip to Ur. We rode in jeeps with guards manning bazookas on all sides. Iraq was a comparatively safe place at the time, but the American Ambassador still required security.

We were travelling to see the famous Ziggurat at Ur, built in the 21st century B.C., but there was very little to see there but sand—endless sand in every direction—with only a lopsided mound of crumbling bricks to interrupt the flat brown monotony. The building there now is mostly a reconstruction built long after George and I left Iraq. The lush gardens and babbling brooks of this "cradle of civilization" were obviously long gone. Suddenly, out of nowhere, nearly 7,000 years of civilization vanished into a mirage. There in front of me was a shimmering sea of water, engulfing me from every side. It was the mother of all mirages. In fact, I never saw anything close to it in any desert in the Middle East in all the decades since.

Agatha Christie had written in a 1928 novel that the heroine "fell in love with Ur, with its beauty in the evenings. The ziggurat standing up, faintly shadowed, and that wide sea of sand with its lovely pale colours of apricot, rose, blue, and mauve, changing every minute. . . . The lure of the past came up to grab her. To see a dagger slowly appearing, with its gold glint, through the sand was romantic." It was two years later, on another trip to Iraq and Ur, that she met Mallowan, who once discovered just such a dagger: "intact in its lattice-work sheath, the elegant lapis lazuli handle embellished with golden studs."

In 1949, Mallowan and his "wonderful helpmate" Agatha retraced the steps of the 19th-century archaeologist Sir Henry Layard to Nineveh in the north. Mallowan's enthusiasm for the sculptures of Nimrud was contagious. I saw some of those wonders—gigantic winged creatures—when I visited the museum in Mosul years later. Some of the creatures weighed as much as 20 tons. Layard had written that to see one of these gigantic figures "rising from the bowels of the earth" frightened workmen into fleeing, adding that "the task of removing vast sculptures... by pulley ropes which crackled with static electricity and sometimes burst into flame was hazardous. Then came the problems of loading them on to the native rafts of the Tigris, *kelleks*, kept afloat by inflated goatskins, and sending them down river to Baghdad and Basra for dispatch to Bombay and then onto Europe."

No wonder that what has happened in Iraq since the 2003 invasion has been called "the death of history." The looting of the Baghdad Museum immediately following the capture of Baghdad, in which 15,000 of the museum's 200,000 treasures were stolen and never recovered, was a loss not just to Iraq but to humanity.

But I didn't have to take archaeological trips for lessons in civilization—I didn't even have to look outside our own four walls to find an amazing variety of languages and religions. Jahangir spoke Farsi and Turkish with Sophie, truncated English and Farsi with me, Arabic and hand gestures with Mansur and Abed. I tried a mixture of Russian, Farsi, Arabic, and English with Sophie. And our household contained as many religions as it did languages. George's Kiefer family was Syrian Orthodox. I was an Episcopalian. Jahangir and his wife Razi were Shiites. Abed, our self-appointed watchman, and Mansur were both Sunni. Sophie was a Syrian Catholic.

In Iraq, politics was just as complex a mixture. I once asked George why a single large extended family we knew included a member of every political party. "It makes sense here in Iraq," he said. "Having a communist, a monarchist, a secularist, and a fundamentalist is a kind of insurance. No matter which party is in power, the other family members will be safe."

As a nation state, Iraq was a Western construct, an area of the Middle East carved into a country by British bureaucrats. Tribe still trumped country, and family still trumped tribe. When you met a stranger in Iraq, the first question you asked wasn't "What do you do?"—our first question in America—but rather "What family do you come from?" So on the wall behind the desk in his office, George hung an enormous and magnificently framed photograph of a 1954 Naifeh family reunion—a reunion of at least 200 Naifehs. He wanted the Iraqi students who came to him by the hundreds for help applying to college in the U.S. to know that he came from a big, and therefore apparently powerful, family back in the States.

Muthir Fattah was an Iraqi applicant who came to George for help. The Fattahs, who owned the Fattah Spinning and Weaving Factory, asked him to help place their youngest son, Usama, in an American college. The eldest son, Muthir, who had graduated from MIT, told George frankly that his youngest brother, however bright, was ridiculously spoiled. Usama needed to realize that his family name was not going to propel him through an education in the U.S. So instead of sending Usama to an Ivy League school, George sent him to Southeastern Oklahoma State University in Durant, Oklahoma, far from the distracting temptations of a major city. Within a year, Usama had become class president. Within another, he was accepted at MIT. A dozen years later, when George was passing through the airport in Tripoli, Libya, a tall, distinguished gentleman in a fine cashmere coat, carrying a walking stick, and wearing a homburg, called out, "Howdy, partner," in a fine Oklahoma accent. He was working in Switzerland for Proctor & Gamble, overseeing sales in Africa. The Fattah family legacy was intact.

George did that for hundreds of Iraqi families.

In his work, George mostly dealt with the country's educated elite, but he knew how to deal with Iraqis at all levels of the economic ladder. I still laugh at the scene that took place one morning in the main bazaar. Just as in Tehran, George got as much pleasure haggling in the bazaar as some men get from playing golf. That morning, he went to buy some *hazirs*, or woven window shades, for an American who had just been assigned to Baghdad. George dickered happily in fluent Arabic in the *hazir* stall. He bemoaned his inability to meet such a stiff price for such mediocre *hazirs*, opening his empty pockets.

Eventually, the seller had enough.

"If you are so poor and needy, just *take* the *hazirs*! You need them more than I do. Take them and *remove yourself from my sight*."

"Just load them up," George shouted to a passing *hamal*, or porter.

To the proprietor of the stall, he said, "I thank you for your generosity. You are a kind man, a fine man, and I thank you."

The poor man started trembling at the sight of his day's profits heading out the door with George and the porter.

George did an immediate about-face, returning the *hazirs*, to the owner's considerable relief—and then to his amusement. The delighted man ordered two "Bebsis"—"P" is pronounced "B" in Arabic—for his new-found friend and himself, after which they complimented each other on their bargaining prowess.

Not every encounter ended so happily.

George accepted an invitation to a religious Sheikh's retreat on the Tigris for a *musgouf* dinner. *Musgouf*—fish barbequed over slow-burning coals—is Iraq's prized cuisine. But ever since his days in Kiefer, George had foresworn fish. The Sheikh was blind, and George assumed that he could get by without eating any *musgouf*. He was wildly mistaken. The Sheikh's two bodyguards had their rifles pointed at George throughout the entire meal. When the Sheikh inquired whether his guest was eating, George looked at the guns, looked at the fish, and started eating.

To help George win hearts and minds for America, AFME sent prominent people from a variety of fields to speak to Iraqi audiences. One was Edith Sampson, the first African-American to be elected as a judge in the U.S., the first African-American delegate appointed to the U.N., and a friend of Adlai Stevenson for over 25 years. George arranged 30 hours of speeches for her at the Women's Union, Queen Aliyeh College, Baghdad College, King Faisal Hall, and the Law College, among other institutions. She was lucky he let her sleep.

Mrs. Sampson was incredible. Her black eyes were hypnotic. Her voice ranged from a *soto voce* when speaking to an audience of one to a thundering roar when addressing a crowd of 2,000. She came to us from Cairo, where she had held a 40-minute meeting with President Gamal Abdel Nasser. I am sure she gave him the same lecture on civility that she gave her Iraqi audiences. She was well aware of the political jockeying among the several new Arab nations formed after World War I. She gained an audience's sympathy first, then fired away: "You Arabs need to keep calm. Don't be so hot-headed and emotional with each other. Damn it, we African-Americans bicker among ourselves, just like you, but when we open the door to the outside world, we come out smiling." Riding to one of the Baghdad venues, she had me laughing. "They wonder where in hell I'm from. Ethiopia? The Congo?" All heads inevitably turned to stare at her wherever we went.

Then came Rabbi Elmer Berger and his elegant wife, Ruth. Scholarly and reserved, Elmer was Executive Director of the American Council for Judaism and a member of AFME'S Board of Directors. Ruth, a distinguished lawyer in her own right, wore the latest in high fashion. I was horrified for her—and for her wardrobe—as one of the packed schedules that George had arranged for them came to a perilous end. We had a cocktail party at our home, but one of the guests, an Iraqi diplomat the Bergers had known in New York, insisted with great pride that they take a midnight tour of Baghdad. Already exhausted, but always game, Ruth admired every plaque, praised every monument, and climbed every step. This included crawling to the top of the new football stadium, a feat that covered at least a foot of her gorgeous green taffeta gown with drying plaster. After 1 a.m., to hasten an escape, I complained that I was hungry and we left.

Elmer had come not only to lecture but to visit the Jewish

Affairs Section of the Ministry of the Interior. The Ministry still held the properties and frozen funds of 5,000 out of the 165,000 Iraqi Jews who had emigrated to Israel after 1948. Jews had been a minority in Mesopotamia since Nebuchadnezzar captured Jerusalem in 599 B.C., but they had remained an integral and vibrant part of Mesopotamian society until the founding of Israel and the diaspora of Jews from throughout the Arab world to the new state.

Bridging all these worlds was a challenge, and Dr. Samim's best friend, Abdul Rahman Al-Bazzaz, would pay the ultimate price for it. Just as Aliyeh had her Wednesday morning "gabuls," Samim had his Friday afternoon gatherings. Being a Western woman, I could join either group without raising an eyebrow. I was there the Friday when George first met Bazzaz. Bazzaz was Dean of the College of Commerce at the time, and it was the Commerce College students George was having the most trouble placing in American universities. Who better to talk with than Bazzaz himself?

Bazzaz, who was a graduate of the University of London, agreed with George that the students lacked adequate preparation and immediately initiated stricter guidelines for bursary students. That same spring, Bazzaz was transferred to the College of Law, the next step in a brilliant career. He later served as Iraq's Ambassador to Egypt and the United Kingdom, as Secretary General of OPEC, and, in 1966, as Iraq's Prime Minister. But before all of that, he was one of the Iraqis George sent to the U.S. on an exchange program. On his return from America, Bazzaz commented that "Americans should seek a greater knowledge of foreign countries, particularly those inhabited by the Arabs." Although he praised the American people for their good intentions and their generosity, he said those two qualities "were often negated by the fact that Americans often came to conclusions on international affairs with only half truths before them."

In 1968, when Saddam Hussein initiated the coup that brought him to power, Bazzaz was one of the first victims. Bazzaz was arrested and sent off to Al-Nihaya prison. A fellow prisoner, Shao'ul Sassoon, son of the last Chief Rabbi of Baghdad, reported seeing Bazzaz hanged by the throat in a dark corridor. He had clearly been badly tortured before he was killed. The image of Bazzaz's dead body with his feet dangling on the floor haunts me.

Another prominent Iraqi we got to know well was Tahsin Qadri, the Protocol Minister in the Royal Court. His Excellency had just returned from the first wedding of King Hussein of Jordan to an Egyptian Hashemite cousin, Sharifa Dina 'bint Abdul Hamid, on April 19, 1955. By the time we moved to Jordan many years later, King Hussein had married his *fourth* wife, the American Lisa Halliby—a Princeton classmate of Steve's who changed her name to Queen Noor. Qadri was a slight, graying man, always immaculately groomed and impeccably mannered. He made me nervous. I was terrified I might spill champagne on his prized antique Qashan carpet, the soft-muted blues and silvery whites of which literally shimmered. I had to force myself to step onto this treasure.

The Qadri home, like those of all prominent Iraqis, was nestled amid towering palm trees on magnificent green lawns along the banks of the Tigris. The clutter and clatter of Rashid Street and Sheikh Omar Street, although only blocks away, didn't intrude on the quiet of the elite.

We watched as this aristocratic family was fumbling its

way into the 20th century. Usama, the second son, a Foreign Ministry official and George's close friend, was loath to admit to his father that his Western-educated older brother was a soil analyst. To earn one's living testing dirt, actually rubbing one's hands and fingers in it, was an occupation for an illiterate Bedouin, not for a member of Iraq's upper class. Usama simply told everyone, especially his father, that his older brother was the manager of the enormous date plantations in the Basrah area that they had inherited from their mother.

Our entire time in Iraq, the present was constantly merging into the past. One night, we went to Sheikh Mohammed Bekr Suheil's village for dinner. We drove under a cornflower blue sky past the dust of Kadhimain and the stench of a slaughterhouse on the village's outskirts. The Sheikh, another of George's friends, was about 60—swarthy, solid, with a smartly trimmed goatee. He welcomed us warmly, then promptly escorted me to the women's quarters, where I joined the women who were squatting on carpets on the floor. The Sheikh's eldest daughter and two of his eight daughters-in-law enjoyed eyeing me as much as I enjoyed eyeing them. Each wore the expected gold bracelets, but they had multiple gold ankle bracelets, too, and slippers with bunches of pink feathers. I was lost in a sea of long, multi-colored dresses, as tray after tray of meat and rice was placed before us. Once dinner was over, and I stood up and used my fractured Arabic and elaborate hand gestures to thank my hostesses, out of the blue came a silver flask pouring perfume over my outstretched hands. I yanked them out of the way but not before they got a full dousing of a heady fragrance.

That turned out to be a relatively tame leave-taking

ceremony. The Political Officer H. R. P. Dickson described leaving a party during the 1920s thusly: "An incense burner is filled with burning camel dung and a piece of incense laid on it. At once a white, pleasantly scented smoke rises, and the burner is passed round by the host, the guests holding it under their noses, inside the ends of their head cloths, or under the fold of their abbas. The guests now depart in silence."

Although the British were no longer completely in control of Iraq as they had been during the 1920s, they were clinging to as much control as possible, just as they were in Iran and everywhere else. We had been swept into their political machinations in Tehran just two years earlier. Here in Iraq, the British had placed King Faisal I on the throne in 1921. Now, with his grandson King Faisal II sitting on the throne, all was quiet—at least on the surface.

I met few Britains socially, other than those at the Alwiyah Club, where we qualified for admission: "The ordinary members shall be British Subjects or Citizens of the United States, of suitable social position irrespective of occupation, not less than 20 years of age and in possession of their civil rights." There was an amendment stating that "Iraqi nationals of suitable social position and standing, irrespective of occupation, but not exceeding 150 in number" could also join. Freya Stark, the irrepressible British writer, had added her own pithy addendum: "If Christ were living now and were proposed for the Alwiyah Club . . . not only would he not be elected, but the proposal would be generally considered absolutely bad from every point of view."

From my point of view, the Alwiyah Club was just fine. Steve learned how to swim in the clear, chlorinated water of the club pool, no Tigris brown anywhere. And the Christmas party for 102 children was perfect. The mothers, their noses powdered, their bodies arrayed in festive holiday finery and stout stockings, supervised the waiters serving trays of some sort of unrecognizable juice, sandwiches spread with jelly or with mayonnaise slathered on so thick it looked like shaving cream. At the appointed hour, Santa Claus burst into view, crawling through a cleverly draped red cloth over the opening of a chimney. There was also a movie—*Cinderella*—Steve's first. And at the end, hundreds of helium-filled balloons were allowed to float into the sky. Steve was beyond thrilled, and so were George and I.

As the New Year arrived and its weeks flew by, it was becoming clear that I was pregnant again. After what we had been through with Roger, our plan was difficult but unavoidable: Aunt Mina and Uncle Roy were too old to handle us, so George would take Steve and me to his family in Tulsa, Oklahoma, then he would return to Baghdad. George found a rental apartment for us, and his brother Benny and his pregnant wife Tillie would keep an eye on us. At 3:30 a.m. on the morning of March 9, I called Dr. Lindstrom, my obstetrician, and then Benny. He alerted a prearranged babysitter to come to stay with Steve. He then raced over to take me to St. John's Hospital. The next moment I was conscious, I was holding a beautiful baby girl in my arms. Carolyn was alive. She was calmly listening to me and to the world around her, cuddling, stretching, and yawning. Within what seemed like seconds we were back at the apartment with Steve.

Poor Benny became the stuff of legend at St. John's Hospital a few days later when he showed up with a second

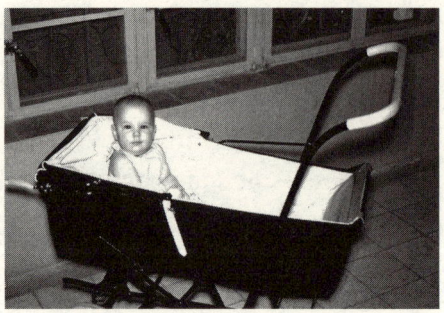

Carolyn on our return to Baghdad.

Mrs. Naifeh, also in labor, to give birth to a baby boy.

We couldn't depart for Baghdad until Carolyn was two months old. Steve was becoming used to living in America and, even though he missed his father terribly, he shared with me several times his deep concern about the availability of "chocolate cake in Baghdad."

When we finally began to make our way back to Iraq, we had a layover in New York before settling into a British Overseas Airways berth for our 15-hour trip across the Atlantic. Despite the luxury of that flight, I was beyond exhausted by the time we landed in London, where we had yet another layover of a few hours. I promptly lay down on the floor of a new special nursery for "tired travelers with infants," to the embarrassment of the airport manager. He was showing off the new facility to the visiting Nigerian Transportation Minister. Swathed in tribal splendor, the dignitary had to step over my sleeping body.

I don't think George had stopped to catch his breath while we were gone. He and Princess Rajiha's husband, an Air Force pilot named Abdul Jabbar Mahmoud, were making the Baghdad Rotary Club a resounding success. Having founded the Boy Scouts in Tehran, George now founded the Cub Scouts in Baghdad. He had turned our roasting-hot, Bauhaus glass cube of house into an enlarged AFME office and had whisked us across the parkway to a house more like a cement fortress. This time, the windows were so small and the walls so thick we might as well have been living underground. But we were supremely cool.

I sorely missed the easy dash next door for my morning coffee and gossip with Aliyeh. We visited her and Muthir as often as we could, since I had Razi, Jahangir's wife, whom he had brought back from Iran, to keep an eye on Carolyn—and to boil everything in sight. Samim found me a pediatrician, Dr. Koumunjian, who assured me that boiling everything but the child herself would be useless: "The bacteria are in the Baghdad air." I was constantly reminded of Freya Stark's comment that Baghdad was "a city of wicked dust. Every scratch turns septic if you are not careful ... and what they call a 'Baghdad tummy' is unassimilated dust . . . ."

Even though our new home was much cooler than our old one, summer in Baghdad was still unbelievably, hellishly hot. I once heard someone say that a Baghdadi goes straight to heaven because he has already endured the heat of hell on earth. One day, walking down Rashid Street, I stopped to chat with an acquaintance. My heels were only an inch high, but they stuck to the asphalt so firmly that I almost couldn't yank my shoes loose. An Iraqi friend told me she tiptoed as fast as she could across Rashid Street to avoid the same fate. And we faced the same problems driving. If you stayed at a red light too long, your tires might literally stick to the asphalt.

Meanwhile, Steve continued to learn vocabulary at an astonishing pace, in both English and Arabic. He would hear a word and it would become his favorite for a day—saying it over and over. I think the word "kerosene" was his all-time favorite, and it lasted more than a week. Unfortunately, one of the evenings that the Prime Minister Fadhel Jamali and his wife Sarah were over for dinner, he had just learned the word "silly" from an American girl named Suzy. They had run around the house all day yelling the word at each other. Later that evening, when Steve was asked to come say goodnight to us and to our guests, he went up to the Prime Minister and said, "You are a silly man. A silly, silly man." For a moment, I thought he had undone all the diplomacy that George had effected over the past couple of years, but fortunately the Jamalis thought it was funny.

Another evening, we were invited to the American Ambassador's residence for a black-tie dinner with all of the country's elite, including Jamali, who had just stepped down as Prime Minister, and Nuri Al-Said, who had been appointed to take his place.

I was happy to meet the famous Nuri. Thirty-five years earlier, he had served under the command of Lawrence of Arabia in the famed Arab revolt. Lawrence had written in *Seven Pillars of Wisdom* that "Nuri Pasha Said offered to command the Deraa expedition, for which his courage, authority, and coolness marked him as the ideal leader."

Another prominent new acquaintance soon became a friend—Jawad Salim, perhaps the leading Iraqi artist of his day. Having studied in Paris, Rome, and London, he had returned to Baghdad with a British bride, Lorna. After World War II, together with his fellow painter Faiq Hassan, Jawad had started the two most important Iraqi art organizations, La Société Primitive and the Plastic Artists Society. I can still hear the two artists in our living room discussing the place of art in culture and politics. They often came with an intense young architect, Rifat Chaderchi, whose grandfather Kamil was the founder of Iraq's secular National Democratic Party. Rifat had studied architecture in Great Britain. He was, we were told, among the first generation of foreign-educated architects to come back and help build a new Iraq. The Central Post, the Telegraph and Telephone tower, and the Federation of Industries building in Baghdad were all his.

Nuri Al-Said was right in the midst of all this activity. As Chairman of the Development Board, the task of which was to develop the country's new infrastructure, he was commissioning roads, bridges, and public buildings throughout Iraq. Among the Western architects asked for their advice were Frank Lloyd Wright, Gropius, and Le Corbusier.

We had left Tehran aware of the fierce political undercurrents around us, but unaware of the political turmoil that would emerge soon after we left. The same was true of Baghdad. Ambassador Gallman had stated that the "United States does not play a decisive role in Iraq, economically or politically." He described our role as "modest and self-effacing." When Nasser nationalized the Suez Canal on July 26, 1956, the Cold War heated up again. Secretary of State Dean Acheson had warned that the Middle East was a tinder box.

The tinder box erupted into flames on July 14, 1958, when Abdul Karim Kassem and Colonel Abdul Salam Arif overthrew the monarchy. The bodies of King Faisal II and Nuri Al-Said were dragged through the streets until nothing was left of them. Fadhel Jamali was sentenced to life in jail.

In the days of the British Mandate and in the days that followed, a "perplexing predicament" prevailed. In 1921, when Great Britain placed King Faisal I on the throne of Iraq, the people were asked to vote. They thought they were voting for a larger sugar ration—not for a new government. Jafar Pasha Al-Askari, another distinguished Iraqi who fought under T. E. Lawrence during the Arab Revolt and who was married to Nuri Al-Said's sister, writes in his memoirs that British efforts to dispense justice during the Mandate were laughable—literally making their verdicts dependent on the results of tests and riddles. A political officer once "tossed a coin and ordered the defendant [in a trial] to call heads or tails. Conviction or acquittal depended on him guessing correctly!" Iraqi nationalists argued that there were actually two governments in Iraq, one foreign and the other national. Early on, George had said that Iraqis wanted to run their own affairs more than they wanted paved streets.

Things didn't improve when the nationalists took over the country, or when Saddam Hussein took over from them. Our friend the architect Rifat Chaderchi was imprisoned by Saddam Hussein in 1978 in Abu Graib prison—a prison built on agricultural land where we had bought our Christmas trees when we lived in Baghdad. Rifat survived his imprisonment and was quoted in the *Christian Science*

The Naifeh family back in America between assignments abroad.

Monitor in 2008 saying, "For more than 2,000 years there has been no stability in Iraq. We have either had tyrants or feuding gangs. Every new group that comes demolishes everything and starts over again." In 2016, Iraq is still a collection of ethnic groups, tribes, and families, not a nation. And there is still turmoil.

But most of that turmoil was yet to come when we left Baghdad in November 1956 for reassignment to the United States. All of our friends had come to the airport to wish us farewell: Fathers Jolson and Fallon, Jahangir and Razi, Mary Routh, Usama, Mohammed Kashif Al-Gita, and the entire Saffar family. I had said goodbye to Aliyeh earlier, since she had said she wasn't going to come to the airport. Yet there she was, and, as a sign of affection, without her *abaya* clutched around her. We both burst into tears.

Reassignment was not to be. While he still had a chance, George decided to resign from AFME to try politics. He wanted to run for Congress. His huge family in Tulsa would give him a head start in building a political base. But knowing that he would need to earn a lot of money to run a political campaign, he bought a southwest franchise for a home-delivery juice company called Home Juice.

Within two years, it was clear that we were in over our heads bottling and selling fruit juice. We were scurrying around, chasing our shadows.

George called a friend at the State Department and asked if there was a place for him back in the Middle East.

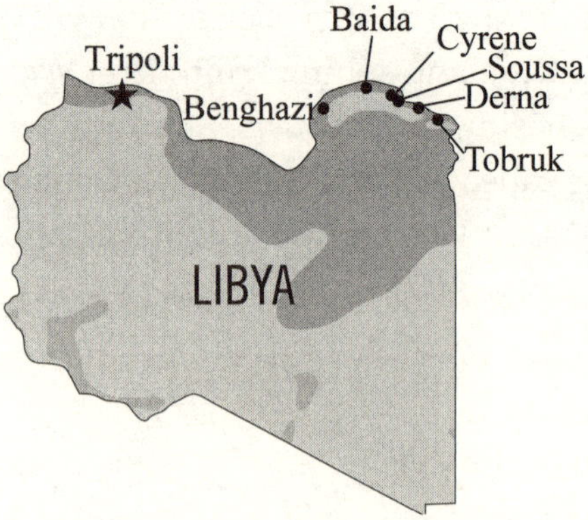
Baida
Cyrene
Tripoli
Soussa
Benghazi
Derna
Tobruk
LIBYA

LIBYA

It wasn't even on the map. George went to Washington in January 1963 to talk about our new post overseas, and called Tulsa with the answer: We were going to Baida, one of two capitals of the North African country of Libya, a place which was literally not on maps yet. George would be the Public Affairs Officer in a new town in the Jebel Al-Akhdar, the Green Mountains. I couldn't quite believe him about the map thing. The name sounded as though there might be a "b", an "e", maybe a "d" in it. I scoured the atlas to no avail. No Baida anywhere in North Africa. I had two students from Libya in my English for Foreigners class at the University of Tulsa and my two heroes rushed right over when I called for help. "Oh, yes, Baida is the new administrative capital of the entire country. Brand new. You know, like Brasilia new."

I decided that this was going to be perfect. I had always admired the Brazilian architect Oscar Niemeyer, who worked with Lucio Costa on the plans for Brasilia. Baida would be perfect even if it was in the middle of nowhere in Libya. It would have the same clean lines, the same progressive thinking, and the same "the future is ours" mentality of Brazil's modern capital.

Then George added, "But, honey, there is one problem. There are no international schools, no schools for non-Libyans. You will have to teach the children."

George was so pumped up he didn't need a put-down from me. Steve was doing very well in the fifth grade and Carolyn in the first. They were in Americana heaven: Cub Scouts, softball, and church acolyte for Steve; Fourth of July parades and swarms of friends for Carolyn.

Reality struck the minute George hung up the phone. We would be leaving before the end of the month. Missionary kids in China who didn't go off to boarding school used the "private school in a box," the Calvert system of homeschooling that was invented in 1905. I didn't have time to properly research the entire subject of home schooling, but I did secure the syllabus for their current school year. I guess we would be starting from scratch—just like Libya itself. Libya was only six months older than Steve.

To my surprise, the children accepted another move as a matter of course. The reality of school with Mom had probably not sunk in yet. However, Carolyn had one serious

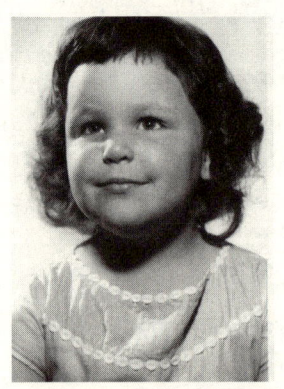

Carolyn, reassured that life would be all right outside of the U.S.

problem. Her seventh birthday was not until March. She was justly terrified that she wouldn't know a single person in the entire country of Libya. "You can't have a birthday without a birthday party," she informed me. Presents weren't essential, but friends were. So we had a party for her three months early. Each child in her class drew what they would give her to take to Libya if they could—lollipops, dolls, games, books, a puppy, three kittens, and a unicorn. And Libya became acceptable. Steve, who was ten, decided that being the only student in a class would be a great thing: He could complete a year's material in two months.

The minute the plane took off from Tulsa, I was terrified that I might scar them for life if I didn't keep the family's focus on schooling for the remainder of their school year. So I had the kids write essays on all of the places we visited. Washington was the Capitol, the Lincoln Memorial, the Smithsonian, and the White House. In Worcester, to say goodbye to Aunt Mina and Uncle Roy, we read about the Boston Tea Party, the Midnight Ride of Paul Revere, and Bunker Hill. Paris was a boat ride on the Seine, the Eiffel Tower, and the Louvre. Heidelberg was the Castle and the Old Bridge over the Neckar River. Rome was the Vatican, and standing in St. Peter's Square, receiving the blessings of Pope John XXIII as he spoke from that high pontifical window.

When we arrived in Libya, there was an unexpected delay in moving to Baida—a six-week delay. There was a week in Tripoli, then five more in Benghazi. The Embassy housed us in a staff apartment building located next to the only movie theater in town, the Rex Cinema. Steve could hear the movie speakers from his bedroom and went to sleep at night to the soundtracks from "Spartacus" and "The Swiss Family Robinson."

George drove up to Baida every week to check on our new home, which was in the "finishing stages" of being built. He returned to our temporary apartment laden with gorgeous red poppies and mounds of purple thistle. I should have been suspicious. The house was taking a very long time getting sorted out.

Eventually, George decided that the house was in good enough shape for us to move in. George thought he had taken care of the plumbing, heating, and electricity during those five weeks of racing back and forth up the Green Mountains. He had left the finishing touches in the hands of Shamedu, the landlord.

I had good reason to be suspicious. Our new home was a concrete nightmare, with a sliver of garden, about five feet wide, circling it. The floor plan was fine enough: It addressed Muslim propriety by positioning the living room, dining room, kitchen, and guest bath on one side of the house, and the bedrooms on the other, separated by frosted glass doors. The house itself was primitive. My childhood home in Wuhu was a marvel of sophisticated architecture by comparison.

Even though it was brand new, the house was covered in mold, partly because the only heat came from a single kerosene heater in the middle of the building. And that one heater spewed out a lot of toxic smells, but very little heat. "We'll have fungus in our lungs," I wailed. George had asked Shamedu to install a fireplace in the living room. Scruffy, unshaven, and pot-bellied, Shamedu was cashing in on Baida's sudden desperate need for housing. He had apparently said, "A fireplace? No problem." He had a hole cut in the living room wall and a firebox put in it, but the chimney didn't function. When we set a fire, all the smoke billowed into the house. George told Shamedu that the problem lay with a

The U.S. Embassy compound at bottom, with the new Parliament building above it, in Baida, a city that barely existed.

blockage in the chimney vent, so the landlord tore down the chimney and rebuilt it. Same problem. Smoke still billowed into the house. So we gave up on the fireplace, and more or less gave up on heat. To control the mold, we had the interior of the house painted several times, which cured the mold, but left the walls a motley mess of uneven paint layers.

The plumbing didn't work, either. I soon discovered that the only water that came out of the tap in the kitchen was scalding hot. Occasionally, the children would forget and howl in pain when turning on the faucet. Shamedu finally tracked down a plumber after George tracked down Shamedu. The plumber discovered a labyrinth of ill-sorted pipes, and admitted that, without a blueprint, he was at a loss. Only the plumber who laid the pipe could untangle the mess, and that plumber had disappeared from town. The only solution was to install an extra pipe to the kitchen faucet and connect it to the garden faucet, the only supply of cold water he could find.

Only one of the two bathtubs was usable. The other had been used to mix cement. George decided to brave the

The replacement plumber standing, perplexed, outside our home in Baida.

other tub the night we arrived, but the water running into the tub stopped after it filled less than an inch of the tub. George jumped out, dried himself, put on his trousers, and mounted a ladder still propped against the side of the house, strode across the roof, and saw that the water tank was minuscule—and, somehow, despite the fact that the house was brand new, already rusty. As George wrestled the tiny tank loose from its tiny pipe, casual evening strollers were paralyzed in their tracks. Shamedu magically appeared.

"My tank, my tank, what are you doing to my tank?" he wailed.

In impeccable Arabic, George repeated what he had already told Shamedu more than once.

"This tank is not big enough to do the job. I want a new one!"

"But the tank is *good!* It is *new!* It is *big!*"

"*You* like it? *You* take it." George hurled the tank to the ground, to the entertainment of the neighborhood.

A new tank, 10 times the size of the original, was delivered and connected the next day.

With enough water to fill the tub, we discovered that the drains backed up—another Shamedu plumbing disaster. I hesitated to complain, fearing it was my fault. Maybe I had used too much laundry detergent. An Embassy nurse and friend, who had been stationed in Cairo, had warned me that unless you washed everything you ate, every fruit and vegetable—every leaf of lettuce—with laundry detergent, you could contract parasitic flatworms, or bilharzia, a serious health threat. But George had no such hesitation. He called the Director of Public Works, who discovered that Shamedu had connected all of the drainage pipes—including the sewer pipes—to the city water supply.

The next day, the neighbors—they were Syrian and he was a professor at the small local university—invited us for tea in their house, which was a carbon copy of ours. Another Shamedu construction.

I stared at one of the living room walls as unobtrusively

Our garage turned into a one-room schoolhouse.

as possible until I couldn't stand it any longer.

"Why do you have a microscope slide scotch-taped to the wall?" The slide was taped across a crack in the wall.

My limited Arabic, combined with some finger-pointing, got the question across. "Oh," my hostess replied, "the landlord told us that, when the glass cracks, the house will be falling down, and we should leave."

The house was one thing; school was another. Libya had been cobbled together by the United Nations on December 21, 1951, under the rule of King Idris. Henry Villard, our first American Minister to Libya, said, "It is difficult to conceive of a kingdom starting off with such serious handicaps . . . ." The literacy rate was 10 percent. The per capita income was $30 a year. The other statistics were equally dismal. Even now, the country only had 16 university graduates.

In 1953, President Nasser of Egypt had been asked to loan a few lecturers for Libya's primitive educational system. Now that I was going to have to teach Steve and Carolyn, I needed every bit as much help.

The first help came at the hands of a Greek Cypriot named Chris, who worked for the British construction company Costain. Chris taught Steve French until Jean-Marie, a French-speaking Belgian architect, showed up. He, too, had been told that Baida would be another Brasilia, which, he told us as often as possible, couldn't have been further from the truth. Jean-Marie was excruciatingly bored, and teaching Steve alleviated a bit of his daily tedium. A young Palestinian science teacher at Baida's middle school procured diseased liver cells for Steve to examine under a microscope. Another Belgian at the Ministry of Post and Telegraph helped rig up a telegraph set. Tony Bersa, a young Yugoslav biochemist who worked at the tuberculosis sanitarium outside of town, which was staffed by 24 Cold War Yugoslav doctors and nurses, introduced Steve to quail hunting. That left social studies and history. Cyrene, which was the breadbasket for the Greek and Roman Empires, was only 13 miles away, and its port city, Apollonia, was only a couple of miles farther down an escarpment to a wide and gloriously empty stretch of Mediterranean beach. About 631 B.C., Battus, a young Greek settler on the island of Thera, suffered from a dreadful stammer. He consulted the oracle of Apollo at Delphi, who told him: "Battus, thou camest for a voice, but the lord Apollo sendeth thee to found a city in Libya, which giveth good pasture to sheep." According to *The Histories*, Herodotus says that friendly Libyans led Battus and his group to Cyrene: "Here, O Greeks, ye may fitly dwell, for in this place is a hole in the heavens"—meaning that there was enough rain there to grow enough wheat for the Greek Empire.

After Battus arrived in Libya, he encountered a lion and was so terrified that he yelled frantically, curing his stammer instantly. That "hole in the heavens" also grew silphium plants, the most effective birth control agent known at the time. It was exported back to Greece in such vast quantities that it became exceedingly rare. Cyrene was named after the nymph Kurana, who Apollo married and brought to Libya. Her hobby was going out into the countryside to find wild animals to strangle with her bare hands.

That same Cyrenaican silphium was lauded even in Roman days. The Roman poet Catullus suggested to his lover Lesbia that they should exchange kisses numbering "as many as there are grains of sand on Cyrene's silphium shores."

Despite its vast and majestic ruins, Cyrene was empty of all tourists. We had the place to ourselves. There were no souvenir hawkers and no throngs of camera-clickers. There was only the wind skittering through gnarled pines and scruffy junipers. We wandered through the Forum, which was thickly carpeted with red poppies and purple and white anemones. In our minds, we could hear chariots thundering down the cobbled road beside us. We walked across what had obviously been a mosaic floor in the house of a rich Roman. We could imagine a man, sitting in a corner on a bench, taking off his sandals, happy to feel the cool tile under his sore feet.

We did need a classroom, to differentiate, at least in some way, "school" from "home." The only reasonable solution was to turn the garage into a schoolroom.

"Can't you tile the garage floor and put in screens?" George asked the landlord. "And we need another electric outlet."

"No, no, no! What will happen to your car out on the street?"

"What will happen to my children if they never go to school?"

"No, no, no! Who ever heard of a garage with a tile floor? The answer still is NO."

However irritated he was by our constant complaints, Shamedu regularly brought his friends by to ogle these strange foreigners. He particularly enjoyed showing off George's five-by-twelve-foot patch of grass at the back of the house, probably the only lawn in town. Once, when Shamedu was passing the open school door, he heard Steve and Carolyn reciting their Arabic lessons for Abdul Gader Mansoury, George's office assistant. He listened incredulously as they recited the "ba-be-bu" of their Arabic grammar. Early the next morning, before our 9 a.m. salute to the flag and Pledge of Allegiance, workmen showed up to lay a tile floor. So we finally had a tiled floor—and a small refrigerator. All for one teacher and two students, or three, if you counted the dog, which always joined us.

The people who lived on the street were all members of the faculty at the local Islamic University—except for us and the Wongs. Ambassdor Wong represented the Republic of China (Taiwan). He spoke fluent Arabic and English, in addition to Chinese, but his poor wife spoke only Chinese. The only person she could speak to within 500 miles was her husband.

She was so stir crazy that she usually accompanied him on our minuscule cocktail-party circuit. She developed a way of shaking her head—not up and down, to indicate agreement, or from side to side, to indicate disapproval, but sort of in circles, to indicate whatever the speaker wanted to think. One evening, she was seated next to an American visitor from Tripoli, who chattered at her so incessantly—without ever asking a question—and Mrs. Wong moved her head so ambiguously in reaction, that the visitor had no clue that Mrs. Wong hadn't understood a single word of what she had said all evening.

One afternoon, the quite sizeable wife of the professor of the Preservation of the Faith who lived on the other side of our house caught sight of Steve, who had climbed up on the roof of the garage-turned-schoolhouse. Within hours, several workmen had barged into our yard and headed to the wall between our two houses. They trampled George's beloved flowers with the oil drums they positioned to use as ladders, then started to build the wall higher, dripping cement with abandon.

George was beyond irate. "Who gave you permission to

build that wall and destroy my flowers and drip cement everywhere?"

"Your neighbor gave us permission. Your son was looking upon his wife. We cannot build on his side because the owner does not want us to look upon his wife."

"*His* wife," yelled George. "And what about *my* wife? Shame be upon you."

"*Haq ma-aq.* You're right." They loaded up their buckets and trowels and left.

Meanwhile, George was having a problem at work. His normally hyper-efficient assistant, Abdul Gader, was sitting hour after hour in the USIS office doing absolutely nothing but staring into space.

Day after day, George came home for lunch railing against Abdul Gader.

"He sits there doing nothing, nothing at all."

"Turn your chair so you don't have to look at him."

"I tried that, but I can still tell what he's doing just by the way he holds his head, by the way he slumps in his chair. It's driving me crazy."

"You're exaggerating."

"No, I'm not. You come look for yourself."

I did, that very afternoon. On the pretext of looking for a special book, I scanned the library shelves—and Abdul Gader. George had not exaggerated. The normally cheerful Abdul Gader sat with his chin cupped in his hands, his brow furrowed.

George met me in the hall for my assessment.

"You're right. It's serious."

"But what's wrong with him? He manages to get his work done, but he just sits there. It's not normal."

Soon enough, however, the answer became clear: Abdul

Gader had fallen in love. George discovered that he was feverishly placing calls to Benghazi whenever George had an appointment. The first phrases from Abdul Gader were formal, but as soon George left the room, the call turned dreamily romantic.

It was unusual to see a romance unfold in such a Western manner. Virtually all Libyan marriages were arranged by the two families, and the bride and groom were not allowed to meet until the day of the wedding. Abdul Gader was a university graduate and had traveled once to a conference in Nairobi, but he was from an isolated village near Baida and remained close to his roots. While still at the university, Abdul Gader had begun tutoring a classmate named Hussein in English. During one of his visits to Hussein's home, Abdul Gader had caught a glimpse of Fawzia, one of Hussein's sisters. The door had been left slightly ajar, and Fawzia crossed his field of vision against a background of gerunds and past participles.

During the next English lesson, Fawzia had sent a much younger sister—still young enough to be exposed to a man outside the family—into the dining room to serve the young men tea. Amal reported back to Fawzia on the handsome young man's height, his build, the color of his eyes, the size of his pupils, the sharpness of the crease in his trousers, the state of his socks, the shine of his shoes. In turn, Abdul Gader had his sister find a friend who knew the family and thus could pay a social call and extract similar information on Fawzia. If Fawzia had been a modern girl, or if she had at least gone to school, Abdul Gader might have been able to see her himself as she walked between classes with her classmates. But her father had brought her up as conservatively as possible. When she finished the Sixth

Form—approximately the 8th grade in the U.S.—the outside world was closed to her except for weddings and wakes—and then only with maximum-security chaperones. It sounded like house arrest to me.

When she got engaged to Abdul Gader, Fawzia had three wedding parties—one each in Benghazi, in Baida, and in the village of Ghuba. And not a single man in sight.

George received an embossed engagement announcement —addressed to him alone. I wasn't invited. After the two fathers had signed papers before a sheikh at a mosque, a reception was held in the best coffeehouse in Benghazi, attended exclusively by male relatives and guests.

I wasn't invited to the engagement, but I was invited to all three weddings. At each one, the bride received her guests in solitary splendor. Enthroned in a large overstuffed armchair on a raised platform, Fawzia sat alone facing her guests the entire evening, the expression on her face emotionless all evening. Fortunately, she did get to move twice, both times to go and change her gown. When I arrived late at the Ghuba party, she had changed into the Libyan national dress, replete with a sparkling dowry of gold jewelry. After an hour, keeping the gold on, she changed into a white satin Western wedding gown with a veil. A smile never crossed her frozen cheeks.

Meanwhile, the guests continued to chat and exchange morsels of gossip. I missed the nuances, but the gossip was pretty much like that of any group of women the world over. A singer and a professional dancer performed songs that bestowed blessings on Fawzia. Each blessing ended in a series of shrill, soaring trills, at which point the entire audience would erupt in ululations. They puckered their mouths into round "O"s and flicked their tongues back and forth to the

Abdul Gader's mother at left, with a professional dancer, at the bride's party.

roofs of their mouths, cutting the passage of air from deep in their throats. Herodotus, writing in the fifth century B.C., had commented on the ululating of Libyan women: "The crying of women at religious ceremonies also originated in Libya—for the Libyan women are addicted to this practice and do it beautifully."

Abdul Gader's tiny mother was heavily tattooed and covered in shawls and veils—her wide smile baring several missing teeth. She greeted me warmly to the Ghuba wedding party. Most of the guests were Bedouin women, sitting on thick carpets. They pulled aside their leather boots to let me pass to the front of the room and, more specifically, to the only chair. Loops of gold circled their necks and wrists and fingers and hung from their earlobes.

Most of Fawzia's guests had faces and hands battered by the elements and worn from lives of endless labor and unremitting harshness. In tribal life, it is the women who not only raised the children but who also followed their goats and sheep to their seasonal grazing grounds, helped set up tents, gathered brush for firewood, and spun goat hair held by a big toe and fastened to a spindle. Every gram

George playing a drum at the groom's party.

of gold they wore had come to them through their dowries or had been earned by their own labor.

I think I looked more bizarre to them than they to me. They had had almost no contact with Westerners. Some had battery-powered radios or sons who attended school, and had heard of lands that existed beyond Libya. If I was the first live embodiment of that land beyond Libya, I was not a propitious sight. My glasses were bad enough. Much worse was that the only bit of gold on my body was a pathetic gold wedding band. Even the tiniest Libyan baby, its ears pierced and wearing gold earrings, had more value than I did. Never before had I been so overwhelmed by pity.

When I returned home, I told George how much the Bedouin women pitied me for my poverty. George didn't really comment, but the next Christmas there was a glittering gold bracelet under the tree from Santa for me—the first of more than 50, each one celebrating a year of our marriage.

There was a bizarre coda to the story suggesting just how stifling a life Fawzia had led before she married Abdul Gader. One afternoon, quite a while after they had been married,

Abdul Gader asked George, who had planned a trip to Benghazi, if he would take Fawzia with him so that she could attend her uncle's funeral. George had long since learned not to be surprised by Abdul Gader, although the idea that Abdul Gader would let him ride unchaperoned for three hours with his wife did startle him a bit. Abdul Gader retracted the request the next morning, a few hours before the scheduled departure, and George looked at him knowingly.

"No, it's not what you think," said Abdul Gader.

George nodded in disbelief.

"No," Abdul Gader replied. "Fawzia doesn't know where she *lived*. She doesn't know the neighborhood where she grew up. The directions are very difficult and she wouldn't be able to help you out."

My limited holdings in gold jewelry soon rescued George from a serious diplomatic conundrum. A Libyan farmer, a friend of George's, had invited the entire family to spend a day on his farm. Steve, Carolyn, and I watched spellbound as a sheep was skinned by blowing air into it like air into a balloon, separating meat from skin, then strung on a pole and roasted over an open fire. We did nothing much except practice a little of our Arabic to much general amusement. Steve, Carolyn, and I were already proficient at mixing up the assorted food on our plates, so we were able to avoid eating even a bite of the sheep, which had won our considerable sympathy. We followed George as he went to express his appreciation to our host for the lovely day. The farmer told us to wait a minute so that he could go into the house and retrieve an important gift for George.

"Here is my 13-year-old daughter, to be a second wife for you."

The three of us were all ears, waiting for George's

response. It took George a second or two before he figured out what to say. Pointing at me, he said, "Look at the wife I *already* have. She doesn't have a single bracelet or necklace. Not even earrings. Just a pathetic wedding band. I am very grateful, but as you can see, I can barely afford even one wife. Two is impossible."

Speaking of gold, from the minute Steve heard that the Greeks and Romans had left coins—including gold coins— strewn throughout the ruins, he looked diligently at the ground every time we visited Cyrene. He never found any. But it was hard not to keep on trying when we heard the local lore that the lighthouse keeper at Apollonia—modern-day Sousa, just up the beach from where we would go swimming—had found gold coins by the hundreds.

Every afternoon, we were told, Saad, the lighthouse keeper, used to walk into town from the lighthouse on the northernmost heap of rocks of the Sousa coast. Sometimes, he went for provisions. Other times, he went to visit the coffee house and play backgammon.

One afternoon, on his way from town, he noticed small footprints.

"Did anyone come while I was gone?" he asked his wife. No one had come by.

The footsteps were always washed away every morning, but they reappeared every afternoon for three days. His wife assured him again that no one had come to visit. The suspense was too much. The next day, Saad hid behind some rocks to wait out the footprint maker and eventually, from the far side of the lighthouse, a small boy appeared, gold coins glittering in his open hands. As he darted by, Saad grabbed him by his leg. The boy tumbled and the coins dropped. "Don't beat me," he whimpered.

"What's this?" Saad asked as he picked up a thick coin, rubbing off its oil and grit with his thumb and forefinger. "Where did you find this?"

Still caught fast in Saad's grip, the boy nodded in the direction of the beach. Saad released his hold, and the two walked to a small cove. At first, Saad could see only the shimmering blue sea. The boy held out his arm. "There it is. See the plane. The gold comes from there."

Sliding off his sandals, Saad threw himself into the water. The boy was right. A plane lay off the coast, its wings had fallen off and the door was unhinged. There on the floor of the plane, spilling out of a Jerry can, were coins, hundreds of them, dull in the shaded water, but each one just like the one the boy had just held in his hand 10 minutes earlier. He surfaced and swam to the boy waiting on shore.

Saad asked the boy if anyone else knew, and the boy claimed that no one did—not even his father. "I showed him a coin," the boy said. "But he beat me and called me a thief. I haven't shown him any others."

That same afternoon, after he had sent the boy away, Saad swam to the plane. Before the sun had set, he filled five Jerry cans with gold coins. Back at the lighthouse, he hid them in a storeroom before his wife returned from gathering firewood.

Within a week, there was not one person in Sousa or for miles around who had not heard of Saad's treasure. Like goats scrambling over the rocks, they came singly, in pairs, and in herds. The sands were dug, sifted, and washed. The rocks were scraped and scrubbed. But Saad sat inside his lighthouse keeping his Jerry cans hidden. When the fury subsided and the last disappointed treasure seeker had given up, Saad left one afternoon for the coffee house, but he did not stop. He passed through Sousa and kept on going.

I wanted to think that, with his two million pounds, Saad played his way through Europe's most exclusive resorts with a new pretty young woman on his arm every day.

But a retired Libyan diplomat and friend corrected me. "Saad found gold coins by the hundreds in the wreckage of a submerged German military plane about a kilometer off shore. He used a 5-gallon German gasoline container to recover all the gold. He announced his candidacy for the Libyan Parliament and succeeded. He bought a second-hand Cadillac from an American Air Force officer. He ran through his money in Libya and returned to his former occupation."

We eventually gave up looking for gold coins ourselves, although we never stopped marveling at the unspoiled Mediterranean beach, as far as the eye could see. On the way to the beach, we had to pass the Sousa Post Office, where we often saw the aging lighthouse keeper sitting on the steps, his shoulders hunched up with sadness.

Steve and Carolyn, 11 and seven, could only take so many trips to Cyrene, and there was nothing else for a child to do. Nothing. There were no friends. There was no TV—only an erratic radio. School was tolerable, I think. Carolyn did prefer writing her new address to the old one in Tulsa. Now she lived on a street called Rommel's Cave. At the end of our street, there was indeed a huge cave where Field Marshal Erwin Rommel, the "Desert Fox" commander of Germany's Afrika Korps, had often sought safe haven with his senior staff.

Friends kept us supplied with books. Carolyn read 200 books in one year; Steven read 400. For years, George would brag about that. I tried to tell him how abnormal that was for children their ages, but he didn't listen. Carolyn did have a Barbie collection, and George and Steve spent months building a doll house for them. We sent photos to Aunt Mina of this architectural masterpiece. There was a sunken living room, functioning electric lights, running water, and a miniature bookcase filled with books individually bound by Steve, and, to Uncle Roy's delight, a splendid bathroom with Barbie sitting on a toilet crafted from a pink Joy detergent bottle. Uncle Roy, who obviously didn't look at the photographs too carefully, apparently said, "What is Marion always complaining about? That's a fine bathroom."

Really, nothing about living in Baida was "normal" for two American kids. There were only two other expatriot kids in town, the two young Bentley boys, and they were in Baida only when they were home on break from school in London. One year, the two boys were home during Halloween, and the four kids decided that they wanted to go trick-or-treating. Chris and Kevin Bentley had never done it before, but they thought it was a great idea to dress up as cowboys and pirates and knock on doors demanding candy.

Of course, we couldn't just show up at Libyan houses with children in costumes, so George tried to explain the mores of Halloween to Ambassador and Mrs. Wong, to the Missons—

Carolyn and Steve trick-or-treating at the home of the Chinese Ambassador.

the only other diplomats posted in Baida, from Belgium as it happens—and to Tony Bersa, the carefree young biochemist with the group of Yugoslavs running the T. B. hospital. Cherif, the USIS driver, drove the carload of cowboys and pirates to the carefully selected homes. All of Carolyn's fears were realized. Tony gave them jars of plum jam. The Missons gave them a ham. Ambassador and Mrs. Wong gave them huge boxes of Perugina chocolates—very expensive Halloween treats, but unsatisfactory to kids who wanted candy bars.

The biggest surprise to unfold that year was the arrival of the newly appointed American Ambassador, E. Allan Lightner, who arrived to spend much of the summer in the ambassadorial residence in Cyrene, an old Italian colonial villa, along with his wife Dotty and their three children: eight-year-old Ned, six-year-old John, and four-year-old Babette. Carolyn was thrilled.

"Do they speak English, Mama?"

"Of course they speak English, Carolyn. He's the American Ambassador, and they are Americans."

But I was wrong. Ambassador Lightner had been Assistant Chief of the U.S. Mission in Berlin, and the kids had been raised with the help of a German governess who spoke only German.

By this point in Steve and Carolyn's lives as children in a city as unusual as Baida—a capital city with a population of only 2,000 and virtually no one to play with—nothing seemed unusual to them.

On the other side of Sousa, opposite the lighthouse, was a site called Ras el Hilal, a promontory that stuck out into the sea. The Italians carved a tunnel out of a rock cliff on the promontory to safeguard their wartime submarines. It was extraordinary and beautiful and an almost surreal place to spend the day swimming.

Not far up the escarpment was another Cyrenaican character: Miss Olive Brittan, the King's beekeeper. Apparently, in the 1950s, when King Idris was on a visit to Jordan, he had met her and tasted some of her honey—and had heard that eating honey could enhance longevity. So the King brought her back to Libya with him. Technically, she worked for the Department of Agriculture. In fact, she worked directly for the King. Her house, which was located on a long dirt track off the main road from Baida to Derna, had served as a mess hall for Rommel's officers during the war. Colorful murals of Aryan German soldiers, giant swastikas, and caricatures of Churchill, graced her living room walls, while an enormous, dignified portrait of Queen Elizabeth and Prince Philip hung over the fireplace.

Sir Peter Wakefield, who served as the British Consul General in Libya from 1965 to 1969, described Miss Brittan's departure from Libya a few years later, about the same time we left the country. The day after Colonel Qaddafi's coup, a detachment of Royal Irish Rangers was sent to rescue her. The officer in charge wrote that they returned "with a charming but reluctant beekeeper." Sir Peter, who accompanied them, wrote that Miss Brittan "insisted on a proper ceremonial leave-taking, and marched the colonel of the mission and myself to the top of 'bee hill,' where she unfurled the Union Flag for us to salute. The flag was then folded away and carried back down the hill, past the hives of the slumbering royal bees."

We always stopped to see Miss Brittan on our way to the coastal city of Derna, further to the east. There, we loaded up on fresh produce in the markets, including lemons, apples, and eggplant. Another stop was at the clinic of Dr. Khalif, a

Palestinian, our dog Wendy's veterinarian. I had to laugh when he said giving Wendy food from a can was just *wrong*. Didn't we know that a dog needed fresh food? I didn't bother to tell him that most of our own meat was also canned. Our beef and chicken came to us in huge cafeteria-sized cans from Wheelus, the U.S. air base in Tripoli at the other end of the country. In Derna, we also visited Dr. and Mrs. Kreshel, not for medical treatment, but stamps. A German citizen, Dr. Kreshel had been practicing in Derna for 15 years. All that time, he had been amassing an extraordinary stamp collection. George and Steve, who also collected stamps more casually, were spellbound as he showed them examples from his collection of every Libya-related stamp ever issued. His collection went back to Ottoman days. The bulk of it, worth thousands, was in a bank vault in Switzerland.

The American Embassy in Baida was not just one of only three embassies in the country's new "capital"—it was also the smallest American embassy in the entire world, with only two officers, George and Ralph Stephan, the Political Officer. Ralph and his wife Catharina were, to put it mildly, colorful. Ralph was a Yale-educated scholar and an athlete—he rowed for a U.S. Olympic crew team—whose family disowned him when he married Catharina, partly because she was 20 years his senior. They rarely saw a convention they weren't willing to flout. One night they showed up to a formal dinner at the T. B. hospital wearing their bathing trunks—they had been swimming and saw no reason to come all the way back home to change—to the serious consternation of the head of the hospital, who was presumably also the head of Soviet intelligence in the area. He called George up afterwards to ask if this was a common practice among Americans. George tried to assure him that it was not, but he may have seen it as evidence of the decadent American way of life.

The Stephans also loved animals and, when you went to their home for dinner, you had to step over dogs, cats, and rabbits. George and I couldn't begin to imagine what the Libyans thought about this menagerie, all inside the house. When a tribal friend of Ralph's gave them a baby goat, Catharina insisted that the "darling" be allowed to frolic freely in the yard of the next-door guest house, which was used by the Ambassador's flight crew when he flew into town. Ralph wrote our administrative officer's efficiency report, an assessment that was usually critical to an employee's career advancement. The administrative officer had faced combat in the Air Force, but nothing like the combat he faced with Catharina, who refused his request that the goat be transferred to the Stephan yard when the Ambassador arrived with his flight crew. Catharina simply moved the goat into the Ambassador's bathroom, making for one very surprised American Ambassador.

In Berlin, Ambassador Lightner had achieved some recognition by overseeing the transfer of the U.S. spy Francis Gary Powers from the Soviets at Checkpoint Charlie. The rest of us soon called Catharina's goat "Checkpoint Charlie."

Ralph's replacement, Hume Horan, had also rowed, but at Harvard. It was as if rowing at an Ivy League school was a requirement for the position. Much more importantly, Hume also spoke Arabic. He was the best Arabic-speaker in the history of the State Department for whom Arabic was not his first language. His career would skyrocket from his post in Libya to ambassadorial posts in the Sudan, the Cameroons, the Ivory Coast, and Saudi Arabia. Hume credited his Arabic to having studied with the renowned British Arabic scholar

H. A. R. Gibb at Harvard, which he described as "equivalent to being taught Latin by the Pope." In Baida, Hume enrolled in poetry classes at the Islamic University. It was reliably reported that not just his fellow students but also his professors literally wept at the beauty of Hume's Arabic.

Hume also used his language skills in more practical ways. The Horans' gardener planted strawberries in their small garden, but every time, just before the strawberries were ready to be picked, they were being stolen. Hume casually told his gardener that the actual word for the fruit was Arabic for "pig berries." Pork being forbidden to faithful Muslims as unclean, the tactic worked, and the great strawberry robbery was foiled.

When they arrived in Baida, Hume and Nancy Horan—Nancy had also attended Harvard—had one child, a son named Alex, who was one. But soon, Nancy was pregnant again. She was terrified that, if the new baby was born prematurely, there were no facilities to handle it. The only hospital for hundreds of miles was the T.B. hospital. What if a plane from Wheelus, the American Air Force base in Tripoli, couldn't make it to Baida in time? What was she to do? Clinging to our copies of Dr. Spock, she and I fashioned a makeshift incubator. As it turned out, the pregnancy came to term; a plane did make it in time, and Margy was born at the Wheelus hospital in Tripoli.

We had a fright of our own in the form of a car accident. Every weekend possible, we drove down the steep escarpment from Cyrene to Apollonia. The zig-zag turns down the escarpment had been laid out in 100 A.D. To Carolyn's delight, on that particular day's drive down the twisted road, George was singing her favorite verses of "When I was in the Army" at the top of his lungs. He had progressed from "the coffee tasting like iodine" to a "biscuit" had just fallen and "killed a friend of mine." At the next sharp curve, the sun shot a blinding light into his eyes. George's reflexes were excellent, which was fortunate, for there was only one option. To the left was an immediate drop of hundreds of feet. He swerved right, and we fell into a grave: The entire escarpment was a necropolis with openings to caves where the Romans buried their dead.

So we only fell three feet, but our car, a 1956 Chevy, was stuck in the opening to the grave. Fortunately, the Wongs' driver happened by not long after and rescued us. The car was retrieved at some point, but was beyond repair, so we had to make do for the rest of our stay in Baida with the USIS panel truck, which had only a front seat. The passengers in the back had to sit on the truck's flatbed.

Once, when George was driving to Benghazi, he ran across the American Ambassador's wife, Dotty Lightner, who had been driving with two distinguished elderly guests from the States when their vehicle broke down. So Mrs. Lightner gamely spent the next two hours lying in the flat bed of the truck.

When our first Christmas in Baida rolled around, Carolyn was tremendously consoled when she saw the Parliament Building lit up with red and green lights: "Now Santa will find us!" I didn't have the heart to tell her that the lights were for Libya's Independence Day celebrations, not for Christmas. Up in the mountains, there were fir trees, so we had a proper fir Christmas tree instead of the palms we had to make do with in Baghdad. George took the children and Cherif, the driver, with him to choose a perfectly shaped tree, and they chopped it down themselves—all sticky sap, prickly needles, and Christmas fragrance.

That year, we actually had two Christmases. The Sears order did not come until December 26, so George took the pictures of all the toys he had bought in the Sears catalogue and wrapped them up. The kids opened those on Christmas day, then opened the actual toys a few days later, when the order finally arrived.

There was a new Christmas challenge the following year. Dotty Lightner had sent George a gross of boxes with United Nations Christmas cards to sell. One hundred and forty-four boxes of Christmas cards to sell in Muslim Baida! The Yugoslavs were Communists. The Wongs were Muslim. That left our three American Embassy families, the Bentleys, the Missons, and a few Cypriots who worked at the construction company. George was undaunted. He had the brilliant idea of holding a Miss U.N. Christmas card contest at the Cyrene Hotel and invited all of the young officers from the Libyan Foreign Office to the party. The Cyrene Hotel had seen better days—under Mussolini. It hadn't had so much as a paint job since Il Duce stayed there during World War II. For parties, the hotel manager would put detergent in the fountain that was the centerpiece of the lobby, and it gushed frothy soap bubbles the entire evening, lit with flashing colored lights.

The Cypriots put up one of their single secretaries to compete against Shirley Cowger, our branch Embassy secretary for the title of Miss U.N. George told the guests that they could vote as many times as they liked, but each vote cost a box of Christmas cards. Young, vivacious, and pretty, Shirley Cowger was the Libyan officers' favorite—so much so that George soon ran out of cards to sell. Shirley won by a landslide.

Meanwhile, we were running out of time. Our two years

in Baida were coming to an end. George was to continue to run the Baida office, but his new principal assignment was Benghazi.

Compared with Baida, Benghazi was paradise on earth. After two years living in a village of 2,000 people, we were suddenly in a cosmopolitan metropolis of sorts. Everywhere, we could see oversize trailer trucks carrying oil pipes and rigs headed to the Zelten oil fields some 200 miles to the south. There were trucks crammed with flocks of sheep from Turkish and Syrian ships on way from the dock to the slaughter house. We could see those ships and the brilliant blue Mediterranean from the roof of our apartment building when we hung the laundry. We could see the twin-domed cathedral that had been built by the Italians in 1932. The chimes from the cathedral took turns with calls to prayer from the minarets of the profusion of mosques surrounding us.

After a year in that apartment house, we were given a large spacious home in a lovely suburb, with rooms that stayed heated during the winter, fireplaces that worked, and a kitchen with faucets that ran both hot and cold with a turn of the handle. There were also rambling colonnades covered with an exuberance of hibiscus blossoms and a garden with poinsettias and olive and fig trees. And there was a school, a proper American school with American teachers and American kids—most of them the children of the people working in the new oil industry.

George adored working in his magnificent new garden.

That same garden proved useful to some friends, a Canadian couple who taught business at the Benghazi University. One morning, the wife, Jo Ann Wedley, came over weeping. She and her husband Bill had invited a new

French colleague and his wife to stay with them until they could find adequate living quarters of their own.

Apparently the French guests were appalled at the precautions Jo Ann, who had a new infant, took with fresh produce. She washed her vegetables and her fruit in disinfectant. "I even use permanganate, and sometimes, like you, Clorox. I can't let my baby get sick." At this point, she was actually sobbing. "What can I do? My houseguest Michelle says we will die because we won't develop immunity to Libyan germs."

"Invite her to tea," said George. "I'll take care of her."

George gave Michelle a tour of his garden with its eggplant, cucumbers, and tomatoes. "I water these vegetables in the garden myself," George said. "See that water tank behind the fig tree? I keep it filled with boiled water. You know, the germs here in Libya are so bad, most Libyans die young. They just die from all of the germs everywhere. They just die."

I'm not sure Michelle believed what George said, but she stopped giving Jo Ann trouble. We learned two months later, after they had found a home of their own, that the husband contracted a virulent case of amoebic dysentery, and they had to return to France.

Our first year in Benghazi seemed like perfection. Everything was perfect: no riots, no mud, and, most importantly, Carolyn and Steve had friends their own age. After two years of attending cocktail parties with George and me in Baida, they had something approaching a normal life.

Except that the American school stopped at high school. That meant sending Steve away to boarding school, something that I had promised myself would never happen, ever since the time that I was deposited at age seven at a boarding school in Kuling. We had heard that George might suddenly be transferred to Khartoum, where there wasn't an adequate school, and boarding school seemed the only safe bet. Except for the boarding schools that I had attended in China, we didn't have any experience with such institutions. Hume Horan had attended St. Andrew's before going to Harvard and had enjoyed his time there. So we were sending Steve to the only boarding school we had any awareness of. I sobbed that entire day in September 1966 as we took 14-year-old Steve to the Benghazi airport to board a plane for New York City and St. Andrew's in Middletown, Delaware. Standing there with me, every one of them dry-eyed, was a group of British mothers watching their four- and five-year-olds happily boarding the same plane.

Carolyn was dry-eyed, but she was crushed in a different way. Steve had a check for thousands of dollars in his pocket. I don't think she understood the concept of tuition. And, in addition to being lucrative, she thought going off to boarding school would be a terrific adventure. Her day would come later.

No longer running a one-room schoolhouse in Baida, I was available to help out in the very "English" English Department of the Faculty of Arts at Benghazi University. (By now I was beginning to lose my conviction that I would never be a teacher.) It was there at Benghazi University that I learned an important lesson about Arab women and the veil.

I was already quite well-acquainted with the topic. I had marveled at how Iranian women could hold the corners of their *chadors* with their teeth when they bent to pick something up, without dropping whatever they happened to be holding. It was also in Tehran that I met the mother of a young man who had just returned from studying in the U.S., who was driving her crazy, insisting that she join the 20th century and remove her *chador* when she left the house.

"Just you listen to me," she reprimanded him. "This *chador* of mine is important. I can wear a nightgown under it if I have to when I dash to the market. I don't have to comb my hair if I don't want to. Just leave me alone."

One of my fellow teachers at the university in Benghazi told me that, in Mecca, at the time of the Prophet Mohammad, tribal leaders and merchants gathered annually from hundreds of miles around for a major trade fair. They used to dress their unmarried daughters in all their finery, their faces unveiled, to attract suitors as they paraded around the Ka'ba, then a shrine to a pantheon of idols. The comments from the men were, as one might expect, raw. When the Prophet told his female followers that they should cover their hair and faces when they went outdoors, he was asking for modesty in order to protect their honor. God's message as delivered to the Prophet by the Angel Gabriel was clear: "O Prophet, tell your wives and daughters, and the women of the faithful, to draw their wraps a little over their faces. They will thus not be recognized and no harm will come to them."

At Benghazi University, which was only 11 years old, most of my students were male. Young girls had only begun going to school under a UNESCO program in the early 1950s. The first day of classes, I watched as one of my female students approached the gate to our building heavily veiled. But the minute she entered the gate, she flung off her veil and her black *abaya*; underneath, she was dressed like any

Western female college student. Modesty and propriety had been served by wearing the veil to school. The minute she entered the school, she entered the 20th century—without the slightest apparent dislocation.

Toward the end of my year at the University, with Carolyn at the American Community School and Steve at St. Andrew's, George was reassigned to Washington, not Khartoum. It had been quite a change from our little schoolhouse in Baida. My Libyan students never said things like "my brother is mean" and "my sister is silly." But unlike my two children, my Libyan students sometimes went on strike—in particular, when the administration announced that there would now be quarterly exams as well as semester exams. One of my second-year students, back from the strike, and confronted with a test, had an interesting excuse: "I do reply these questions, because, I went to meet my mother and my brother who were in Mecca. When I say this for you, I find myself very agr and sorry. Be truste and comfortable I shall be clover in the future. Your pupil."

I'm sure if my students reacted to my Arabic the way I reacted to their English, they would have been even more amused than I was.

We all were so absorbed in the daily activities of life that last year in Libya, 1967, we had no inkling of yet another political storm about to engulf us. Just as we were packing to leave Libya, President Nasser of Egypt was pitting the Soviet Union and the United States against each other—to Egypt's benefit. He decided to block Israeli traffice from the Gulf of Aqaba and demanded that the United Nations withdraw the force that was monitoring the Gaza border.

Israel beat him to the draw.

We left Benghazi the morning of June 5, and the trip to

the airport was uneventful. The entire Consulate was there to say goodbye—and their return to the city was uneventful. But total chaos was building in Benghazi. Rumor had it that the U.S. had joined forces with Israel and that U.S. Navy planes had bombed Cairo. The Consulate group rushed into the chancery just as many of the Libyan staff rushed out. The detachment of guards from the Cyrenaican Defense Forces that was assigned to protect the Consulate was no match for the onslaught of hundreds of rioting Libyans. They were joined by a contingent from the 2,000 Egyptian laborers building a pan-Arab Olympic stadium on the outskirts of Benghazi.

Fortunately, before it was turned into a consulate, the chancery building, which was on the Cathedral Square, had been a bank. The staff went to the roof to burn classified documents in huge steel drums until the barrage of rocks became too lethal, which sent them running to take refuge in the bank's steel vault. The vault successfully resisted attempts to ram the door open with a long steel sewer pipe. All around the vault, fires raged. George's spanking-new Cultural Center across the square was reduced to ashes in seconds.

In the meantime, the Consulate wives waited nervously. Miraculously, the phones worked, and the wife of the Commercial Officer, upon hearing her husband's voice, knew that she was not yet a widow. They had hosted a farewell party for us the night before. She learned of the trouble in town when two Embassy drivers brought an Embassy truck to the house for safekeeping as they ran off on stored bicycles. "I've never seen men so scared," she later wrote me. "And I never hope to see that look in anyone's eyes." She had a young American friend from home staying with her and helping her with their young children. Although the wife did not know how to load her husband's two rifles, she got them out to use as clubs if needed. She even contemplated handing her young visitor a birth control pill in case they were raped, but decided that would only terrify her more.

It was hours before the troops from the British Army D'Aosta base were able to rescue the American men and their families. An armored car that had earlier tried to reach the Embassy had been destroyed by screaming men pouring gasoline down the hatch.

In the air, we had no idea what was happening on the ground. But as we rode from the airport into Tripoli, we noticed people gathering on the streets. We were stopping in Tripoli for another farewell party before a scheduled flight to Rome and then on to the States. We drove straight to the apartment of our hosts, Mohammed and Wedad Salah. Palestinians from Jerusalem, the Salahs had been with us throughout most of our stay in Baida, where Mohammed served as adviser and interpreter for the Ambassador.

"Put your heads down, both of you," Wedad yelled as we stepped into the apartment living room. George was taken to the Tripoli Embassy to help destroy classified documents. He would remain there two days and nights until we were evacuated in an Army transport plane from Wheelus to Spain.

In the meantime, across the street, girls from a secondary school had caught sight of Carolyn and me. They were screaming that Carolyn and I were "American dogs." Wedad yelled back at them that we were from Holland. She then had both of us sit down with some of her neighbors who had congregated to sew Palestinian flags and toss them from the apartment balcony to crowds below.

The Arab armies met swift defeat in the Six-Day War. Nasser's decision to block Israel from using the Suez Canal had proven reckless, and his martial rhetoric against Israel had proven empty. The Egyptians, Jordanians, and Syrians were no match for a much better-supplied Israel. In the Six-Day War, Israel not only gained additional territory, amounting to one-third of its original size, but also the trophy of Jerusalem. Once again Arab unity had proven to be an illusion.

Our view of the Middle East as a stable region had also proven illusory. No longer could the United States be isolated from the turmoil throughout the region.

FOREIGN SERVICE | 201

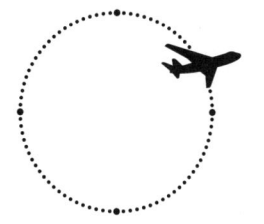

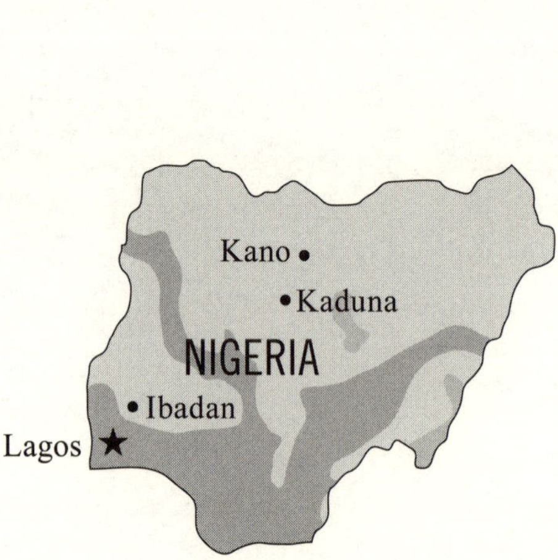
Kano
Kaduna
NIGERIA
Ibadan
Lagos

NIGERIA

We were only in Washington briefly, but long enough for George to serve on the African desk at USIA on Pennsylvania Avenue and for me to take a job teaching at a high school in Silver Spring, Maryland.

I was teaching history in the red-brick, white-columned Montgomery Blair High School when I announced that January 4 would be my last day—because my husband had been assigned as Cultural Affairs Officer in Lagos, Nigeria.

For an entire semester, Allan, a sullen heap of a boy, had been excruciatingly painful for me to watch. He sat slouched in the back row, sliding further and further down in his chair every time I glanced in his direction. He turned a deaf ear to my questions. In desperation, I actually sought help—for me, not for him. The school counselor told me his IQ was low. I just needed to be patient.

"Nigeria—that's where you *belong*," Allan said.

The class gulped. What would I do? Happily, my survival instinct kicked in. "This is wonderful," I said, leading the class in applause. "Allan knows how to *speak!*"

Sarah Lee Owens, the Assistant Cultural Affairs Officer,

met us at Ikeja Airport, amidst deafening shouts and frantic scurrying about. Sara Lee—nearly six feet of impeccable grooming and Baha'i serenity—blazed a trail through the airport crowds. She dismissed our jet-lagged pleas for mercy, however, insisting that we stop to call on various dignitaries on the way to our assigned Embassy house, located in the newest part of Lagos on prestigious Victoria Island. At each home, all three Naifehs—11-year-old Carolyn included—were welcomed with a gift bottle of Johnny Walker, either Red or Black.

"I don't even drink whiskey," mumbled George on our way to yet another home.

"You can't refuse," Sarah Lee scolded. "That would be very rude. But don't worry. You can use this cache when you have to welcome someone to *your* home. It all works out very well. You'll see."

Carolyn decided that all adults were completely addled.

Working our whiskey-laden way along Ikorodu Road on the mainland, our car had to edge over to the shoulder for the open-air passenger lorries. Packed with people, the lorries had boldly painted signs: "Who Can Tell?," "Friends before Money," "Destiny," "Never Say Fail," "Thank God." We drove below and around giant billboard signs for Golden Penny Flour, Fanta Orange, Guinness Beer, Samco Milk, and Dunlop Tyres, while passing Honesty Stores, Bobby Benson's Bamboo Room, Doctor Motor Automobile Workshops, Omodumi Maternity Homes, Vono Best Mattresses, City Girl Pools, and Nigerpools. The latest juju hits blared deafeningly loud from the loudspeakers at record and radio shops.

By the time we passed Oyingbo Market, the traffic had quieted a bit. We drove over the newly-opened Eko Bridge to our new home. Sarah Lee informed us that here, some 300 years ago, the sons of the Ife hunter Ogunfuninire planted their crops on land now bequeathed to their descendants, the white-capped chiefs, or *obas*. I was sinking rapidly in a quicksand of names, riddled with vowels, names like Ogunfuninire. Sarah mentioned that putting the accent on the second syllable would help. It never did. If nothing else, Nigeria was going to be a linguistic challenge.

A century earlier, the famous British traveler, Richard Burton, had found Lagos "detestable . . . as if a hole had been hollowed out in the original mangrove forest that skirts the waters, where bush and dense jungle, garnished with many a spreading tree, tall palms, and matted masses of fetid verdure rise in terrible profusion around." He added that the British Consulate in Lagos was a "corrugated iron coffin or palm-lined morgue, containing a dead consul once a year." In 1960, not long before we arrived, Wole Soyinka, who later became the first African to win the Nobel Prize for Literature, had called Lagos a "descent into imagined hell."

Happily for us, the British High Commissioner's "coffin" had been replaced with an air-conditioned glass building. It fronted the harbor on the marina just before the bridge to Victoria Island and our new home at No. 1 Waziri Ibrahim Crescent. Surrounded by the overpopulated bluster of the mainland, Victoria Island was still a pristine open space— not yet fully developed—and if one stood still, one could hear the muffled roar of pounding surf in the distance. George and I were enchanted.

In the 1960s, Nigeria was still proclaiming its proud, boisterous new posture as an independent country. The country had a contagious joy and enthusiasm that even the raging Biafran Civil War could not completely extinguish.

As a consequence, settling in was effortless. Once our

Godwin, the gardener, at our home on Victoria Island.

household effects arrived, I placed our Chinese embroidered screen in a prominent corner, which was my way of announcing that this house was "home." The house was already functioning, since we had inherited the previous occupants' servants, who lived in a small village at the back of our lush green lot. There was Monday, the cook, short of stature and large of belly and voice. His two-year-old son Kenny, already large of belly, wandered all day into the kitchen, stark naked except for a pair of shiny, oversized blue plastic shoes. If I happened to enter the kitchen, Kenny fled screaming in pure terror. The only other white person he had ever seen up close was a mission nurse in Calabar who had given him a shot. Monday and his wife, I later learned, threatened Kenny with a return of the white lady with the hypodermic needle whenever they had to make him behave.

Emmanuel, the bearer, was lean, almost emaciated, tall and quiet. Emmanuel spoke only when spoken to, and then in the softest of voices. Godwin, the gardener, was a teenager with a great smile who happily cut the grass with a machete. He was a serious worker and as proud of his handiwork as he was of his good looks. George was delighted: Godwin would prove to be the best gardener we ever had at any post. Our living room had enormous and highly impractical glass windows, just like our first house in Baghdad. I often saw George and Godwin standing side by side, admiring the wonder of our small corner of Lagos's floral exuberance, which seemed to grow by the inch as they stood there watching it.

It was not uncommon for Nigerians to name their children after the day they were born, so, in addition to Monday the cook, we had Friday the driver. Monday's day off was Sunday, while Friday's was Saturday. It was more than a little confusing at first.

Whatever the day of the week, it made me nervous having so many men living in and visiting our compound. I hired Emmanuel's wife Philomena to stay in the house when we had to go out to an exhibit, cocktail party, or any other official reception. On one of our first nights out, Carolyn talked Philomena into tying her hair into cornrows. It usually takes an entire spool of thick black thread for a single new hair-do. The average Nigerian woman's tightly woven cornrows lasted from three to six weeks, but, to Carolyn's disappointment, her soft hair, tightly bound, lasted in place for only 24 hours. Oh, the trials and tribulations of fashion.

George and me at a reception in Lagos.

However, Philomena had more serious problems. Small and slightly anorexic, her nerves were constantly on edge. She was deeply in love with Emmanuel, and wanted to provide him a family. Seldom did a day go by without her pouring her heart out to me. On the verge of tears, she would wail: "I have no issue, Madame. I have no issue." She was terrified that no one would be there to bury her when she died.

I did not appreciate the full magnitude of the "issue" issue until my first Nigerian wedding, which took place at the Lagos Cathedral. Sarah Lee had brought me along with her. I was sitting in a pew next to the aisle with a clear view of the bride—unmistakably eight months pregnant under her folds of satin and lace.

The bride, Victoria, was marrying the head of state, Major General Yakubu Gowon, and far from being horrified at her obvious pregnancy, the congregation was vastly impressed. "Vicki," Sarah Lee told me, "has proven her fertility."

Two years later, when I was packing up the household and the ubiquitous Chinese screen at the end of our tour, Philomena was helping me. Philomena eyed a three-foot-tall Libyan doll that had been presented to me as a gift when we left Baida. Philomena sighed plaintively as I pulled the doll out of its tissue wrappings to re-pack it. The doll, with a head of intricate blond curls, was dressed in holiday finery, with a cascade of fake gold chains around her neck.

"Oh, Madame," cried Philomena. "Please. She can be my issue."

It was a never-ending, always unexpected course on Nigerian fertility. Once, when George visited Ibadan, his host, who was a prominent city leader, invited him home for lunch. The lunch took place on a second-story balcony which overlooked an enclosure the size of a football field. George complimented the man on opening up his field to some 100 of the neighborhood children.

"*Neighborhood* children? No, no—these are all *my* children."

An American volunteer at the Lagos Handicraft Center later told me that pregnant women often refused to work on the cloth dolls she had designed. They informed her that the spirit of a doll might affect the sex of their next baby and their husbands would beat them for bringing home trouble.

I was soon volunteering myself, although not at the Handicraft Center.

I was attending one of Naomi Matthews's morning coffees for Embassy wives. Mrs. Matthews, our Ambassador's wife, was a lady of the first order. Slim, greying, and impeccably groomed morning, noon, or night, I never saw Naomi Matthews flustered. Her husband, Elbert, who had also served as the U.S. Ambassador in Liberia, was of the same fiber. When Embassy officers in staff meetings complained that Nigerian guests sometimes accepted invitations to formal dinners then didn't show up, Ambassador Matthews told them how he had invited the Liberian Foreign Minister to dinner to meet G. Mennen Williams, then Assistant Secretary of State for African Affairs. The Minister never showed up. Ambassador Matthews called him the next day to ask if there had been a problem the night before and the Minister replied that he wasn't hungry.

When Mrs. Matthews asked you to do something, you didn't hesitate—even when she asked me to take on the literacy program sponsored by the Lagos Women's Club. Before I knew what had hit me, we had over 100 students and more than a dozen volunteer teachers in three centers—at the YWCA, at St. Gregory's Catholic Church, and in Falomo. The students were predominantly market women. The teachers were predominantly friends and acquaintances I could enlist before they had a chance to say no. I decided to teach the first class myself to learn something about illiteracy. The students were eager villagers, male and female, whose schooling was either nonexistent or had been interrupted when they had flocked to the big city to find work. Our classroom was a tin-roofed, open-air enclosure. I had a propped-up blackboard and chalk—but no text.

One particularly muggy afternoon, it began to dawn on me that literacy was about a lot more than reading and writing. I was going on and on about Nigeria being a country, your country. "It is bordered on the north by Niger . . . ."

Hands shot up. "A border? What's a border?"

"It's where Nigeria ends and Niger begins."

To my delight, on graduation day, I was asked to sit at the head table with officers of the Lagos Women's Club. I arrived early and had a front row seat for a fashion show as well as proximity to a running commentary—a fashion show that celebrated the latest cotton head-ties, or *geles*. These luxurious creations were riotous in color and size and ranged from velveteen and silks to intricate brocades. In the privacy of my bedroom, I had once tried to fashionably wrap a three-foot head-tie around my head. I failed miserably, just as Carolyn had failed with her cornrows. I remain to this day in awe of an effortlessly perched head-tie, with its precarious twists and folds. Each one has a name, and they are mostly very creative. The name for my head-tie, if I had one, would have been "Foreign Failure." I soon recognized that the stylish twirls around me that day were political statements. They spoke of the war that was raging in the Niger Delta region: "Crush the Rebellion," "Shh! Don't Talk," "Keep Nigeria One."

Head-ties were a proud statement about Nigeria's rich cultural past. More concerning was a continuing legacy of its British colonial days—a focus on various shades of skin color and hair conditions. The stores and market stalls were heavily stocked with skin lighteners, brilliantine, hair fixatives, wigs, pomades, Vaseline, and talcum powders with exotic names like Saturday Night, Sahara Flower, and Maliki Dancers. I was just becoming attuned to the variations in skin color when I overheard a lady seated to my right comment to a friend on the arrival of a mutual acquaintance: "Take a look. She just put herself through the bleach cycle of a washing machine."

There was an especially graphic Yoruba word for a white man—*oyinbo*—one whose skin has been peeled off. In the late 18th century, a Scottish doctor named Mungo Park had had been searching for the source of the Niger River. In 1795, he wrote that the ladies in the King of Bondou's court "rallied me with a good deal of gaiety on different subjects, particularly the whiteness of my skin and the prominency of my nose. They insisted that both were artificial. The first, they said, was produced when I was an infant, by dipping me in milk; and they insisted that my nose had been pinched every day till it had acquired its present unsightly and unnatural conformation."

But Nigeria was such a glorious confusion of contradictions that the effort to look more white was often mixed with a pride in the beauty of being black. When Dr. Park praised "the glossy jet of their skins, and the lovely depression of their noses," the ladies informed him that flattery, or "honey milk," would do him no good—although they immediately sent to his quarters a large jar of honey. Their own honeyed words were that "a perfect beauty is a load for a camel." And their descendants still defined a well-proportioned buttock as "plenty of cloth," a symbol of wealth and a source of sexual appeal. Clearly, beauty had more than one definition.

The other aspect of Nigeria that I found endlessly fascinating was the intensity of the activity everywhere around us. No matter the direction or the hour, something or someone was always moving. Fishermen were restringing their nets by the low grass on the banks of the Five Cowrie Creek. Washerwomen were flattening the wet clothes they had brought from a thorough scrubbing at public fountains. Everywhere, women were walking with astonishing loads balanced on their heads—not only clothing, but heavy tins filled with money and long-tailed fish stuffed into calabashes. And walking like that for miles. Men from the race course were bringing horses for a run on the sand. Down at the fish market in Apapa, sellers were dipping fish in the sand for preservation.

Maybe George was Nigerian at heart, because he was always on the move. He never stopped. Now that Sarah Lee Owens had been transferred to Sierre Leone, George had a new guide to our new home—his Cultural Assistant, Mrs. T. N. O. Sodeinde, a genuine Yoruba Princess. There may be some 250 ethnic groups in Nigeria, but the Yoruba of the West stand out, along with the Hausa of the North and the Ibo of the South, as the most numerous and most powerful. Like so many of the educated people we met in Nigeria, she had more generations of college education in her family than most Americans do—the only really good legacy from the British colonial years. Mrs. Sodeinde was a third-generation college graduate.

When she told George that she needed a bigger office to counsel students who wanted to study in the U.S., he hesitated until she invited him to sit in on a meeting. Her office was crowded indeed: crowded, because every member of the applicant's village was squeezed in. Mrs. Sodeinde gave George a knowing look as he stared in disbelief. Then he heard her wise invocation: "This fine young man of your family and village will gain great knowledge and real skills to help you. Can you not help him now?" She went round the room one by one: "And how much will you give?" "And you?" She did not stop until she had received pledges for the tuition and board she needed for the young man or woman.

She got her bigger office.

George focused much of his attention on young people, as well. He earned a Man O'War badge for helping with the Citizenship Training Centre for young men, where they learned agility through something called the "commando crawl" and balance through a swift-moving "Eskimo" kayak. On JFK Memorial Day, he asked the hundreds who participated in an essay contest "what they could do for their country." I tagged along whenever I could. I loved the Police College graduation—known as the Passing Out Ceremony—for the name alone. On well-clipped lawns, marching cadets strutted by the reviewing stand. A deafening chorus from a bagpipe band filled the air. Next for me was the Golden Jubilee Celebration of the Nigerian Girl Guides. Lady Baden-Powell herself attended—it was her husband Robert who had started scouting in 1920.

Part of George's job was to bring American dancers, singers, and artists to Nigeria from the U.S.—Cab Calloway and his dancers were a particular hit. But it was also his job to lend support to Nigerian artists, and, luckily for us, Nigeria was a font of world-class talent in the arts when we were there.

Of course, Nigeria has a long and splendid cultural

history. The illustrious Dr. Ekpo Eyo, Director of the Nigerian Department of Antiquities, became such a good friend that he allowed us to visit the storage rooms of the national museum and hold the precious Benin bronzes, Ife terra-cottas, and other masterworks in our hands—with gloves on, of course.

But the current art scene was every bit as exciting. Nigerian artists were just beginning to make major contributions to international contemporary art. It helped that for some time, major artists in the West had been so enamored of traditional African art, especially Picasso, who had a profound and lasting reaction in June 1907 to the collection of African and Oceanic art at the Ethnographic Museum of the Trocadero in Paris. Picasso claimed that African art helped him understand for the first time that painting "is not an aesthetic process: It's a form of magic that interposes itself between us and the hostile universe, a means of seizing power by imposing a form on our terrors as well as our desires."

In the late 1960s, a new generation of Nigerian artists— notably Yusuf Grillo, Erhabor Emokpae, and Bruce Onobrakpeya—was using the Western absorption of African art to make works of their own that brought together the art of Africa with the art of the West. They were engaged in a search for cultural identity almost identical to the one that I had witnessed as a student in Mexico among the muralists Siquieros, Rivera, and Orozco. Grillo, Emokpae, and Onobrakpeya were not only bringing the art of the West into their own art, they were using Western art based in part on African art to capture Nigerian myths and legends.

When I met Emokpae for the first time at his show at George's USIA Center, I literally gasped. His paintings, such as *Olokun, Song to the Unborn*, and *12 Gods in Transition*, which were painted in an Abstract Expressionist style that combined Jackson Pollock and Willem de Kooning, were only part of what made him an icon in the Nigerian art world. Bassey Ita, critic at the *Morning Post*, commented on George's May 1969 show for Emokpae: "Standing before his sculptures generates the same experience it would be standing before a god." Ita may have been referring as much to the artist as to the art. Slowly waving a frayed bamboo fan, Emokpae stood six feet plus. His muscular physique was draped in a vermillion velvet Dorothy Lamour-type sarong, one shoulder bared. He was the son of Chief Ogieva Emo, the vowel-rich Inguosadoba of Benin.

Then there was the wiry and soft-spoken Bruce Onobrakpeya. His mischievous grin masked a fiery intensity. I have one of his etchings, an abstraction of three musicians beating drums. Bruce's etchings, engravings, and intaglio work have brought him world fame. In 2006, UNESCO gave him the Living Human Treasure Award. When we met him, and first became close friends, he was still teaching at St. Gregory's College and had just finished his massive *Stations of the Cross* for Saint Paul's, a massive church in the center of Lagos. A set of the etchings that he made from those 14 *Stations* is hung every Lenten season here in Aiken, South Carolina, at the First Baptist Church. Bruce took Steve—who was making paintings and sculptures of his own—under his wing when Steve came home for Christmas in 1968, becoming his first real art teacher.

We fell in love with one of Bruce's relief sculptures—a series of panels with images of turtles, fish, calabashes, and palms, each of which illustrated a Nigerian folk tale. One evening before we left the country, Bruce and his wife were having dinner with us and admired our pottery dinner

George and me with the son of Ade James.

service, which had been made in Oklahoma. We said it was his. No sooner had he taken the pottery set home than he returned with his spectacular relief sculpture—the very one we had fallen in love with.

George's right hand at the Embassy was a wonderful man named Ade James. Early on, we were invited to a crack-of-dawn naming-day ceremony for his eight-day-old daughter. Ade, his wife, and their two other children had two rooms at the rear of his uncle's house, which we and assorted relatives completely filled. Even at that hour of the morning, a goat had already been slaughtered and was being prepared in the courtyard for a celebratory meal. The baby wore a bracelet of tiny white beads on each wrist and two strings tied around her lower abdomen. Ade explained that the strings represented a chastity belt. We all watched as the baby was sprayed with a calabash of water so that "she will walk through rain in her life and not get sick." She was held briefly under the sun for the same symbolic reason. Whiskey was spread on her lips so that "she will have a life of material comforts." Our material comfort at 7 a.m. was a shot of vodka to toast the newest member of the James family.

Thanks to our daughter Carolyn, Nigeria also introduced us to polo, a sport that had been wildly popular in Nigeria since the British brought it to the country in 1930. Carolyn had a legion of friends at the American International School, so her schedule was as hectic as ours. But sleepovers, swimming at the Federal Palace Hotel, regular outings to Tarkwa Bay, guitar and piano lessons, and even a Sadie Hawkins Turkey Hop were not enough. She was desperate to learn how to ride. We were only a short distance from the posh Lagos Polo Club, where we managed to rent half a pony, "Gulab." We never knew which half. Because he was a thoroughbred, I was terrified of his speed. The horse came with a groom, a knowledgeable young man named Samuel who tolerated my anxieties, and Carolyn thrived after one or two falls.

Polo may have originated in ancient Persia, but we had never watched a polo match in Iran. In Lagos, we soon fell in love with the sport ourselves. We rarely missed any of the regular games and none of the tournaments, each richer in pomp and circumstance than the one before. Brigadier Hassan Katsina, from the North, like so many of Nigeria's polo players, was Captain of the Polo Club. The finale of a weeklong tournament was better than a movie. The Police Band played with gusto, and an Army honor guard marched in fine step. They were followed by a contingent of mounted police, splendid in their red jackets and white helmets. They put on a full display of synchronized riding before the match began.

Mrs. Troels Munk, wife of the Danish Ambassador, and heiress to the Tuborg Beer fortune, was intimately involved with the Lagos Polo Club. I ran into her once in the French grocery store where she pointed out with delight some fresh asparagus, just flown in. Two bunches lay in her shopping cart propped up next to the drugs she had just picked up to take to the Club to put down a horse.

The international community in Lagos was wonderful. Almost every embassy had active cultural programs. There were also piano concerts at the residence of a retired British colonial officer, Major Allen. He had spent 46 years as a District Officer in Eastern Nigeria. He taught piano and had late afternoon concerts for his most accomplished Nigerian piano students. His residence, next to the American Ambassador's, had an expansive lawn reaching out to a serene lagoon. As twilight fell, there was a reflection of the moon on the surface of the unruffled water that spread across the horizon. Thick jasmine vines, spilling over an upstairs balcony, filled the air along with the Mozart and Brahms.

There was no such serenity, however, in the music and politics of Fela Ranikulapo Ransome-Kuti, arguably the most important 20th-century African musician. In 2003, six years after Fela's death, Lisa Phillips, the Director of the New Museum in New York, would call Fela "the most important cultural figure in Africa in the past 100 years." The director and photographer Bill T. Jones described Fela's life as "mythic in scale." A musical based on his life and music made its way to Broadway in November 2009. "Fela!" the musical earned a glowing review from *The New York Times*, which wondered why the people on the street after the show were not "gyrating, swaying, vibrating, in thrall to the force field" of the music's "visceral" spirit of rebellion.

The first time we saw Fela, we saw a scrawny figure dressed in cotton briefs. He was on stage in a jam-packed high-life hall, giving his saxophone a life of its own. Everyone was listening, watching, dancing, swaying, and drumming on the tables.

Fela's entire family was almost as amazing as he was.

His mother Olufunmilayo was Nigeria's first major feminist. She was the first Nigerian woman to drive a car. She was the first to organize and lead women into serious, effective political action. Before one of her indignant marches in Abeokuta, she changed into men's shorts and a shirt. She told her sons that she had to dress like a man because it took a man to fight a man.

Fela was sure that he and his brothers were disciplined more often than any of the other boys in their mother's classes—she beat them regularly—just to set an example. Fela reported that his only relief came when their mother became distracted with politics.

Fela's older brother Beko was a medical doctor. He was also Chairman of the Campaign for Democracy and a passionate human rights activist. For speaking out against the government's outrageous sentencing of prisoners of conscience, he received a life sentence for being an "accessory to treason." The sentence was commuted before he died in 2006.

Fela risked even more government wrath because he had the biggest megaphone of all, in the form of his seditious music. "Soldier Go, Soldier Come" spoke to the revolving door between the military and commerce. In 1974, his commune was raided, and Fela was arrested on suspicion of marijuana possession. The following year, he renamed the commune the "Kalakuta Republic," declaring it an independent zone, free from Nigerian law. In 1977, there was a second, more deadly raid by over 1,000 soldiers. The Republic's 60 inhabitants were beaten or jailed. His mother fell from a balcony—or was pushed off it. Fela's very public mass wedding to 27 women the next year, less than two months before his mother died, shocked some of the nation, but not her. She blessed the marriage from her hospital bed. He was her son and a humanitarian, and she was not going to question God's will.

Twenty years later, Fela's years of unbridled sex led to his death from AIDS. Lagos came to a standstill. More than a million people attended his funeral. Twelve years before, his brother Olikoye, who was then Health Minister, had tried to alert the country to the danger of AIDS, but no one had listened. This time, however, his words had potent meaning to all of Nigeria.

While we were in Nigeria, Fela traveled to Los Angeles, which was still reeling from the Watts riots, where he learned first-hand the struggles of black Americans. Fela attended Black Panther meetings and absorbed the writings of Malcolm X. He also felt the impact of Miles Davis's restless jazz. He recognized, probably for the first time, not only the full risks of his activism but also the full potential.

Even Fela's flaunting of convention—wearing the skimpiest of briefs and smoking marijuana while on stage, marrying more than two dozen women at the same time—was a political statement.

Increasingly, George's work was leading him into close contact with activists in every branch of the cultural world. The professors at the University of Lagos were no exception, and it was there that he met Fela's older brother, Olikoye, a pediatrician and medical professor. It was Olikoye who took us to Fela's dingy throbbing nightclub. Couples on the crowded dance floor worked themselves into a frenzy of pure rhythm. Fela was a classically-trained musician—he had studied at Trinity College, London, in the late 1950s—but he had devised his own style of music, which was called Afro-beat, a unique mixture of Yoruba percussion, blues, and jazz.

At the time, I didn't understand his lyrics, which were in a combination of Yoruba and Pidgin English. I had no idea they were so potent. Like Wole Soyinka, Fela's unending personal and professional struggle was for the disenfranchised and dehumanized.

In fact, Soyinka, the future Nobel Laureate, was a Ransome-Kuti cousin.

I had never heard of Soyinka until George brought home a leaflet of his *Poems from Prison*. Soyinka had been in solitary confinement since August 1967, when he was charged with aiding and abetting the breakaway southeastern province of Biafra. But his real crime had been to call attention to the crimes of the Nigerian government. As the American Cultural Attaché, George was one of the Embassy officers who worked—successfully, in the end—for Soyinka's freedom from prison.

Soyinka was not the only brilliant Nigerian writer of his day. Chinua Achebe, who taught at the University of Ibadan, shared his passion for individual creativity, personal freedom, and respect for human rights. Achebe's great novel *Things Fall Apart* had been published in 1958. Achebe took the title from Yeats's *The Second Coming*: "Things fall apart; the centre cannot hold."

Nigeria's independence from Great Britain two years later, in 1960, had not resulted in the justice that Nigerians had hoped for, and the political situation had only gotten worse year after year. A military coup in 1966 just continued the turmoil. Lt. Colonel Yakubu Gowon, the least controversial military leader at the time, was made head of state, but even he was unable to put down the three-year-old civil war.

Nigerian religious life was as complex as Nigerian politics. It was not at all unusual to find a Christian, a

Muslim, and a Pagan in the same family—or to find all three in the same person. The immense Nigerian world of Pagan deities, or *orishas*, served as intermediaries for solving all of life's problems.

Wole Soyinka writes that his "preferred haven for meandering is within tropical lushness... One is enfolded in the amplitude of Nature, where the incongruities of essence are dissolved or absorbed into numinous forces of which deity stands a wordless medium."

I don't remember why George and I joined a group venturing into the jungle not far from Lagos, but at one point during that trip, I found myself totally lost in the "tropical lushness," and it was very scary. I was squeezed into a sliver of clearing, standing on a bank of tangled tree roots, surrounded by glistening tree trunks. Within a minute I had lost all composure. It was not hard to understand why Nigerians had developed a pantheon of gods to provide them with protection from the terror of human existence. The words of the Nicene Creed, first etched into my consciousness in the St. Mark Chapel in Wuhu, still give me pause: "I believe in one God, the Father Almighty, Maker of heaven and earth, And of all things visible and invisible..."

The Yoruba—the most numerous of Nigeria's 248 ethnic groups—are adept at handling the invisible. They enlist their ancestral spirits to help sort things out. One not only enters life but also leaves it in a kind of purgatory: There is no end and no beginning. All blends into one.

We were living in Nigeria in the middle of the Biafran Civil War, and even though much of the time it seemed far off, it also seemed very close at times. On Sundays, we often drove beyond the airport to load the trunk of the car with a bounty of fat, fragrant oranges and grapefruit sold at roadside stands. Quite suddenly, at an intersection, you could be randomly stopped by a group of drunken federal soldiers. You could smell the fumes of cloying palm wine around these men—boys, really, some of them teenagers. George often found himself ducking a carelessly-handled rifle. I can still smell that sickeningly sweet wine and see those inflamed eyes.

Carolyn remembers the rehabilitation camp for amputees and wounded soldiers that bordered the compound of the American International School. Soldiers on crutches lined up along the fence watching the students during PE.

Carolyn also remembers riding bikes with a friend past the home of Odumegwu Ojukwu, the general who had led the Biafran secession. The home was located on Ikoye Island. "We both knew it was Ojukwu's house," Carolyn said. "And any idiot, even a seventh grader, knew it wasn't a place you should go in, definitely something in the trespassing category, which made it even more enticing. The house was vacant, with stuff strewn about. But in a closet on the first floor was some wiring, including some very pretty multicolored wires for the telephone or for electricity. We swiped some and then went back to my friend's house and made some necklaces with it."

That's how the completely abnormal becomes normal in times of war.

Nathiagali
★ Islamabad
Lahore
•Quetta
PAKISTAN
Mohenjodaro
•Karachi

PAKISTAN

Our arrival in Karachi was not auspicious. The Embassy shipped our effects from post to post in large cargo containers. It was always a very exciting day to see our things again—it helped to make each new house a home. But the day the container arrived in Karachi, there was altogether *too much* excitement. When the front of the container was removed, a shocking amount of water gushed out onto the street. I can't remember how we found out what had happened, but apparently when the container was being transferred from one ship to another at the port of Bombay, the crew had dropped it into the sea. Our earthly treasures—Steve's early paintings, Carolyn's dolls, our scattering of small Persian carpets, and most important, our family scrapbooks—were all but destroyed by the combination of water and salt.

George tried to be philosophical: "Now, be honest, Marion, what haven't you been able to live without since we left Lagos?"

The house in Karachi didn't come with a team of servants. I never quite got used to the idea of having all

The lorries in Karachi were decorated exuberantly.

these people around, but with 20 for lunch and 30 for dinner on any given day, it would have been impossible to cope without them.

The only person we did inherit from the previous occupant was Mohammed, the *chowkidar*, or night watchman. He looked terribly frail for someone whose job it was to protect us from harm, but the house was built like a fortress, with iron bars on every window, so there wasn't much protecting to do.

It took me nearly six months to find a cook who lasted more than a day or two. I ended up trying out more than a dozen supposedly talented chefs, including some from other diplomatic missions. The Norwegian Ambassador's cook was excellent. He had even served with the Ambassador in the U.S. But he didn't get along with the other servants. I finally hired a man named Razi, who was a cousin of one of the other servants. Razi sported a thick leather belt with a huge "007" buckle around his thin midriff.

It turned out that he could have used some James Bond-like powers. We bought a cocker spaniel puppy that came to us from Amsterdam. The dog, which we named Alfie, was reasonably tame most of the time, but he morphed into a snarling, ferocious beast if he was in the kitchen when someone opened the refrigerator door. One day Razi opened the door and Alfie leapt into the refrigerator, turning his head back to Ramzi with bared teeth and a spine-chilling growl. Terrified, Razi leapt with superhuman strength onto the kitchen counter to escape the monster.

Razi saved my life more than a few times—creating a meal for dozens with almost no notice. He was a master chef who could turn nothing much into something memorable with only the most basic of kitchen tools. Thirty to dinner with only an hour's notice? "No, problem, Memsahib." And his pastries were wonders to behold, especially his cakes. Razi could turn spun sugar into intricately decorated buildings with columns, porticoes, and balustrades—even bridges across ponds surrounded by willow trees—all on top of a three-layer marvel of a cake.

The *mali*, or gardener, was assigned by the Consulate General but paid for by us. We also had to have a *dhobi*, or laundryman. In Benghazi, we had at least owned a ringer washing machine. No such appliance here. Our *dhobi* looked even more frail than the *chowkidar* and I started to worry about his ability to do some of the heavy lifting required in the job. But it just so happened that the *dhobi* had a son who could also be added to the payroll. The son could lift the heavy baskets and hang the wet clothes on the roof's clotheslines, allowing the *dhobi* himself to concentrate on actually washing the clothes.

To accommodate as large a payroll as possible, the delineation of all the duties was equally narrow. At times, it seemed as if we had one person to sweep the dust into the dust pan, a second person to pick up the dust pan, a third person to actually empty the waste into the trash, and a fourth person to get rid of the trash. I was the *dalit*, or "unclean one," in the caste pecking system. I was the one who ended up doing what everyone on the staff thought was beneath them.

The *dhobi* had another son who served as our in-house tailor. If the *chowkidar* was thin and the *dhobi* was thinner still, the tailor was emaciated. Despite his size, however, he was a coil of energy. He single-handedly salvaged two chairs I had ordered from a local merchant soon after we arrived in Karachi. When we received the two items, each turned out to be an oversized throne that could accommodate all three Naifehs at the same time. Astonishingly, and in record time, he hacked away at those thrones and shrunk them to human proportions. He also made all of our clothes, even George's suits.

The last member of the staff was Ahmed, who immediately became the bane of my existence. But George liked him. Ahmed bowed and scraped for George *ad nauseum*. He hurried out to the car in the morning to check if George's shoelaces were properly tied and to hand him his briefcase. This did not make me particularly happy with either George or Ahmed, but I had to admit that Ahmed was always willing if not always able. He labored intensely, his brow matted with sweat, trying to master the phrase: "What would you like to drink, Sir?" Inevitably, it came out as "You would like to do what, kind Sir?" More than once I became "Mother" rather than "Memsahib," which startled more than one guest. To her intense displeasure, Carolyn was, more often than not, addressed as "Babee."

Once, exasperated beyond my limit of accumulated irritation, I sputtered loudly, "Your name is mud." He answered, "No, Memsahib," my name is Ahmuuud."

It was hopeless.

First Lady Jacqueline Kennedy meeting Archbishop Cordeiro during her trip to Karachi in 1962. Ahme Stone, our friend who introduced us to the Archbishop is at the far right.

Among the first friends we made in Karachi was the Catholic Archbishop—our friend Ahme Stone, who was a devout Catholic, had served in Karachi before us, and she made the introduction. The Archbishop, Joseph Cordeiro, was an amazing person: brilliant and humble. After we paid an official call on him at his office at St. Patrick's, he often dropped by our house just to chat, driving himself in his little yellow Volkswagen Bug.

Archbishop Cordeiro explained our new home to us. Especially helpful for us was his assessment of 1947, the horrific year when India was broken into two pieces: India and Pakistan. Pakistan itself ended up in two pieces separated from each other by a thousand miles, one on either side of India: Pakistan, where we were living, and East Pakistan, today's Bangladesh. Two far-flung pieces making up one country was a political time bomb.

A year after we left Pakistan in 1973, the Archbishop became the first Pakistani Cardinal ever. Before we left Washington for our next assignment, Cardinal Cordeiro called to say he was in town and would like to drop by. I called the Vatican Embassy to learn how to address a

Cardinal and was told, "Your Eminence." I was so surprised when he arrived at the house, I blurted out, "Oh, my God!" To which he responded graciously, "Not yet, Marion."

In Karachi, yet again, poor Carolyn had to start at another school. Leaving Tulsa for Libya had been heartbreaking for her. She had cried bitterly again at leaving Benghazi and its American School: "Oh, my friends, I will miss my friends. This isn't fair!" There was still more heartbreak when she arrived at North Bethesda Junior High: "I'm not going to know *anybody*." Then, a few months later, when she left: "I don't want to leave my new friends." Constantly changing schools—and friends—is one of the highest prices that kids pay for having parents in the Foreign Service. Happily, the Karachi American School was only a three-minute walk from the house. It took Carolyn only a few days to join all the activities the school had to offer teenagers: swimming, volleyball, drama club, yearbook staff, dances, carnivals, and more.

Carolyn and I also joined an Indian yoga and dance class under the direction of the renowned Mr. Ghanshyam Jaynagarkar. George was the instigator. "Those women are amazing, Marion," he said after seeing a group of female dancers perform at the Pakistan-American Cultural Center, the PACC. "You might want to take a class—they are so graceful they seem to float on air."

So off Carolyn and I went to the Ghanshyam school. Thanks to the tailor, we were properly accoutered in cotton *shalwar kameezes*, which are wonderfully loose—loose enough to let in cool air. I always raced to the class's back row, Carolyn to the front. I was fine during the yoga sessions when we had to clear our minds and focus on something beautiful. In my mind, I was usually in Switzerland, a country we had visited during a family vacation from Libya. But if my mind strayed, as it often did, the sight of row after row of squatting Buddhas before me made me laugh. Unfortunately, the laugh was audible, and Mr. Ghanshyam was not amused.

Carolyn, of course, mastered every intricate movement of every dance. My coordination was abysmal. I labored painfully to emulate the better students and follow the instructions of an exasperated Mr. Ghanysham. But as soon as I had arrived at some approximation of the foot, arm, and neck positions, Carolyn insisted that I demonstrate to George what a graceful creature I had become. George was resting on the couch on the Sunday afternoon that Carolyn had chosen for me to demonstrate my newfound grace and rhythm for him. George laughed so hard he literally fell to the floor. Carolyn started going to class by herself.

It was just as well, since I had my own qualifying exams to prepare for. I had been accepted as a Ph.D. candidate in Medieval Islam at the University of Maryland. George obtained permission for me to use the library at the University of Karachi. The librarians, wielding intimidatingly large keys, unlocked padlocked shelves to assist me. They practically required armed guards when

The lorries were often overloaded, too.

they escorted me into the rare books section to read a book I could not otherwise access. More than once, when George took me down to an Urdu bookstall on Elphinstone Street in the commercial heart of the city, I unearthed a treasure from a moldy heap of books discarded from a personal library.

The most terrifying aspect of my new enterprise was having to master classical written Arabic, nothing at all like my morning gossip sessions with my next-door neighbor Aliyeh in Baghdad. Hume Horan, who knew classical Arabic perfectly, had marveled at the delights of what he called Arabic grammar's "crystalline, baroque structure, whose genius was organized in patterns described in the eighth and ninth centuries." But what he found marvelous, I found mystifying. In Arabic, every verb has 15 derived forms, plus participles. It is baroque, all right, and crystalline, but almost impossible to learn properly, especially at my advanced age.

George engaged a Mr. Rauf, an announcer on the local radio station, to help. Mr. Rauf had complete command of classical Arabic. A portly, dignified, middle-aged gentleman with proper thick sideburns and an untrimmed beard, Mr. Rauf was a devout Muslim. When he arrived at the door the first time, I instinctively offered him my hand, which, of course, he refused. No self-respecting, devout, old-fashioned Muslim male would shake hands with a female outside his family. At the center of his forehead was a raised round bump of calloused skin, the result of years of kneeling in prayer and bowing his head on the floor towards Mecca five times a day.

George expanded the programs, lectures, and courses at the Consulate American Center and at the Pakistan-American Cultural Center. He added much to Karachi's already rich cultural life, including a Festival of Silent Films—"The General" (Buster Keaton), "The Tramp" (Charlie Chaplin), and "Two Tars" (Laurel and Hardy)—and a series of amateur theatricals. He even got into the act himself, playing the lead role in a PACC production of Muriel Resnick's "Any Wednesday." Carolyn was delighted to see her father in the play, keeping company with a gorgeous young blonde—who happened to be her school principal's secretary.

George also produced numerous art exhibitions, including one by the Native American artist Oscar Howe, and another by Steve, who was home for the summer after his first year at Princeton. Steve's exhibition earned kudos from art critic Fayza Haq in the Karachi *Sun*. Haq praised Steve's "message of aestheticism and almost perfect pitch" while citing a "mingling of the Op Art of the West and the oriental aspiration of the East."

George also reactivated a branch of the American Center in Hyderabad, repeating programs that had proven to be rousing successes in Karachi. I loved George's answer to one visiting American lecturer who asked what the size of his provincial audience might be: "Maybe up to 80, but never more than a handful at a time." George knew what he was talking about. At a PACC reading of Arthur Miller's *The Price*, 95 Karachi citizens picked up tickets. Thirty-seven came. Fifteen left at intermission.

One weekend we decided to visit the ruins at the ancient site of Mohenjodaro, the site of an Indus Valley Civilization in the heart of Sind province. Like the Nile in Egypt, the Yellow River in China, and the Tigris and Euphrates in Mesopotamia, the Indus River sustained life for one of the world's earliest civilizations. In 2000 B.C., Mohenjodaro was a city of some 35,000 people living in elaborate two-story houses built from bricks of baked mud. The city was a marvel of early urban planning, with a logical arrangement of streets, each one lined with brick drainage gutters, and with houses organized around courtyards for relief from the fiery summer heat. In winter, the citizens took heated baths in a public bath area. The civilization was rich enough for many of the women to wear lapis lazuli jewelry.

When we retired to the guest house, we ate box lunches while a band of musicians performed and a magician devoured flames of fire.

Muharram, the first month of a new Islamic year and a time of intense mourning for Shiite Muslims, was commemorated in Pakistan as aggressively as it had been back in Meshed. Our first year in Karachi, we stood on the roof of a first-aid station on Bunder Road. Hundreds of men surged forward in a human tidal wave. Stripped to the waist, their arms flung in erratic syncopation, the men flailed themselves with thick iron chains and slashed themselves with long, sharp knives. Blood and sweat streamed down their faces, shoulders, and arms. All of this was to commemorate the death of the Prophet's grandson Hussain on the plains of Kerbala in 680 A.D.

In the complex of religions that is contemporary Pakistan, there were not only Shiite and Sunni Muslims but Christians, Jews, Hindus, Buddhists, and Sikhs. There were also Parsis, followers of Zoroaster from the seventh century B.C. They brought to the subcontinent a reverence for fire, but also a belief that demons enter the bodies of their dead and that the corpses contaminate everything with which they come into contact. This led them to build their haunting "towers of silence."

Permeating all these religions was a reverence for nature,

which, even in the dusty countryside around us could be magnificent. One night, we went to Hawkes Bay Beach, outside Karachi, where we had been told to expect the marvel of giant turtles. But nothing could have prepared us for what we saw. Giant female green and olive ridley marine turtles were crawling steadily out of the surf onto the wet sand. They used their large flippers to dig out body pits in order to lay their clutches of ping pong ball-sized eggs, ranging in number from 60 to 200. Sensitive to the earth's magnetic field, these incredibly patient creatures spend up to 40 or 50 years of a nearly 200-year life span reaching sexual maturity. Now they were returning to their birthplace to give life to a new generation. Their clutches laid, the exhausted mothers returned to the ocean. They count on the sun to hatch their young. Few would survive predators to emerge from those eggs and make their way back into the warm water and perpetuate the cycle.

Human life followed similar rituals, which George and I occasionally upset, to the serious chagrin of the household staff. One day, I went to the Empress market—a wholesale fruit market—and I was quite pleased with myself, since I had almost gotten lost in the chaos of rickshaws, camels, donkeys, and other shoppers. A kind rickshaw driver had come to my rescue.

Back home, however, I was considered a saboteur of the rigid prevailing social order. I may have been the mistress of the household, but I did not know my place. No question about it, I behaved like a *dalit*, an "untouchable." Even the *chowkidar* was horrified when I shamelessly began to unload from the trunk of the car a huge basket of yellow mangoes. Ahmed rushed out of the house crying that he would be laughed at by every "bearer" on the block for permitting the *memsahib* to carry groceries into the house in public.

I was still consumed by my daily routine when someone from the Consulate General called me in early March 1971 and asked if I would organize a group of volunteers to help at the Beach Luxury Hotel on Chundrigar Road. American evacuees from East Pakistan were flying in and needed assistance.

I was certainly aware of the strife taking place in East Pakistan, the site of the most recent tension between Pakistan and India. The Indian Mutiny of 1857 had marked the beginning of the end of Great Britain's "Jewel in the Crown." The next year, 1858, saw the exile of the last Muslim Mughal ruler and the end of a Muslim upper-hand over the Hindus—the British had elevated the minority Muslim population over the majority Hindu population. The losers under that system were now to be the winners.

The unraveling took decades, and it was not until 1947, when the catastrophic losses of World War II were making it impossible for Britain to maintain control over its vast empire, that Prime Minister Clement Attlee instructed Lord Louis Mountbatten, the newly appointed Viceroy of India, to prepare for a June 1948 withdrawal. Fearing civil war, Mountbatten speeded up the proceedings to August 14, 1947. He enlisted his attorney friend, Cyril Radcliffe, who had never been to India, to accomplish the impossible within 40 days of his arrival on the subcontinent. Radcliffe's task was to draw the borders between two new independent countries, Pakistan and India, taking into account the majority areas of the three main religious groups: Hindus, Muslims, and Sikhs.

It would have been an impossible task even for someone

better prepared than Radcliffe. After the separation, Hindus and Sikhs in what was now Pakistan emigrated to India, and Muslims in what was now India emigrated to Pakistan. Sikhs went to the North. Fourteen million people were displaced during the partition and between 250,000 and 500,000 people died in the violence.

But history was not my concern at the moment. I just wanted to make sure that the evacuees were comfortable. Evacuations were nothing new to me. I had watched British women packing to get out of Tehran in 1953. I had been evacuated from China, and we had been evacuated from Libya. Evacuations from Foreign Service postings during the Cold War were to be expected. We always kept a suitcase packed with basic essentials if we had to leave in a hurry.

Within hours, I had corralled enough willing volunteers to deal with the needs of the Beach Luxury Hotel evacuees from East Pakistan.

Which was fortunate because I was off on a vacation. An old Foreign Service friend had asked me to join her on a trip—to *India* of all places—and Nepal.

I felt a little guilty leaving, not because of the political and religious rivalries raging around us, but because we had just returned from an extravagant family vacation in Madrid the previous Christmas. Instead of flying Steve to Karachi, we had flown him to Madrid, and joined him there ourselves. That way we all got a two-week vacation. We had met him at the Madrid airport and spent a wonderful time in a rented apartment on a very high floor of the Atlantica Hotel. At midnight on New Year's Eve, we had joined the happy crowd of Madrilenos in the main square and popped grapes into our mouths at each peal of the main cathedral's mighty bells. We had even flown down to

Barcelona to visit the splendid Picasso museum, which had only recently opened.

With two tuitions to come up with, a second vacation seemed very indulgent. But when else might I have the chance to see India and Nepal?

New Delhi was Karachi multiplied. Coming at us from all directions was chaotic activity: horn-blasting motorized rickshaws, slowly-moving ox carts, screeching monkeys, the echo of calloused bare feet pulling human-powered rickshaws, exhaust-spewing buses lopsided with bodies and overstuffed crates, lumbering cows, sleek honking cars, beggars with legs walking—and beggars without legs careening about on skateboards. It was chaos, but chaos that miraculously seemed to sort itself out somehow.

We dutifully visited the tourist spots: the Red Fort, Jama Masjid, Humayun's Tomb—a blur of sandstone cupolas, high fortress walls, and formal Mughal gardens.

Nepal was the opposite. We were enveloped in quiet from the moment we landed in Kathmandu. The distant mountain ridges were perfectly framed by the window of my room at the Soaltee Oberoi Hotel.

We mingled with the Nepalese, the orange-capped Japanese tour groups, and all the beasts of burden trudging behind their drivers. All seemed to move on padded feet, barely making a sound. Even the all-seeing eyes of the Buddha at the Bouddhanath Stupa shrine swept pilgrims and tourists alike into reverenced silence. Another moment was frozen in time as we inched past the majestic beauty of Mt. Everest on a Royal Nepal Airlines "Daily Flight." Then back to dinner at Kathmandu's Yak & Yeti Bar. The owner, a White Russian, was actually named Boris. We sat sipping hot borscht under the warmth of an enormous fireplace's copper canopy while Boris turned up the volume of his scratched Beethoven and Shostakovich records.

No sooner than we had flown back to Karachi, I was off again—this time with George. He had been to Quetta, the capital of Baluchistan province, before, but this time he let me tag along on his appointments. We boarded the "Bolan Mail" train early one afternoon. The train was new and comfortable, even luxurious, with its purring air conditioner and private bathroom.

Before dusk, we passed Hyderabad, which was astonishingly green. Its canal complex seemingly provided enough water to irrigate every field and orchard. By morning, however, the drought that was Baluchistan was all too obvious. The desert was a parched gray, framed by desolate hills, more stone than earth. From the train, we saw straggling camel caravans bringing tribal families, Baluchi and Pashtu, and their flocks north on an unhappy search for greener pastures.

In Quetta, the days of the Taliban were very far off. We visited a relative of a Pakistani friend of ours. We called him on our arrival, and he came to pick us up from the Quetta Club for tea. His father had been the Governor of the Northwest Frontier Province as well as a wealthy merchant dealing in fine carpets. His family was one of Pakistan's oldest and most prestigious. New York may have had its Four Hundred, but Pakistan still had its Twenty-Two. Our 30-something host was one of them. He was extremely handsome in his Brooks Brother's suit and tasseled loafers, and had a passion for golf, fine cars, and porcelain. Our host's cars were ones that I never heard of: a '29 Studebaker and a '27 green Hupp. He took us for a ride through the countryside in the Hupp, driving past camels, turnip patches, crumbling mud walls, and careening lorries.

We also knew two of the other Twenty-Two Families, who together owned much of the country. Faruq Rahimtoola was a Karachi business tycoon and ardent polo player, whose wife collected antique prints of pre-independence Pakistan. Rafiqa Kirdar's father had been the Emir of Bahawalpur. Always lovely, Rafiqa was one of those elegant women who seemed to glide in her sari. She and her husband Irshad lived in what had been the Emir's enormous hunting lodge on an extensive property on the outskirts of Karachi. Along with the gazebos and gigantic banyan trees, there was a vast and wonderfully fragrant rose garden. A significant percentage of the local markets' roses were grown on the grounds of the Kirdar home, providing the seemingly infinite number of rose garlands and baskets of rose petals that were scattered around the city on special occasions.

Also on the social register were the Nanas. Judge Feroze Nana, a chain-smoker, was also the Chief Justice of the Sind High Court. Mrs. Nana, who was not a chain-smoker, moved smoothly through space in a thick cloud of her husband's fumes. The jingle of the 15 glass bangles on her right wrist announced her every step. She made her own clothes, including the long, silk gypsy skirt and brocade vest she was wearing the night we met her. Fellow guests at the Nanas that night were the poet Ahmed Ali and his unforgettable wife. Mr. Ali read his poems, then Mrs. Ali sang old classical Indian songs. Once, she stopped for a breather and opened her silk purse to pull out an antique gadget to crack betel nuts. She cracked and chewed the nuts with gusto before continuing her diva solo. In the garden, the Nana's 14-year-old son tended his personal petting zoo—a gazelle, a falcon, and a squawking flock of ducks.

The story of Karachi extravaganzas would be incomplete without a mention of the weddings. The night before a wedding, I was invited to the bride's henna party, a singular honor. A professional henna artist etched intricate floral arbors and bouquets in deep reddish-brown henna on my hands. The next morning at the breakfast table, George glanced at my hands and said, "My God, what is that? What did you do? I don't care what you did. Just go and wipe it off." I tried soaking my hands in Clorox, kerosene, Ajax, and various combinations thereof. None of it worked. The decorations took two weeks to wear off, by which time both George and I had grown rather fond of them.

At the wedding, we sat in traditional Pakistani wedding chairs. With fretwork backs studded with large, round, mercilessly hard wooden balls—six rows with seven balls on each row—the chairs were incredibly uncomfortable. Three older women wailed blessings in Urdu with an occasional Arabic refrain. After the singing, the bride, I was informed, was to be rubbed with saffron and herbs.

The second wedding George and I attended together, he was in one of the five rooms in the enormous *shamiana* ceremonial tent, and I was in another. In yet another space, visible to us all, sat the bride and groom. Two priests sang blessings for 20 minutes while rice was sprinkled all about. Most of the guests went up to the couple and handed them envelopes of money. The groom wore a gold turban and at least five garlands of flowers around his neck. The bride wore a splendid red silk sari that was generously embroidered with gold thread.

Life in Karachi was getting hectic even as trouble continued to brew in the East.

A charming young girl in Karachi.

When you are in a danger zone, the outside world is sometimes more keenly aware of what is going on than you are yourself. We had several visits at the time from U.S. Naval destroyers, none of which had anything to do with unrest in East Pakistan. The sailors brought a wealth of movies that we showed to grateful Pakistani audiences. A rock band from one of the destroyers entertained at Carolyn's 14th birthday party. She remembers the evening as one of the most embarrassing moments of her life. When she asked the drummer if he needed anything, he asked for a "screwdriver," and Carolyn promptly brought him a screwdriver from George's handy red toolbox.

We heard that, at another gathering for sailors from one of the U.S. ships, the Naval Attaché's wife hired an all-male Karachi band for a touch of authentic local color—without a trial run. She got more color than she counted on when one of the musicians put down his instrument and darted behind a colleague to put on a sari. When he reappeared, gyrating his body in the most suggestive possible feminine hip and body motions, it was too late. We happened to drive by their house, which was in our neighborhood, and every *chowkidar* for blocks had abandoned his post to peek over the wall at the spectacle.

The next spectacle was my doing. I was appointed coordinator for the dessert table at a Women's Club benefit dinner at the Hilton. At the last minute, the night before the dinner, I decided that we didn't have enough cakes and pies. Razi had gone home, the shops were closed, and the only flour in the pantry had weevils. George and I sat in the kitchen carefully sifting out weevils before I baked a walnut cake. At the dinner, I added our hastily baked cake to the pyramid of confections on the dessert table: delicate chocolate swirls, beautiful tarts with perfect berries, and elaborate curlicues of puff pastries. The Hilton chef strode to the desserts in full uniform, his toque adjusted to perfection. With great drama, he sampled each of the 20 delicacies before him. When he had finished, he walked back to number 18—our mess of a walnut cake—and pronounced it the winner. George burst out laughing from across the dining room, although no one knew why. I was awarded the silver measuring cup I myself had commissioned for the winner of the best dessert.

But not everything was a laughing matter. Each summer day as the heat and humidity increased, George was steadily losing what remained of the hearing in his right ear. The Consulate General doctor finally ordered him to leave the steam bath that was Karachi in July. The damage to his hearing had begun on a short airplane flight in Nigeria when a Lagos doctor repeatedly punctured the eardrum in his right ear to relieve the pressure. Before we left for Karachi, a doctor in Washington had tried to replace the damaged stapes with artificial ones, but his knife slipped, severing the nerve completely. With a new infection festering in Karachi, the doctor wanted us to find a less humid place for George's inflamed ears. Only Nathiagali, in the mountainous north—which Henry Kissinger would later call a "hill station"—would do.

The world thought Kissinger was there at the same time as George and me; he was said to be recovering from a stomach ache in President Yahya Khan's guest house in the mountain retreat. On July 9, as we sat relishing a fire in the fireplace of our Natiagali Hotel Pines International bungalow, Kissinger was secretly flying to Beijing on a PAI Boeing 707, flown by Yahya's personal pilot. Six days later, President Nixon announced a "new relationship with the People's Republic of China" from an NBC television studio in Burbank, California.

That same summer, George, Carolyn, and I met Steve for a quick trip to Iran, the first time we had visited the country since Steve was born. Visiting the bazaar in Tehran, we saw a beautiful Nain carpet, which seemed out of the question, given our modest government income. George haggled with the merchant for the pure joy of it, only to find that we could almost afford it, but only if we paid in installments. On nothing more than George's word and a small deposit, the merchant let us walk away with the carpet.

As Thanksgiving approached, we travelled—without Steve, who was still at Princeton—to spend the holiday in Amman, Jordan, with the Horans, our friends and colleagues from Libya. We first flew into Beirut and then drove the magnificent mountain road to Damascus. The route was all twists and curves and offered sweeping vistas

Aunt Wadia.

of the Mediterranean behind us as we drove through steep hill passes covered with rich forest. George agreed that we had to stop at the Al-Umayyad Mosque in Damascus, one of Islam's finest, a star of the Golden Age of Islam. Over the years, from its space at the east end of the Souk al-Hamidiyeh, the mosque had first been a Roman temple for the god Jupiter. Then, with the spread of Christianity after 330 A.D., it became a cathedral. For a brief period after the ascendency of Islam, Christians and Muslims shared the prayer space. In fact, the mosque still has a shrine reportedly containing the head of St. John the Baptist.

Often, when Foreign Service people share posts, they become family. The Horan family still is family, but George had an actual relative living in Jordan, where his father had been born: his father's younger sister, Wadia. While still in kindergarten, George had taken his father's letters to the Kiefer post office to be mailed back to Wadia, who lived, he was told, in the "old country." But by now his father had been dead for nearly 20 years and contact with Wadia had been lost.

"Come on, let's go," suggested Nancy when George mentioned that he had an aunt living in Ajlun, which was only 40 miles north of Amman. "You only have a post office box number, but we'll find her. And if we don't, at least you will have seen Ajlun."

The driver of our Embassy car stopped once to ask for the post office. That was all it took. Word was out and racing ahead faster than our car as we drove through the thick olive and pine groves on the outskirts of Ajlun.

We found Wadia at the Baptist Church just down the hill from her granite-block, one-room house. Standing in obvious disbelief inside of the simple wooden church was a tiny woman, wrapped in black from head to toe. A thin black shawl slid over her thinning white hair to reveal a pale face creased with age. Nieces, nephews, neighbors, and the curious had already gathered to ululate as George swept her into his arms. She barely reached his chest. Hand in hand, they climbed up the path to her room, which was located across a small courtyard from a family house now occupied by a niece and her brood of young children. The children scampered in and out, squeezing through the crowd at the open door. Inside, George, Wadia, Nancy, Carolyn, the Embassy driver, and I sat weeping and passing a box of Kleenex. As soon as one of us stopped to wipe our tears, the others started crying even harder.

We didn't know at the time that George's last Foreign Service assignment would be Amman, and that we would get to know Wadia well. Now, it was enough that George promised to send her a monthly check.

Three quarters of a century earlier, Wadia had waved goodbye when George's father, their sister, and their brother-in-law left by donkey for the port of Haifa and a boat to America. Wadia had stayed behind, growing up, getting married, and bearing seven children, only to watch each child die before reaching the age of 10. Her mother-in-law made Wadia's husband divorce her so that he could remarry and produce a living grandchild.

Upon our return to Karachi, life went back to normal, but tragedy lurked there, too. It was beginning to be more and more difficult to ignore the rumblings of war.

Although West Pakistanis and East Pakistanis were all Muslims, they had different cultural backgrounds, physical traits, languages, and traditions. Ever since the partition, India had kept an uneasy eye on both the West and the East. Disputes over the lush Kashmir valley had resulted in a war in 1948 and again in 1965. Only UN-sponsored ceasefires quieted the conflagrations. By 1970, there was more trouble. This time the more populous East Pakistan felt short-changed in an elected National Assembly that was to have drafted a new constitution. President Yahya Khan of West Pakistan postponed a scheduled meeting of the Assembly and sent the army to quell the Easterners. This led to riots and civil war.

At 4 a.m. on December 3, 1971, Carolyn was screaming at the top of her lungs: "Under the staircase! Quick, get under the stairs!"

Anti-aircraft guns were firing. Bombs were exploding in the port area where many of the local oil installations were located. We huddled together in the dark front hall under the stairs, the safest place in the house. India had entered the war, joining forces with what would now be called Bangladesh.

Fortunately for us, neither country wanted foreign casualties on their hands. So both India and Pakistan actually agreed to a two-hour ceasefire to allow all of the consulates to get their citizens out of Karachi. *They actually agreed to stop the war for us.*

I still don't know the particulars of how the ceasefire was secured for those two hours, but I can imagine that heated diplomatic conversations were held around the globe.

It took 48 hours to arrange the ceasefire, but there were enough lulls between the bombing attacks that we did not have to stay under the stairs the entire time. The house was under a "brown-out," with drapes and blinds pulled to prevent any light from escaping. A girl Carolyn's age from across the street dashed over to play pinochle with Carolyn for one day. They snacked on pickles. George went to the office as if life was normal. Every member of the Consulate staff was making frantic efforts to inform all American citizens of their option to leave. George marveled that they were able to track down an impoverished American woman living with her Pakistani husband and children in a warren of trash-filled streets by the port. The home was filled with the stink of rotting fish. She declined evacuation because she had no place to go. But at least she had been given notice. All Consulate wives and children as well as any American citizens who wanted out were to meet on Sunday, December 5, at the American Commissary, and from there we would all leave for the airport.

And fly where? The notice never said. It did, however, say: "For your personal comfort, it is suggested that you bring two blankets and/or a sleeping bag, one pillow, and a filled water container." Carolyn also brought her guitar. The Consulate's male staff stayed behind—all except George, who was put in charge of shepherding the evacuees out of the country. To Tehran, as it turned out.

With Carolyn and her friend Jeanne Duerbeck strumming their guitars, the evacuees sang—at least the ones under 18—throughout the packed Pan Am flight with about 250 American passengers and another 100 Germans, Italians, and Lebanese. I heard more than one teenager say, "Evacuation was really rather fun"—reminding me of my own teenage evacuation from Kuling to Shanghai.

More than half the evacuees booked ongoing flights to stay with family in places ranging from Australia to England.

We were trying to figure out what to do with Steve. Just a few days earlier, George had sent him tickets to come home for Christmas vacation via Vienna. We almost had to camp out at Tehran's Central Telephone Exchange to reach him. The call finally went through, and he was called out of his English Lit class by campus police to take it.

Obviously, he had to stay in the U.S. The best answer we could come up with was Worcester with Uncle Roy. I frantically tried to enroll Carolyn in a decent American school in case the Karachi American School didn't reopen. It worked. She was accepted—with a sizeable scholarship—at Abbot Academy in Andover, one year before it merged with Phillips Academy.

The Embassy had secured rooms for the official American evacuees at the Soraya Pension, a few short blocks from the Embassy and its cafeteria. We traipsed over for every meal. The pension was cramped, so George found us all a new furnished apartment and managed to negotiate a one-month lease, which the special per diem evacuation allowance covered.

Carolyn happily played a George Harrison record incessantly. It had been banned in Karachi because of his very vocal support for Bangladesh. I had to buy a warm pantsuit since mine was still at the cleaners in Karachi after our Thanksgiving flight to Jordan. I prowled through the subterranean passages of the Tehran bazaar for a present for George. I found an antique carpet-covering for a teahouse bench. I terrified the poor merchant when he hesitated to guarantee that I could return it should my husband not like it. Speaking so little Farsi, I ran my fingers across my throat to show him what would happen to me if George wasn't pleased. George and I attended a Christmas open house at the residence of Ambassador and Mrs. Douglas MacArthur II, where I overheard one guest explaining to a friend that, when she and her husband were evacuated from Paris to Lisbon during World War II, she had made sure to take her calling cards.

George found hundreds of evergreen Christmas trees propped up against the wall of the Soviet Embassy for us and our fellow evacuees. Each family set about winning an informal competition for the most imaginatively decorated tree. Without our ornaments, we made paper chains and strung popcorn.

Apparently there was only one more really bad night in Karachi after we left, but the bombs and bullets wreaked havoc anyway. On December 19, Pakistan had no choice but to surrender and accept the loss of East Pakistan. It was time to go back home.

Our return was delayed until December 29 to make certain the fighting had stopped. Our Jam Street landowner watched, horrified, as 10 of his 11 new apartments emptied in less than two hours. At the airport, light snow was falling as we waited for our flight. Fifteen of our young boys rushed out onto the tarmac to make the muddiest, most forlorn, but most admired snowman I ever saw. Our 44-pound baggage limit from the trip to Tehran had quadrupled for the trip home.

Back in Karachi, to all appearances, there was little damage outside the port area. Our cars were at the airport, and we simply got in and drove home. Many of the houses on the way were splattered with mud, which the occupants had used as a form of camouflage. Ahmed was at the door to greet us. George's yellow, white, and orange chrysanthemums and zinnias were blossoming in full splendor.

But tragedy was all around us. More than half a million had died. Hundreds of thousands were displaced. Archbishop Cordeiro worked with the Vatican to intervene with India to secure the release of 93,000 Pakistani prisoners of war.

George's assistant, Husnara Shameem, a man of great dignity, added some chilling words to a note thanking George for a New Year's gift: "We have been unhappy, very unhappy indeed after all these ugly past few weeks. We had no fear then or now. But we are still unhappy with the destruction outside, and also with the destruction inside, not knowing what to do, what to say. The blinding blackouts and booming bombs have come and gone, but the dark, mean smoke seems to have sealed itself into our hearts. It is funny to have stayed alive. Some did not. Our hope did not. Some of us carried glass houses in our hearts. They broke down, inside. Strange feelings haunt."

Traumatized, he would sometimes just stand and stare into space.

Somehow, despite the British prejudice in favor of Muslims over Hindus during the colonial era, it was India, not Pakistan, that had inherited the essential functioning institutions of an army, a well-trained police, and a seasoned bureaucracy. Benazir Bhutto wrote, shortly before her assassination in 2009, that in the two-week war in 1971, Pakistan lost half its Navy, half its Army, and one quarter of its Air Force. It was her father, Zulfikar Ali Bhutto, who replaced the humiliated General Yahya Khan as head of state after the war. Yahya Khan was booted out of office on December 20 by junior officers of the Pakistan Army.

A Lebanese friend named Aliya fell down a long flight of stairs from her third-floor apartment the first night of the bombing. She was still on crutches and would be far into the future. Aliya was the second wife of ex-Prime Minister Mohammed Ali Bogra, who charmed Washington twice as his country's Ambassador in the early 1950s. Aliya had posed a delicate problem for Washington society. Should social invitations addressed to a bigamous ambassador include one wife, neither wife, or both? The Ambassador solved the dilemma by only bringing Aliya to Washington the second time he was posted there. In January 1972, days after the war ended, Aliya lost her job when her company closed. Now an unemployed widow with two young teenagers, Aliya was preparing to return to family in Canada. Another friend of ours, one of the Twenty-Two Families, lost half of his wealth in the land reforms instituted by Bhutto.

I had the tailor make up countless appliqué cushions, studded in Pakistani style, with small decorative metallic mirrors, to bring back to the U.S. as gifts for family and friends. I laid them out on Steve's empty bed upstairs ready to be packed. We knew that we would be off in July for George's next assignment, a year as Diplomat in Residence at the University of Minnesota.

FOREIGN SERVICE | 253

THE U.A.E.

Abu Dhabi has one of the most poetic names. In Arabic, it means Father of the White Gazelle with the Brown Eyes. According to legend, one day in the distant past, a man from the Bani Yas tribe in the interior of the United Arab Emirates, or U.A.E., was searching for water. As he approached the island of Abu Dhabi, he discovered not only a white gazelle, but also a source of sweet water.

The sight from the plane as we approached our new home was astonishing—empty desert right up to a shimmering sea of blue, green, and turquoise.

The country itself was only two years old when we arrived in 1973, and housing was a problem. The Embassy put us up in a temporary apartment worse than anything we had lived in since Baida. It was still filthy after I had scrubbed it within an inch of my life, and there was no way to camouflage the mass of wires and tangled pipes that purported to provide electricity and plumbing.

I was alone. No children. No servants. No George. He was at his USIS office across from that miraculous shoreline. From my window, I saw nothing but towering cranes, bulldozers, dump trucks, and hard-hatted construction workers balancing perilously on endless scaffolding. What I saw was an entire country under construction.

It had been two years since we had been in Karachi. On returning to the States, George had spent a year at the University of Minnesota and then another year in Washington. In those two years, Carolyn had graduated from Abbott and was now a freshman at Vanderbilt. Steve had graduated from Princeton and was now at Harvard Law School. My acceptance at Maryland had lapsed but I had passed the requirements at our old alma mater, The School of Advanced International Studies at Johns Hopkins, to enter a Ph.D. program in Islamic Institutions. I had also survived the Arabic requirement, much to the astonishment of both my Arabic professor and me.

Each morning, after George drove to the Embassy on the Abu Dhabi Corniche, I walked to the bookstore down the street to pick up a day-old copy of the Cairo *Al Ahram* newspaper. The handsome young Lebanese owner greeted me effusively every morning with a "Sabah al-ful." I responded less cordially, assuming that he was wishing me a day "filled with beans."

One morning, when I had my fill of beans, I asked, "Ful?"

"Why, yes, may your day be full of sweet, fragrant, beautiful jasmine."

Clearly, my Arabic still needed work.

George arrived home one evening with the very good news that we could move immediately into the Mani Otaiba building, not far from the Embassy and, like it, on the Corniche. Because the new apartment faced the water diagonally, and because our apartment was perfectly situated, the only room without a spectacular view of the Gulf was a guest bathroom. Stretched out on the kitchen counter, I felt as though I was literally sitting on top of the Corniche, with nothing between me and the Gulf except a large glass window. Every morning, I had a view of the breathtaking shore: The light danced on the waves, dolphins soared and dove for their pleasure and mine, and seagulls cavorted around. During the late afternoon, before George came home, I returned to the kitchen counter, where I sat mesmerized, watching the sun, an exploding ball of fire, drown inch by inch beyond the horizon of the Gulf.

However, the sea was not always so serene. One morning, propped up on the kitchen counter, I saw a *dhow*, a fishing boat, which had lost its moorings and was crashing in and out of the waves against the wall of the Corniche. I saw a fisherman, obviously the owner of the empty boat, running around in circles, waving his arms in horror. There was a little tug boat that ferried workers out and back all day from the shore to a breakwater being built in the distance. The tugboat pilot saw the fisherman, managed to take him aboard, and reached the *dhow* right smack in front of me. The old man, with a rope tied around his waist, jumped into the tumult and, like a crab, crawled up into his boat. Then the tugboat pilot pulled the *dhow* out of danger—all before 8 a.m.

Now that the U.A.E. is so wealthy, it is hard to imagine how difficult life was before the discovery of oil.

Abu Dhabi is not far from the lands near the Strait of Hormuz that were known as the Pirate Coast in the late 18th century. In 1853, the British government, annoyed by the attacks on its sea route to India, carefully wove all the sheikhdoms by a series of truces into an entity called

Abu Dhabi before oil was discovered in 1958.

the Trucial Coast.

No longer able to make their living by plunder, the men along the coast turned to pearl diving. It is said that, when they first began diving for pearls, one Bedouin wife mistook the handful of pearls her husband gave her for rice kernels, boiled them, and, when they proved inedible, threw them out. During the summer, the men would come to the shore to do their pearl diving from their homes in Al Ain and Liwa, oases in the interior of the Emirate, where they lived in huts called *barastis* made from palm fronds. In 1900, at the peak of the pearl-diving season, a flotilla of some 1,200 boats set out to sea. The divers extended the time they could stay under the water by using *fitaam*, or nose clips, made from two thin slices of goat horn fastened with a rivet.

But by the 1940s, competition from Japan's synthetic pearl industry had wiped out yet another source of income.

Then, in 1958, oil was discovered. Sheikh Zayed's predecessor, his brother Sheikh Shakhbut, did not trust the swarm of British advisers who arrived to "consult" with him on his new-found fortune. He didn't trust his fellow tribesmen either. So instead of investing his money or putting it in banks, he hid piles of paper currency in the empty corners of the historic old palace, a tempting feast for hungry rats.

Sheikh Zayed took over from his brother in 1966, and emerged as a remarkably gifted head of state. When he died in 2004, *The New York Times* called him a "statesman" in their obituary. His obituary in *The Economist* praised his "fabled diplomatic skills," calling him "that rarity in Arab countries, a leader truly loved and admired by his subjects."

According to one of his subjects, as soon as Sheikh Zayed assumed control, he "began taking steps that would bring Abu Dhabi out of the dark ages." Unlike his brother, Sheikh Shakhbut, Sheikh Zayed eagerly sought out advisers. He could handle warring tribes, but he knew relatively little about running a country in the 20th century. When he was 12, he had served as a guide to foreign crews searching for oil. Upon becoming the ruler of Abu Dhabi in 1966, and then President of the Federation of Emirates in 1971, he immediately assembled a group of experts from around the world. There were only three native college graduates at the time.

In 1961, even before he became ruler, Sheikh Zayed ordered Abu Dhabi's first desalination plant to produce potable water. The project was not an immediate success. Either the contractor failed to provide chlorine to purify the water or the plant operators didn't realize they should add it after the water was desalinated. Ironically, the brackish well water long imported from Bahrain in rusty barrels had to be added to make the water drinkable. But eventually they got the process right and, for the first time, the desert country had plenty of drinkable water.

In 1967, *Time* magazine had published an article on a group of scientists from the University of Arizona who were growing vegetables in the desert. "The story so intrigued Sheik Zaid bin Sultan al Nahayan," *Time* later reported, "that he gave the university's Environmental Research Laboratory more than $3,000,000 to build an experimental controlled environmental greenhouse on the tiny island of Saadiyat off the Abu Dhabi coast." By the time we arrived in the U.A.E., Saadiyat was a terrific source of fresh fruits and vegetables—all grown on land that had been desert just a few years before.

Among the new advisors to the Presidential Court—and also translator to Sheikh Zayed—was Zaki Nusseibeh. Zaki had a B.A. and an M.A. in Economics from Cambridge. He was also a descendent of the most famous Jerusalem family. Zaki's brother, Sari, the President of Al-Quds University in Jerusalem—and a professor of philosophy there—writes that four of the 14 tribal leaders who first defended the Prophet were women—including a woman named Nusaybah, the progenitor of the Nusseibehs. She "was a fierce fighter who, on horseback, skillfully defended the Prophet with life and limb. In one battle she lost two sons and a leg, yet continued fighting." In 638 A.D., Omar the Just—the second Caliph, or successor to the Prophet—approached Jerusalem to accept terms of surrender to his army. Omar asked to be met by the Byzantine Bishop Sephronius. Because Omar promised to spare Jerusalem and its people, the grateful Bishop handed Omar the keys to the city. Nusaybah's brother was campaigning with

Caliph Omar, who not only made him the "first Muslim high judge of Jerusalem" but gave him the keys to the Church of the Holy Sepulcher—the different Christian denominations were struggling so fiercely for control of the Church that they preferred to have a Muslim hold the keys. A Nusaybah descendent has kept the keys to the Church for the 1,300 years ever since.

In 1968, Ambassador Najmuddin Abdullah Hamoodi left Iraq as a political refugee and was welcomed as a member of Sheikh Zayed's Ministry of Foreign Affairs. He had served his own country in Moscow, Cairo, and London. He was never without a kind word for his friends, and never without a smile on his face. For years, his wife worked in the Ministry of Education. Today his daughter Aseel works at the Abu Dhabi Company for Onshore Petroleum Operations.

Another Iraqi political refugee was Adnan Pachachi. Not only did his father and uncle serve as prime ministers, but his father-in-law as well. In 2003, after the American invasion of Iraq, he returned to Baghdad to serve in the new Parliament. But I remember him and his wife Salwa hosting quiet evenings in their lovely home on the Corniche. There he sat, next to a magnificent inlaid Damascene chest, talking proudly about their daughter who was studying in London.

Dr. Ezzedin Ibrahim, who came from Egypt, served as Cultural Adviser to Sheikh Zayed. Dr. Ezzedin had a doctorate from England, and his credentials as an Islamic scholar were unmatched. He and a British academic had translated the *Forty Hadith* (the deeds and sayings of the Prophet) as recorded by the 13th-century Syrian jurist An-Nawawi. Dr. Ezzedin grew to trust and appreciate George, who helped Dr. Ezzedin build a national library for the U.A.E. The library was housed in the old palace, which had not long before been the only building of significance in town, but would soon feature a large modern addition designed by American architects.

George and I went to almost every single lecture sponsored by the Ministry of Foreign Affairs and Dr. Ezzedin's Cultural office. The array of academics, scientists and political notables from all over the world was dazzling. But it was James Irwin, an American astronaut, who brought the house down. Irwin was on the 1971 Apollo 15 mission, but he was now an ex-astronaut and leader of a Christian foundation based in Colorado. Sitting in the front row of an audience of 700 were two Catholic priests and the most important Muslim *mullah* in town. Instead of focusing on the technological feat of reaching the moon, Irwin spoke of the awe he felt in God's presence when he got there.

"I know," Irwin pounded his fists on the podium in the packed hall, "I *know* there is a God and He is alive and well!" The room erupted in whoops, hollers, and ululations.

Astronauts were always the stars. A lecture by Stafford,

George and me in our apartment in our apartment in Abu Dhabi.

Brand, and Slayton, who had taken part in the Apollo-Soyuz docking mission in 1975, also drew a vast crowd. They showed slides of the Arabian Peninsula, with a special focus on sand dune formations. Jack Lousma, who was famous for his 1973 Skylab II mission, also came to town. I loved the moment in Jack's lecture when his wife Gratia was asked what she talked about to Jack when he was in space: "Where did you store the storm windows? I can't find them."

Abu Dhabi only had two hotels at the time, and only one of them, the Hilton, was any good. But we had two guest bedrooms. So very soon, we had a virtually endless line of houseguests we hadn't met before they arrived at the apartment to stay with us. This was made more complicated by the fact that Abu Dhabi was the only place we had yet been posted where a cook would have been too costly. So I became both chef and chief bottle-washer. Fortunately, most of our guests were so grateful to have a bed that they happily pitched in. The wife of one USIS technician from Washington spent an entire day scouring every pot and pan in the kitchen.

More often than not, if an American group making an official tour of the U.A.E. included a woman, I was invited along with George for a trip around the Emirates. One evening, Dubai's ruler, Sheikh Rashid bin Said Al Maktoum, hosted a dinner for James Keogh, the Director of the USIS, and his wife—plus two Naifehs—plus *200 others* at his new Jumaira Palace. Sheikh Rashid was probably about six feet tall and very formal. Upon our arrival at the Palace, we were received by his protocol chief, who was better looking than Omar Sharif. We were served Arab coffee in the formal drawing room, a sea of beige and blue with marble walls and gorgeous chandeliers. Then off we went to the dining room with its 200 blue velvet and gold-braided chairs. At precisely 7:30 p.m., our group was seated at the head table facing every important person in Dubai—and their chauffeurs. At precisely 8:30 p.m., Sheikh Rashid stood up, and all 200 guests—finished with their dinners or not—stood up as well and retired to the receiving hall for more coffee.

Ras al Khaimah, the last Emirate before the curve into the Gulf of Oman, was on that same Keogh "tour." We drove up the coast with the Ras al Khaimah-Omani mountain range on our right and the sea on our left. The Emirate's extremely charismatic ruler, Sheikh Saqr, received us graciously. We toured a huge cement factory before we joined the ruler for lunch on a thickly-carpeted floor. A waiter with his sleeves rolled up tore off a strip of lamb and used it to scoop up nuts and raisins. Following suit, we reached our arms in to scoop up our lunch—no fingerbowls or wash basins in sight. The Keoghs loved it. We loved it.

A few weeks later, we returned to Ras al Khaimah to visit Sheikh Saqr again, this time at his farm in Nakheel. It was a palm grove with orange, grapefruit, and lemon trees nestled at the foot of the mountain range, although the fertilizer, made from dried and crushed sardines, obliterated the scent of orange blossoms. We were given an enormous basket of superb grapefruit and lemons to take home.

More and more often, we raced back and forth from Abu Dhabi to Dubai to attend a meeting or catch a plane or just to take a break. One evening at sunset, on the way back to Abu Dhabi, cars stopped to let their passengers out to pray. If their left cheek faced the setting sun, we were told, they were in the correct position facing Mecca to pray. There were no skyscrapers in Dubai at the time, just wonderful wind towers—high above the rooftops with openings at the very top to catch breezes and funnel them into the rooms below. *Dhows*, identical to the boats of centuries past, shuttled back and forth nonstop across the Gulf with commercial goods, making Dubai among the busiest trading centers along the entire Emirati coast. A record located in the Dubai Museum dating from 1908 listed the Emirate's wealth as 4,000 date trees, 1,650 camels, 45 horses, 380 donkeys, 430 cattle, and 960 goats.

George once accompanied Alexander Heard, the Chancellor of Vanderbilt, where Carolyn had just matriculated as a freshman, through the Dubai suq. The Chancellor promised to call Carolyn upon his return, and he actually did early one morning: "Good morning, Carolyn, this is Chancellor Heard." Carolyn thought it was a joke and immediately hung up. Happily, he persisted, and they became friends.

The famous singer Pearl Bailey also paid an official visit to the U.A.E., and I was her escort for a courtesy call on Sheikha Fatima, the wife of Sheikh Zayed. Sheikha Fatima was known to be a kind and demure lady. She received us draped in her robes and wearing her *battula*, a beaked mask, with two slits for her eyes and a rigid peak for her nose. She rose from a large upholstered armchair to welcome us. During my time in the Middle East, I had seen countless *burqas* that covered the entire face, with a mesh screen over the eyes; *niqabs* that veiled the face but not the eyes; and *hijabs* that covered the hair but not the face; and now, in the U.A.E., this beaked mask. Then we all sat down for tea with one of the Sheikha's Egyptian ladies-in-waiting providing the translation.

South Dakota Senator James Abourezk also visited with a small group, including his sister. Because the party included a woman, Margaret Dickman, the Ambassador's wife, and I were invited to dinner at the Palace. Margaret and I were in a quandary concerning proper attire. As far as we could tell, it was the first time American women had been invited for dinner by Sheikh Zayed. Out of respect for Emirati customs, we decided that we should wear long dresses with high collars and long sleeves.

An American reporter was in town, and George had managed to get him an invitation to the dinner. When we stopped at the Hilton to pick him up, his girlfriend was at his side. An extra guest is never a problem at an Arab home—*especially* a palace. The problem was not the lack of an invitation. The problem was the lady friend, or more precisely, her attire; or even more precisely, her *lack* of attire. She was wearing a skintight black décolleté dress—I'm not sure I had ever seen more cleavage. George and I had no idea what to do. When we arrived at the palace, the receiving hall was lined on both sides with two dozen falconers, each one with a falcon perched on his gauntleted wrist. I watched as the two dozen old Bedouin falconers turned to gape. And then as each falcon, on each gauntlet, also turned to gape. Throughout the evening, everyone pretended that the woman wasn't there—no mean feat, given that she sat herself next to Sheikh Zayed on a sofa after the dinner.

Sheikh Zayed's passion for falconry was legendary. In fact, the following year he was to host the first-ever International Conference on Falconry. He once said that "by following this sport, we are, after all, induced to remember our genuine Arab traditions and to hold fast to our ancient virtues and moral code." When a new falcon joined the Sheikh's group, its eyes were still "sealed." Because movement and light agitates an untrained falcon, cotton threads were sewn through their lower eyelids and tied to the tops of their heads, so the birds couldn't see. Sheikh Zayed would order the seals broken when the falcons were ready to feed. When a male hawk came into the group with a broken feather, Sheikh Zayed mended it with "a splint made from two slivers of gazelle horn."

I had another encounter with a falcon, at another dinner. This one was hosted by Mark Allen, a newly-appointed Third Secretary at the British Embassy. In fact, it was his first dinner party. The entire Western community in Abu Dhabi was titillated by the story that he had ridden a camel from Jordan to the U.A.E. and tied it up in the parking lot of the Hilton in Abu Dhabi. Mark had been a falconer since he was 14. He also spoke fluent Arabic, which he learned at Oxford and on visits to Egypt, Syria, and Jordan. He had a silver dish sprinkled with dried rose petals on an entrance table for calling cards. Mark had borrowed a waiter for the evening and, when the waiter spilled some peas, he just scooped them up and put them back in the serving bowl. I was seated next to Mark, whose prize falcon was perched on his left wrist, and, throughout the evening, Mark fed the bird bits of raw meat. The falcon was hooded but it was hard not to think it was eyeing you all evening.

In the late 19th century, Charles M. Doughty, the English writer and traveler, had described seeing Bedouins with their falcons and "carrying their greyhounds upon camelback, lest the burning sand should scald their tender feet." Wilfred Thesiger, a later English traveler not much older than George and me, wrote in 1980 that he wished he had read Mark's book on falconry before he went hunting with Sheikh Zayed in the days before Zayed became ruler.

Mark's 1980 book was called *Falconry in Arabia*. In it, he voiced his concern that, in the sudden rush into modernity, hawking might slip into the past. He needn't have worried. Today there is a dedicated conservation program to protect falcons. And by 1987, there was a falcon hospital in Abu Dhabi which now treats 9,000 birds each year.

Falconry wasn't the only tie to the Emirati past. Near the junction of the Emirati, Saudi, and Omani borders is the oasis of Al Ain, where time seemed to have stopped in its tracks. Enormous thick mud walls—there to keep out goats, camels, and marauders—towered over deep gardens, thick with palms and greenery watered from underground passageways. Sun filtered through the palm fronds. George and I were there on a Thursday, and an auction of cows and goats was taking place across from the Al Ain Fort. A large group of Omani farmers with their silver daggers tied about their waists were keeping an eye on the bidding.

With a guide, we once took a drive deep into the sands of the Empty Quarter—empty but for sand. There was not a sign of life anywhere, just sand in swirls, heaps, mounds, ridges, hills, and mountains—some as high as 325 feet. One moment those mounds were absolutely still. Then, without warning, they were buffeted by typhoon-strength winds. At night, there was some dew, but never more than the equivalent of half a millimeter of rainfall per night—just enough to allow lichens and dew beetles to survive.

Lady Anne Blunt, a granddaughter of Lord Byron, wrote about crossing the Nefud desert of the Empty Quarter with her husband in 1878. They were on "the shore of the great Nefud... At half past three o'clock we saw a red streak on the horizon before us, which rose and gathered as we approached it, stretching out east and west in an unbroken line. It might at first have been taken for an effect of mirage, but on coming nearer we found it broken into billows and but for its red colour not unlike a stormy sea seen from the shore, for it rose up, as the sea seems to rise, when the waves are high, above the level of the land... What surprised us was its colour, that of rhubarb and magnesia, nothing at all like the sand we had hitherto seen."

My days as a tourist, however, were numbered. I was soon asked to teach English at the Umm Ammar Secondary School for Girls. George assured me that I would love the girls, and that they would love me.

I walked through the school's gates for the first time on a Saturday morning in early October. A *firasha*, or janitress, welcomed me and took me to the office of Sitt Manal, the headmistress, who was swaddled in knits despite the still-sizzling October heat. Ten members of the faculty were in her office and one of them, a woman named Faika, leapt up to escort me to the Staff Room, where she introduced me to a dozen English-language teachers. I was bewildered by all of my new acquaintances when Faika took me to the first of my three secondary classes. My students were all *tawjiheh*, meaning that they were in their last year of school preparing to sit for the *tawjiheh* exam.

Umm Ammar had started in 1968, with a shoe-string staff and limited enrollment. Two years later, primary education was made compulsory, and every student received a quarterly stipend above and beyond free tuition, free books, free uniforms, free school lunches, and free bus service. Every year the student was in school, the stipend was increased.

My first few days were not auspicious. All 20 of my students complained both to Sitt Manal and to the Ministry of Education that an English teacher should be English and not American. "We'll flunk, and it will be her fault! She teaches *American*—not English. We are *tawjiheh*. We can't make a change this year."

On the third day, the Undersecretary of Education, escorted by a very nervous Sitt Manal, came to sit in on my classes. He heard the girls' complaints but urged them to be patient.

It was a hard sell.

The students were as much an Arab mix as the teachers: It was their parents who had come to "man" the new government departments, hospitals, law courts, and oil companies. There also were the *wataniyeh*, the nationals: Huda, Badria, Sheikha, Moza, Shamsa, all clothed in their prim uniforms and head scarfs, and all of them shy.

I was expected not only to use a standard textbook but never to deviate from it. The Inspector of Classes required that I have a detailed lesson plan, and she could arrive without warning at any moment to make sure that I was sticking to it. Janet, who was from Oman, and who sat next to me in the Staff Room, warned, "You have to—you absolutely *have* to—write down every word you will utter."

Janet apparently had useful connections in the Ministry: She always seemed to know when a surprise visit might occur.

The problem is that I had no inkling of what I would say in class. The girls were so bored by the lessons that I knew I would have to improvise, so I became adept in writing up my lesson plan, not when I left for a class, but when I returned from it.

I asked for volunteers to read a sentence from the text book, and Nadia eagerly raised her hand to display her mastery of English. She read aloud for those less fortunate than she: "When 999 is dialed and an accident is reported to the main switchboard at Scotland Yard, the supervisor radios roving police cars in the area."

Complete boredom.

So I suggested that we act out the sentence we were reading: "Let's try a play."

"Acting it out is not in the text book. It won't be on the exam. It's not fair."

But then one girl said, "A play, Miss?"

"No, let's act out a movie. You all watch movies on TV. We'll film a TV movie. There, over there by the window. Amal, you're a police car. Huda, you're a responsible citizen reporting an accident to Scotland Yard police headquarters, asking for help. Sumaya, you can be the accident. Yes, just anything. A thief stole your TV. You're helping an old lady cross the street and she falls. Anything, girls. Use your imaginations." I really was just chatting to myself.

"Me, Miss, me," Thawra shouted.

"Nasreen, come on up. You'd better coordinate this. You're the officer at the switchboard. Sit here at my desk. And Thawra, you are our director."

"Me, Miss?" Her brown eyes sparkled. This was going to be fun.

"Yes, yes. Without you, we can't begin. When you shout

'Action,' everything will happen."

Sumaya screamed: "Robbers, thieves, I've been stolen!"

"Not you, dear. A thing is stolen, but a person is robbed."

Sumaya was crestfallen.

"Not to worry. You screamed beautifully. Now wait for Thawra, and then you can scream again. We can't begin without Thawra. We also need a thief. Amal, our police car should be chasing a thief. OK. That's perfect. Now it's time for Thawra."

As I ranted, Thawra, our director, strode purposefully to the door, and, in total command of the scene, bellowed an impressive, "Action."

The next lesson was on Arab Nationalism.

In the Staff Room, Faika had warned me: "You'll never get it across."

There, sitting in front of me was Nadia, with her red hair and freckles, and her eyes glued to her watch, which kept Cairo time so that she could know exactly what her friends back home were doing at every minute. Basma, from Lebanon, sat drumming her long red fingernails. Mirium, scarred with tribal slashes on each cheek, came from West Africa. There was Feryal, from Yemen. And, of course, there were all of the girls from Abu Dhabi.

"What is an Arab, girls?"

Instant muttering, which I interpreted to mean, "Here she goes again, asking us the questions. *She's* supposed to tell *us*, not *us* tell *her*."

"An Arab, Miss, is someone who speaks Arabic," Nadia said.

"Like me?" I asked.

"You're American, we know that. But you like us, and you try to speak Arabic."

I dismissed the praise of my Arabic, or the insult to it, and continued, "Is it your music? Your foods? Your customs? Your traditions? Are they the basis of nationality? Is it a passport?"

"I don't have a passport, Miss. I'm Palestinian. I only have a travel document," lamented Ghada. "I've never seen my country."

"But girls, all of you—Ghada, you too—all of you are Arab. What makes you an Arab and not me?"

"I don't know, Miss. You're making this very complicated," said Mirium.

"Miss, can I ask you something?" Sumaya was stirring. "Do all the teachers in America teach like you? You are asking us what we *think*. We aren't used to this."

But they were getting used to it, and getting used to it quickly. Before long, I was able to ask them to give an oral report on a subject of their own choosing. Instead of the old standbys—"Weddings," "My Family," "My Country," I got "The Occult."

The girls all sat up straighter.

Nasreen said, "You know, Miss. Spirits. I read a lovely book where a French archaeologist takes a mummy back to France from Egypt. Then when the coffin is opened, one arm flies all around the room." The girls nodded in approval.

"Nasreen, that is revolting."

"Oh, no, Miss, it's beautiful," added Mona. "We like stories like this."

"Fine with me, but I need another topic. There is time for two reports. What about you, Sheikha?"

"I can't talk. I don't know anything."

"Of course you do. You wrote a composition for me about

the trip you took to Japan last summer with your father."

"I didn't go, Miss. I just wrote what my father and brother told me. They went. Not me." Sheikha had never left the U.A.E., nor was she likely to unless she married a man who would consider taking her with him on his travels. Her parents were from the Liwa oasis and already went back every Friday for a visit, so the family could reconnect with simpler days.

"I just figured out a topic," I said. "Your grandmother lives with you, doesn't she? I'm sure she has stories. You could translate one. Maybe one about women. You could tell us what life used to be like in Abu Dhabi."

"In the Shamsa family, Miss . . . In the Shamsa family of the Naimi branch of the Bani Yas, there were two brothers. This is what my grandmother says. Each brother had six children. One had all boys and the other all daughters. Everyone in the tribe made fun of the father of the daughters. One day, the oldest daughter, Aliya, who had a chip in her front tooth, was tired of hearing her father laughed at. 'You send me and have Uncle send his oldest son Fuad to seek our fortunes,' she said."

"'But we are poor, my daughter. I have nothing to give you, nothing to prepare you for a journey into the world but the donkey.'"

"Fuad's father provided him with a splendid white horse, new robes, and a golden sword. Poorly clad, but well-provisioned with food and water, Aliya rode out into the desert on the family's old donkey. Fuad soon passed her racing his fine horse. Aliya reached Fuad two days later. He was in a pitiful state, since he had not troubled himself to bring food and water. Without identifying herself, Aliya gave him food and water and her donkey in exchange for his fine outer robe, his sword, and his horse. As Fuad turned back to their tribe, Aliya rode on. Now wearing a man's fine clothing, she soon reached the encampment of a tribal sheikh. But the sheikh's son thought something was amiss—despite her garb, he felt sure that she was a woman. To test her, he had a retainer place a bowl of yoghurt next to her head as she slept. If he was right, and she was a girl, she would not turn in her sleep and the yoghurt, undisturbed, would become solid cheese. Knowing the tribal test, Aliya stayed awake all night, rocking the bowl of yoghurt.

In the morning, the sheikh's son was heartbroken. His father gave precious gifts to the visitor, who returned in triumph to her family. Time passed. The sheikh's son went in search of the visitor with the chipped tooth who had captured his heart. He rode the desert far and wide. Eventually, he stopped by a well where Aliya and her sisters were laughing and filling their containers with water. He saw her chipped tooth and recognized her for the lovely girl he had fallen in love with. Aliya became his wife. When he took his father's place as paramount Sheikh, he sought her counsel before judging tribal disputes. She was known throughout the land for her beauty and wisdom."

I told Sheikha it was a beautiful story.

About the same time, I was invited to the wedding of Sheikh Zayed's daughter Shamsa to Sheikh Tahnoun, Governor of the Eastern Region. We left at 7 a.m. to get to the wedding in Al Ain by 9:30 a.m. We entered a temporary shelter in front of a simple house—it was more like a tent with red carpeting and a tin roof. Bedouin females were streaming into the tent as Sheikha Fatima, the bride's mother, entered. We greeted her with our "salaams," followed her in, and sat down on the carpet. It seemed like thousands of Bedouin women were there. Aside from a small female diplomatic contingent, all were Bedouin, including one of my former students, dressed in a *burqa*. I could not make out her features, but the quiet "Mrs. Naifeh" gave her away. It was Aisha, who had graduated in 1977, coming in third in the country of males and females, in the *tawjiheh*.

Five bands started up. At noon, we were served rice and lamb to be scooped up into our mouths with our fingers. After lunch, another Egyptian band, famous to everyone except me, struck up, this time with both a dancer and singer to provide additional entertainment. Over to one side, some palace retainers ululated, calling our attention to Tahnoun's gifts to Shamsa: four large suitcases, opened to display diamond, emerald, and ruby necklaces; an open briefcase with one million dirham notes; and five footlockers of gowns. The proceedings were over by 1 p.m.—without a single sighting of the bride.

Unlike Aisha, not all our students would even pass the *tawjiheh*. So the school held a graduation ceremony three months before exams. Each girl would receive a commemorative scrapbook from Sheikha Fatima. The girls went all out getting dressed for the event, which was held six hours after the end of the last class. No blue uniforms or long-sleeved blouses. Each girl, according to her family means and her ability to persuade her mother, came draped in varying degrees of revealing white cloth: silk, cotton, polyester, and organza. Even heads normally covered with scarves were bared. Nasreen, who summered with her family in London, wore an enormous white organdy garden hat bordered with white satin.

The girls' families had been told that they could bring two guests for each graduating senior and were warned that no children were allowed. Only males under eight were permitted. But the guests ignored this injunction entirely and came with all of their female children, including toddlers and even infants. Total chaos prevailed until Sheikha Fatima arrived. Even that produced only a moment's silence. The room returned to chaos until a lovely girl named Sumaya went up to the microphone and began singing verses from the Qur'an invoking God's blessings. Her voice was frail but her pitch was perfect.

From then on, it was unadulterated chaos again. Sitt Manal's welcoming speech was followed by two student speeches—the equivalent of valedictory and salutatory addresses—which were listened to only by the two mothers directly involved. Two short plays followed. The first consisted of a family argument over the return of a son from studying in the U.S. Ahmed, the prodigal son, dangled a watch chain as she/he shuffled into the family gathering with a disco song playing on the record player. He agreed to join the family firm, but for one year only. A look of horror registered on the father's face. He

A traditional Emirati dance to celebrate the return of the pearl divers.

really wanted no part of this ruined son, who had been corrupted by the West, but accepted him anyway. Even Sheikha Fatima's coffee-maker, carrying a stainless steel thermos, sat enthralled.

Next came the dancers performing traditional dances, common to much of the Gulf. Ten sequined dancers, chosen as much for their long hair as for their agile footwork, appeared on the stage. I had seen the dances every night when they concluded the evening news on Abu Dhabi TV. The dances involved moving the head from side to side—slowly, at first, then faster and faster—so that the long hair created a syncopated thrashing halo. The dances were originally intended to be an expression of joy from the women of a tribe when husbands, fathers, sons, and brothers returned from long, dangerous pearl-diving expeditions.

This same hair-tossing elation was a little more perilous in the next dance. Six women faced six fishermen. When the head shaking reached its fastest point, if a single girl had forgotten and turned her head right when everyone else in the lineup was turning left, there would have been instant concussions.

Actually, all eyes were riveted on the Adonises: Thawra, Huda, Rehab, Mona, and Hala. With charcoal moustaches and their upswept hair hidden under their keffiyehs, the "male" chorus line was a sensation. Led by the indomitable Thawra, they figuratively rowed to shore and greeted their partners, with flirtatious winks, as they circled momentarily in pairs before drifting offstage.

Sadly, it wasn't long before George and I drifted offstage, too, leaving Abu Dhabi after a very happy four years there.

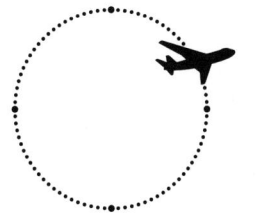

FOREIGN SERVICE

JORDAN

The Foreign Service had a policy against assigning officers to the countries of their ancestry, and it almost never happened, but here was the Embassy's new Public Affairs Officer, assigned to Jordan, the land of his roots. The headline in the *Jordan Times* on Friday, September 10, 1978, two months after our arrival, spelled it out: "George Naifeh Relishes Chance to Renew Links with Past."

Aunt Wadia was the physical embodiment of that link: "Although George's aunt speaks only Arabic, is shrunken with age, and has spent her whole life as agile as a mountain goat among the hills of Ajlun, she remains cool, calm, and collected at dinner party after dinner party, showing no signs of fatigue and behaving for the whole world as if she had never done anything else." The article noted that George, Carolyn, and I had spent two hours with Wadia in Ajlun in November 1971 when we had visited the Horans in Amman for Thanksgiving weekend.

We drove back to Ajlun on our first free weekend in Amman.

Once again we drove past the Roman ruins of Jerash,

halfway between the two cities. The occasional, unexpected clump of olive trees with their twisted limbs was straight from the Bible.

I had read up on Ajlun since our previous visit. Historically, travelers commented on its good markets, the stream of sweet water running through it, and the medieval castle overlooking it. The castle, the Qal'at al-Rabadh, was perched on our left, high on a cliff as we approached Ajlun. The castle was not just another Crusader castle: One of Saladin's own soldiers had built it. It is thought to have been built on the site of an ancient monastery, once inhabited by a Christian monk named Ajlun. In Saladin's days, the Qal'at was one of a chain of castles whose heliographs (movable mirrors that reflected sunlight), fire beacons, and pigeon posts could relay messages from Damascus to Cairo in less than 12 hours.

Eight hundred years later, we drove around yet another wide curve in the road and there Wadia was—waiting in the same spot where we had first met her seven years earlier, just inside the Baptist Church, with the door ajar so that she could see our approach.

Her grand-nephews and -nieces were there again as well. Startled by our black car, they began scampering in every direction, shouting, "He came back! He came back! He came back from America." Wadia clutched George's arm and never let it go the entire visit.

George and I had a hard time convincing her that our visit this time was less ephemeral. We would return soon and regularly. And she would ride back with us to Amman once a month for a week's visit. It turned out that she had not left the town of Ajlun in 45 years, and then it was to visit a friend in Irbid, some 40 kilometers north. She had managed the bus to Irbid, but had been petrified that the maze of streets and the crowds would be too much for her. Amman terrified her far more—but she finally gave in and agreed to let us come get her once a month for a long stay in the capital city.

We had settled easily into Amman's stylish Fifth Circle, where we moved into the solid white limestone house that had been occupied by George's predecessor. The house was split in two by a long hall that separated the formal rooms in the front of the house from the bedrooms in the rear. Our own bedroom had a splendid screened balcony, with a magnificent view of the open countryside at the edge of Amman.

We inherited a terrific housekeeper and cook from our predecessor, a woman named Teresa Joseph from India, who soon became a good friend. Her pungent ginger-and-garlic-infused curries and mountains of whole-wheat chapatis were irresistible. Teresa even produced George's favorite tapioca and bread puddings, whose fragrance and flavor evoked his mother's.

The first weekend that Wadia visited from Ajlun she set about teaching Teresa and me how to pickle eggplant, or *maqdus*. Wadia remembered George having said he liked them. "Here, here on the floor," she pointed. It turned out that *maqdus* had to be made on the floor, not at a comfortable height on a kitchen table.

"No, not like that! Like *this*." Her arthritic, green-tattooed fingers shed the skin from each clove of garlic in a flash.

Teresa and I were quick learners, squeezing, stuffing, and pounding to Wadia's satisfaction. I caught the look of astonishment on an Embassy maintenance staff employee who had come to repair a burner on the stove. It was not every morning that he encountered an Embassy wife preparing pickles on a kitchen floor.

Wadia, who had never eaten a dinner with someone other than a relative—and never with a Muslim, despite living almost a century in a town that was half Christian and half Muslim—somehow took our official dinner parties in stride. She waited until the guests headed into the dining room before she sat herself down at the head of the table, motioning to foreign ambassadors and Jordanian cabinet ministers alike that they were to greet her with a kiss. I can't remember a single one refusing the unexpected familiarity.

It took the bathtub to shake Wadia's equanimity. One look at the porcelain fixture set off alarm bells. She had never bathed in anything but a round, galvanized-tin tub filled with well water heated on a kerosene burner. Pleading for mercy, she informed me that she had scrubbed herself so thoroughly when she was in Ajlun that she would be clean forever. Despite her entreaties, I stood my ground: A bath once a week was in order. Teresa and I held her tightly as we lowered her slowly into the pink tub. As she gradually realized that she was not going to drown, she announced that Amman baths were acceptable.

Wadia was ecstatic to see George day after day. Of course, he left for the Embassy or the American Center every morning, but he returned every evening. As the magic hour of his return approached, she stood by the front windows waiting. "It's time for him to come home from work," she informed me. "It will be like all the lights in the house turn on when he walks in." When he finally arrived and bent down to hug her, she would say, "Your fragrance is that of jasmine." As if that wasn't bad enough, she insisted that every word falling from his lips was a "jewel, a glittering diamond."

George walking with his aunt Wadia in Ajlun, the town where his father was born.

Wadia's monthly visits to Amman became so routine that we were a little shocked one day when we came to pick her up and she announced that she was too busy to come for at least another week. A Bedouin friend had just brought her a year's supply of fresh goat milk to be made into *leban*, or sour yogurt. She had to drain it, knead it, and shape it into round little balls and preserve it in jars of fresh olive oil, and it would take many days. She was unmovable.

Two more of Shahada's sons, George's brothers Jimmie and Sam, made the pilgrimage to Jordan soon after we had settled in. Three nephews—*all at the same time*. This was almost more happiness than one person could handle.

We asked Wadia to take us to the house where she and their father were born in the late 19th century. It was still there, a large free-standing dried mud hut, conical in shape, in an alley of similar primitive dwellings. The house was heated by a fire in the middle of the one-room building. All the food was cooked on it. There was no chimney—just a hole in the middle of the roof. A shelf for sleeping was carved into one wall, a shelf for storage into another. A Muslim neighbor, who had grown up with Wadia and Shahada, came out to see what was going on when we appeared at the house. She was veiled, with a green tattoo on her forehead, and eager to supply any information that Wadia couldn't.

Jimmie had served in an elite Alpine Army troop in the mountains of Italy during World War II. Certainly, he must have seen simple dwellings in those mountains. But his father's childhood home left him visibly aghast.

We had a lunch of stuffed grape leaves, or *dolma*. I sat on the low stone wall of Wadia's and Aliya's courtyard watching a woman named Salwa work her magic with the grape leaves, rolling each slightly-veined, dark-green leaf around a mixture of lamb, rice, and assorted spices, then folding the leaf carefully before placing the finished product into the pot to cook. Salwa was mistress of her world, as she squatted at the opening of her closet-sized kitchen, its walls blackened from decades of sputtering charcoal fires.

After lunch, we attended a family burial. I had met the deceased, a woman named Radijah Rabadi, and a third-cousin, at least once before. On each of our monthly trips, assorted Naifehs and Rabadis always gathered for a short visit in Wadia's small home. I remembered Radijah as a middle-aged, diabetic phantom, occasionally visible through a cloud of cigarette smoke as she choked and coughed her way through another visit.

Unfortunately, the Ajlun Christian cemetery, which was on the other side of town, was full. Radijah was the first person to be buried in a new pine-shaded gravesite not far from the Baptist Church. The path to the gravesite was steep, and we four American Naifehs grabbed onto roots and branches to steady ourselves on the way up the path. The Ajlun Naifehs had no such need. Even Wadia, in her 90s, scampered up the hill as easily as one of her sure-footed grand-nephews. The coffin was a couple sizes too small for the corpse, and Jimmie and I sat there riveted as assorted family members grabbed heavy rocks in an effort to force the lid of the coffin shut. But her body just wouldn't fit, so they left the lid ajar. The Syrian Orthodox priest, oblivious to the grim dilemma, serenely conducted the simple service.

It was during this visit that Sam, Jimmie, and George all heard for the first time how their father's branch of the family had come to Ajlun, Jordan, from Marj Uyun, Lebanon. "There was a massacre," Wadia explained. "They divided Lebanon in half and, in 1860, the Druze massacred us Christians. That is all anyone ever talked about: the massacre. All of the men in Marj Uyun were killed or taken to be in some army—which one, I don't know—there were armies everywhere. The Druze left the women and children alone. The children ran around crying, and their mothers never stopped crying. With all the men gone, the children were being called by the names of their mothers: 'Ibn Halwa' or 'Bint Halwa.' Naifa, which means purity, was the name of your great-grandmother. We all became the children of Naifa.

"Not so many years later, when the bullets stopped, your grandfather, Sa'ad, and your grandmother, Zaweh, fled with their two small daughters, Aliya and Naima. They stopped here in Ajlun, and stayed. It's too bad more did not come. There was always more trouble there than there was here."

Back in Amman, I took Jimmie and Sam on a one-day Bible tour of Jordan. Because George was usually at the office, I was usually the one who took visitors from America on the tour.

We began on the same "king's highway" that Moses had traveled (Numbers 20:17). Unlike us, Moses had started on the king's highway in southern Jordan, heading north; we were in the north, heading just a few miles south. When we reached Mt. Nebo, we were standing on the very ground where Moses had stood—and where he is believed to have been buried. According to Deuteronomy (34:1-7), we were at the exact spot where Jehovah "caused" Moses to "see" the land he was never to actually set foot on.

Then we headed to the town of Madaba for a visit to the Syrian Orthodox parish church of St. George. The building was constructed in 1896 on the ruins of a Byzantine church that dated back to the late sixth century, and it still had a sixth-century mosaic map that was in remarkable condition. The church was on a high promontory, and from there you could see miles across a deep valley to the west—on this day, astonishingly, all the way to Jerusalem. I couldn't quite make out the Dome of the Rock, but it was hard not to feel the history and faith of the three monotheistic religions.

Not long afterward, George and I drove from Amman to Petra. But before you arrive at the ancient city, you pass through Wadi Musa, reportedly the site where Moses, who was looking for water, struck a rock to have an abundance of fresh water spring forth.

Petra was the ancient capital of the Nabatean kingdom, which dates from the third century B.C. to the second century A.D. It was a prosperous trading post with gold, spices, incense, ivory, and textiles from China and India finding their way to the ports of the Mediterranean through the city. T. E. Lawrence, who spent a night in one of the tombs carved into the cliffs, called the ruins "brilliant." Gertrude Bell described Petra as being "like a fairy tale city, all pink and wonderful," adding that "it was the most beautiful sight I have ever seen."

To get to the city, you have to walk a half mile through the gorge of the Petra Syk. On each side, the walls tower 100 feet straight up. Then, after the darkness of the stony crevice, you arrive at an opening with a magnificent view of the sun-drenched ruins. First, the startling 90-foot-tall, two-storied Al-Khazneh, or treasury, with its columns, friezes, and capitals, then market places, a forum, and eventually the necropolis.

A New York lawyer, John Lloyd Stephens, visited Petra in 1836. He was so transfixed, we are told, that he gave up law and began a brilliant career as an archaeologist. Before he ventured into Mayan ruins, Stephens wrote that the "first view of that superb facade [of Al-Khazneh] must produce an effect which could never pass away." He wrote that neither the Colosseum in Rome nor the Pyramids nor the Acropolis in Athens "are so often in my memory."

As glorious as Petra is, what I remember with even greater nostalgia are the much less frequently visited desert castles outside Amman. George and I joined the Friends of Archaeology and accompanied them on their day-long excursions whenever he could take off from work and Wadia was not visiting. Especially when the landscape was at its most desolate, it was astonishing to look across the parched earth and find a patch of poppies or anemones. There must have been an ancient vein of water down there somewhere. And then, out of the desolation, appears the most famous of all the desert castles, Qasr al Amra. The castles were actually country estates, self-contained economic units that served as retreats from the grand metropolis of Damascus. The nobleman who built Qasr al Amra during the seventh century had even arranged luxurious baths in the castle, through an extremely clever system of hydraulic pulleys. All evidence of the baths was now gone, but elaborate frescoes were still there, depicting gazelles, camels, hunting dogs, and a naked woman emerging from one of those long-gone baths.

Life at home in Amman was charmingly simple. There was always an ample supply of Jordan almonds, the shiny, multicolored, sugar-coated almonds that both George and Teresa loved to eat by the handful. When I made egg salad for George's lunch, Wadia showed me how to test the readiness of a hard-boiled egg by spinning it on the floor. When Teresa or I used the clothes dryer, we would let Wadia push the knob on the dryer, and she would giggle uncontrollably at this silly way to dry clothes.

Although Wadia joined us for all parties at the house, she didn't join us when we went out. I had to teach myself not to flinch when she started to cry when we left the house during the evening. It was not unlike the behavior of a child: "Please, don't go! *Pleeease* don't! I won't be able to sleep until you get back home safely!" She would clutch George's arm until, heartless soul that I was, I dragged him away. My guilt was considerably alleviated when my spy Teresa reported that Wadia would fall asleep the moment we left the house.

Our social life was endless, day and night. But some events stood out. One afternoon, we attended a tea party at the home of the vivacious Turkish Princess Fahrelnissa. She was only a princess by marriage, the widow of Prince Zeid. A recognized modern artist, she had draped the ceiling of her drawing room with cloths wildly painted with the reds, yellows, blues, and greens of a shamiana tent. Her bold, energetic canvases were propped up on easels everywhere. The place was so crowded with decorations that we had a hard time finding a spot to put down our gold-plated tea cups and plates. Even the small end tables, each skirted in enormous folds of cloth, were crowded with silver-framed photos of every Hashemite royal who ever breathed. Her bracelets and rings clanked with each gesture and every hearty laugh. Abdul Jabar Mahmoud, our friend from Baghdad days who was married to a Hashemite princess himself—a daughter of King Faisal I—referred to Fahrelnissa as a "19th-century Russian princess."

Also out of the ordinary was the Syrian Orthodox wedding of Rami Khouri, a good friend and a distinguished reporter for the *Jordan Times*.

But not every day was so festive. One day, George and I drove north of Amman to pick up a crate of ripe figs for a luncheon when a car ploughed into ours. Two police cruisers just happened by as we and the careening speeders stopped to check the damage. The police took all of us to file a report at the nearest police station, which was in the Baqa'a refugee camp. We were not at fault, but even with a diplomatic license plate, we and our accusers, two Palestinian brothers, had to explain ourselves. Everything grew complicated because one of the brothers had been arrested for reckless driving before and would be facing a long jail sentence if he was charged with reckless driving again.

"He's lucky," commented the brother. "Jail will be a lot better than what we have at home here in the camp."

I knew that Baqa'a was one of six refugees camps started in 1968 by the United Nations Relief and Works Agency (UNRWA) to house the tens of thousands of refugees who escaped from the West Bank of the Jordan River during the

1967 Arab-Israeli war. And many of them were refugees twice over, having been forced onto the West Bank during the 1948 war—the original *nakhba*, or catastrophe, as the Palestinians refer to it.

Then, only a month later, following up on Egyptian President Anwar Sadat's dramatic November 1977 address before the Israeli Knesset, Egypt and Israel signed a peace treaty in Washington. George watched the March 26 signing on Israeli TV at the home of a Jordanian friend. Palestinian students at the University of Jordan went on a rampage. Their explosion of political rage and a three-week strike that followed may have eased the students' frustration, but their response was futile. Since 1948, Israel had become a permanent "fact on the ground" of the Middle East. Now, Egypt—the most heavily-armed Arab military force in the Middle East—had removed itself from the increasingly deadly Israeli-Arab quicksand.

As a perk, American Embassy employees in Amman were occasionally allowed to serve as couriers to take the U.S. diplomatic pouch from our Embassy in Amman to our Consulate General in Jerusalem. The ride down the rollercoaster of road to the Jordan Valley and the Jordan River was uneventful. At the Allenby Bridge, we crossed between Jordan and the Israeli-occupied West Bank.

It was 10 years after crossing the Allenby Bridge that I read a riveting article by the Israeli writer David Grossman, "The Yellow Wind," in the *New Yorker*. He wrote that he belonged "to the generation that celebrated its bar mitzvah during the Six-Day War, with the occupation of the West Bank and the Gaza Strip." He wrote of the need to "understand how an entire nation" like his could "train itself to live as a conqueror without making its own life wretched."

At the end of our car ride was the extraordinary city of Jerusalem. In his masterpiece, *Jerusalem: City of Mirrors*, the brilliant author Amos Elon credits Sir Ronald Storrs, who was appointed the British Military Governor in Jerusalem in 1917, for decreeing that all new structures in Jerusalem be built with the "ubiquitous" local limestone. Storrs himself wrote that the clear white stone had been quarried and cut "soft" for 3000 years "but [dried] hard" and "weather[ed] blue-grey or amber-yellow with time," helping preserve "through the centuries a hallowed and immemorial tradition." Elon celebrates Storrs's decree as "one of the finest contributions any British colonial administrator ever made to the aesthetics of a historic city."

We set out early the next morning for the Damascus Gate, stopping to buy some sesame seed-encrusted *zatar*, or flat bread. A different vendor was chanting the virtues of the mounds of fat strawberries stacked in front of him. We were swept through the gate in a crowd of tourists, shoppers, and schoolchildren. Young machine gun-carrying Israeli soldiers kept a careful eye on us. We turned left onto the section of the Via Dolorosa leading to the Temple Mount, remembering the centuries of humanity that had walked before us.

Our crowd of tourists walked all the way to the Temple Mount, and each of us—Christian, Muslim, and Jew alike—was stunned silent by the sense of belonging to an ancient religion, of being in real time, yet looking toward the next world, a world that was not yet ours. The majestic gold dome of the Dome of the Rock, capping an expanse of lush blue tiles, was also enough to make you catch your breath.

But the strife between the faiths—and between adherents of the same faiths—was evident everywhere in Jerusalem. When the second Caliph, Omar the Just, captured the city from the Christians in 638 A.D., he promised that all persons and property in Jerusalem would remain unharmed, and he kept that promise. On receiving the keys to the city and to the Church of the Holy Sepulcher, he refused the bishop's offer that he pray in Christianity's holiest of churches, saying, "If I do, my people may appropriate the Church when I am no longer here to protect your rights." He appointed the first Muslim High Judge in Jerusalem and handed him the keys to the Holy Sepulcher for safe keeping.

That first High Judge was a man named Ubadah, the brother of the woman named Nusaybah who had fought alongside the Prophet. As we visited Jerusalem 13 centuries later, her descendants still held the keys to the Church. We knew the family well: not just Zaki Nusseibeh, from our four years in Abu Dhabi, but also now his brother Sari, the Al-Quds University President.

The Church is still holy to many Christian sects—the Egyptian Copts, the Latin Catholics, the Franciscans, the Armenians, the Dominicans, the Greek Orthodox, the Armenian Orthodox—and each group is allotted certain responsibilities within the Church, from fixing broken sewer covers to dusting the chandeliers. Three principal sects take turns setting up the ladder each morning for a Nusseibeh to climb and unlock the ancient iron door lock. An Israeli government official is responsible for making sure that the sects remain within their respective areas of control.

The same kinds of disputes over control exist at the other church that is so crucial to Christianity, the Basilica of the Nativity. When Sir Ronald Storrs took over as Military Governor in 1917, he reviewed the rigid protocol in every church, including the Basilica of the Nativity, concluding:

1. That the Greek Orthodox Community may open the windows of the Basilica looking Southward, for the time of cleaning only.
2. That the Greek Orthodox Community may place a ladder on the floor of the Armenian Chapel for cleaning the upper part of this Chapel above the Cornice.
3. That the Armenians have the right to clean the North face of the pillar on which the Greek Orthodox pulpit is placed, up to the Cornice only.
4. That by mutual agreement the following has been arranged:

   a) That the Greeks should attach their curtain right to the lower nail No. 2 at the foot of the pillar which lies South-East of the left hand set of steps leading to the Manger.

   b) That the Latins should have their curtain fall naturally down the same pillar leaving a space of 16 cm. between it and that of the Greek Orthodox.

   c) That Nail No. 1 be left unused by any of the Communities.

During our visit to Jerusalem, we stayed at the historic American Colony Hotel, which had been built in the mid-19th century. The building had originally been the palatial home of an Ottoman Pasha, who provided each of his four wives with the comfort of her own summer and winter rooms. The palace's outer walls, which ranged from three to five feet thick, cooled the summer rooms, and the windows of the well-insulated winter rooms held the sun's warmth. We had one of those summer rooms, along with its splendid bath, each with 20-foot-high ceilings. The courtyard outside our room was perfectly shaded with majestic palms and fragrant lemon trees.

The American Colony had opened as a hotel at the turn of the 20th century, at the suggestion of the actor Peter Ustinov's grandfather, who managed a hotel in Jaffa. But it was purchased from the Pasha by Horatio and Anna Spafford, the parents of a friend of ours, Bertha Spafford Vester. They arrived in Jerusalem in 1881, when Bertha was two years old, to found a utopian Christian commune, and she lived there for more than a century, not dying until 1986.

Bertha was there to greet us when we stayed at the Colony, reminding us that our lives in the Foreign Service were graced, even more than by the extraordinary places where we lived and visited, by the extraordinary people we met everywhere we went.

Already an old woman when we saw her again at the hotel, with gray upswept hair, her smile was still magical, her eyes still twinkled, and she was still full of stories that carried you back into history. We had drinks with her in the hotel bar, where she told us of meeting General Charles George "Chinese" Gordon—Gordon of Khartoum, famed hero of the siege of Sebastopol and the occupation of Peking. Gordon had been on furlough in Jerusalem in 1883, studying Biblical history, and often rode on his white donkey from the village of Ein Karim to visit her parents in Jerusalem. Her mother had warned her not to bother the famous general, but young Bertha would climb up on the flat roof where he would go to meditate and study. He would catch sight of her as she hid behind a chimney to watch him and would ask her to come over to visit so he could tell her stories.

Bertha claimed that he taught her to swear. He once accepted an invitation from her mother to have lunch at the Colony so long as she was not serving chicken. As he informed Mrs. Spafford, every day his servant Joseph would ask him what he wanted for dinner, and when Gordon asked him what he had on hand, the answer was always chicken. One morning, when Joseph approached, the General beat him to the draw by announcing, "Damn it, have chicken." A few days later, when Bertha was asked what she wanted for supper, she anticipated the inevitable bread and milk by saying, "Damn it, have bread and milk."

Always sensitive to any criticism of my Arabic, I was thrilled when Bertha commented that her friend Gertrude Bell's Arabic "was correct and classical," but that no one "could understand a word she said" and that it fell to Bertha to translate "from Bell's classical Arabic to the Arabic of the ordinary folk." To think that the Arabic of any of those singular Westerners in Jerusalem's modern history may not have been intelligible to anyone was wonderfully consoling.

Another of my happiest memories is that of Sarah and Fadhel Jamali, walking hand in hand into the sunset up the rise of the hill from our Fifth Circle home in April 1979. He may have had a cane in his other hand, but at 76, he seemed as agile as he was in his mid-50s, when we had known them in Baghdad. He still had a neatly-trimmed goatee, now totally white. They had refused our offer to take them to their hotel after having tea with us while in Amman for a series of lectures he was delivering.

Fadhel, a graduate of the American University of Beirut, had signed the Charter of the United Nations in 1945 on behalf of Iraq. He was to become Foreign Minister eight times and Prime Minister twice. When we first met him, he was the Foreign Minister, and had returned from the Afro-Asian Conference at Bandung, Indonesia. I remember being terribly impressed when he offered George one of the cigarettes Zhou Enlai had given him. Fadhel drew the cigarette from a British tin box covered with an elaborate Chinese design.

When the Iraqi monarchy was overthrown in July 1958, Fadhel had been sentenced by the Revolutionary Military Tribunal to 55 years of prison and fined over $100,000. Major world figures had helped get his sentence reduced to 10 years, and he was eventually released after only three. While in prison, he had written a series of *Letters on Islam* to his youngest son, Abbas, stressing that, "besides the feeling of awe for death, I had another feeling, that of comfort and inner peace resulting from a deep faith in Allah the Sublime ... and the sympathy, kindness, and loyalty of friends."

In our living room, he repeated that he had been reprieved and in effect been born again: "How many of us get a second chance?" In all of the countries where we had been privileged to represent our country, we were always amazed by the stunning resilience in the face of adversity that defined so many of the people we met—and gave us hope for the future, no matter how dire the current political circumstances might be.

Our own walks in the Jordanian hills were unexpectedly and abruptly halted by a bureaucratic snafu. The American Ambassador wanted to promote a favorite employee as the principal Political Officer, and she wanted her husband, who was George's assistant, to take George's job—after serving only a year in the land of his father. George, who reacted to this request from the Ambassador with a distinctly undiplomatic, if highly justified, expletive, was offered any post around the world—here was our chance for Stockholm or Buenos Aires or Kuala Lumpur—but George chose instead to retire from the government and move on to a second career. In 1981, he became founder and Chairman of the American-Arab Affairs Council—now the Middle East

Policy Council—a non-profit Washington think-tank. Its goal was to highlight the mutual strategic interests of the United States and the Middle East and to help each gain a better understanding of the other. After a lifetime of explaining America to Arabs and Muslims, now he would help explain the Arab and Muslim world to America.

We were tempted to bring Wadia with us to the United States, but were counseled against it. A rupture in routine at her age would not be a good thing. We opened a bank account for her in Ajlun, and, even though she couldn't write her name—she had to sign the papers with her right thumbprint—she understood compound interest in a savings account. She would be fine without us.

Any qualms I might have had about George leaving the Foreign Service were dispelled during our life back in Washington. He now had an even wider audience for touching "hearts and minds" in the U.S. and the Middle East. And we had a new opportunity to meet and befriend hundreds of fascinating new people from virtually every land.

ACKNOWLEDGEMENTS

I want to thank my daughter Carolyn and my son Steven, as well as my friends Nancy Horan, Kiki Murphy, and Daniel P. Ranger, for reading the manuscript of this book. It benefits greatly from their suggestions.

I also want to thank Elizabeth Petit, who edited the book so brilliantly; Eva Saviano, who copyedited the manuscript so perfectly; and Melissa Spivey and Eleni Tzinakos, who produced the elegant design. Finally, my thanks to Brent Cline, Richard de Combray, Bob Harris, Bennett Lindauer, Riadh Muslih, Bonnie Smith, and Michael Stone—among others—for their wonderful photographs.

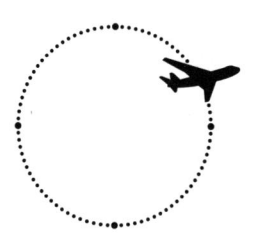